WENDY MCELROY

THE

REASONABLE

WOMAN

A Guide to
Intellectual Survival

Prometheus Books

59 John Glenn
Amherst, New York

Published 1998 by Prometheus Books

02 01 00 99 98   5 4 3 2 1

Library of Congress Cataloging-in-Publication Data

McElroy, Wendy.
        The reasonable woman : a guide to intellectual survival / Wendy McElroy.
                p.   cm.
        Includes bibliographical references (p.   ) and index.
        ISBN 1–57392–208–0 (alk. paper)
        1. Women—United States—Psychology. 2. Women—United States—Intellectual life. 3. Self-esteem in women—United States. 4. Self-help groups—United States. I. Title.
HQ1206.M367   1998
153.4'082—dc21   97–51477
                                                                                                      CIP

Printed in the United States of America on acid-free paper

Contents

Acknowledgments   9

Preface   11

1. What Is a Reasonable Woman?   23

2. Barriers to Being Reasonable   43

3. Overcoming Bad Habits   61

4. Taking Yourself Seriously   79

5. Forming New Habits   101

6. Books and Other Good Friends   121

7. Intellectual Therapy   141

8. Forming an Intellectual Therapy Group   155

9. The Tools of Reasoning 179

10. The Power of Definitions 195

11. Applying Reason to Theory 207

12. Applying Reason to Statistics 223

13. The Psychology of Arguing 237

14. Arguing in an Atmosphere of Good Will 253

15. Arguing in the Absence of Good Will 265

16. Addressing Philosophical Assaults 285

Afterword 299

Recommended Readings 301

Index 307

To Bradford—
my context of everything reasonable
and not.

Acknowledgments

With great pleasure I acknowledge the contributions of many people to this work. Within the text, I have tried to indicate the printed sources from which *The Reasonable Woman* was drawn, but the material gathered from direct personal experiences requires more specific acknowledgments.

First of all, I wish to thank my friend and former agent Simon Green whose patient input improved two rough drafts of the manuscript. My editor, Steven L. Mitchell, offered invaluable advice on expanding the book at the beginning of our association and, then, edited the results of his counsel with a careful hand.

Four people require special mention and thanks. The second time I ran away from home, Ed Paige not only kept me off the streets but, over a period of months, we listened to stacks of tapes from the Nathaniel Branden Institute, which constituted my passage from intellectual infancy to adulthood. (Of particular value were the tapes on efficient thinking by Barbara Branden.) The philosopher George Smith created the intellectual therapy groups discussed in *The Reasonable Woman* and, over the ten years of our close association, we discussed many of the ideas expanded upon within. Computer guru

Bart Kosko provided the spark for the book by challenging me to learn mathematics, thus forcing me to confront my own psychology of reasoning. But most of all, I would like to thank Queen Silver—who was still an active feminist and free-speech advocate at the age of eighty-six—for providing me with that most necessary of all intellectual touchstones, a role model.

My husband, Bradford Rodriguez, critiqued and proofed a series of drafts without ever losing his enthusiasm—an act close to heroism. As always, I offer him my love and admiration.

Preface

Reason is the mistress and queen of all things.
Cicero, *Tusculanarum Disputationum,* 2.21

When I was sixteen years old, I ran away from home and lived on the streets, sleeping in churches to keep from freezing at night. This is the main reason I have no formal education beyond high school. Nevertheless, I have published books through both major popular presses and academic ones. I have written documentaries that have been narrated by George C. Scott, Harry Reasoner, and Walter Cronkite. And I have worked as a scholar for think tanks, such as the Cato Institute.

I do not write the above paragraph in a spirit of self-congratulation. Believe me, if I could have pursued a more traditional path, I would have done so in a flash. As it is, I made the most of the opportunities I had, including some unorthodox steps in learning how to handle myself intellectually. For example, I participated in and helped to organize a long-running intellectual therapy group, which functioned much like a psychotherapy group. It assisted people in dealing with the underlying psychological problems that were blocking their

11

intellectual potential. From fear of error to techniques for dealing with hostility, the group addressed what might be called the psychology of reasoning.

When people I work with learn of my background, they are amazed at where I came from. I am amazed at where I ended up. But the amazement on both sides is unjustified. Throughout most of history, philosophers and others considered to be the "intellectual elite" were usually self-educated, and often from lower-working-class families, such as my own. The amazement reflects their assumption that intellectual achievement has to come from a traditional academic education.

If that were true, however, it would be impossible to explain many of the most prominent intellectuals of our times, from Edison to Einstein. Alongside the accomplishments of such thinkers and innovators, how surprising can it be that I have taught myself how to write a proper sentence and how to footnote articles for academic journals? Yet people persist in believing there is only one path—the accepted one—to intellectual accomplishment.

This is a destructive belief. Many young people, with good minds, are in circumstances that preclude an academic career. Many women who have put husbands and family first for years now believe they are too old to register at the lowest level of entry into college. Still others denigrate themselves as ignorant or even stupid because they do not have the traditional credentials of a "learned person." But colleges and universities have no monopoly on learning, and they have no necessary connection to being a reasonable human being—that is, a person who values her reason and uses her mind to the best advantage.

Yet there is considerably more to the process of becoming what I call a reasonable woman than merely absorbing information. In attempting to reach that goal, I have consciously developed a very specific attitude toward ideas and toward my own reasoning process. I also constructed a philosophy, or psychology, of how I wanted to interact with other people intellectually.

I cultivated what amounted to a psychological approach to reasoning, because most of the barriers I experienced intellectually were emotional ones. In a sense, this was to be expected. Every human being brings emotions, past experiences, good and bad habits—in essence, they bring who they *are*—to every encounter they have. Why should intellectual encounters be any different?

This book embodies and expands upon the approach that worked for me. It offers a blueprint of what could be described as intellectual therapy for the nonacademic, for women who don't have the time or interest to pursue a university degree but who want to overcome intellectual barriers. It is a psychology of reasoning for women who wish to accomplish more intellectually. Their goals may be to argue more effectively, to overcome a fear of error and of appearing foolish, or simply to learn how to reason more efficiently. All of these can be learned in a step-by-step commonsense manner.

This book is addressed specifically to women, even though most of the information and techniques can be used readily and as easily by men. I believe society throws up unique psychological barriers in the path of women who try to make it intellectually. The barriers may not be unique "in kind"—that is, both men and women may experience ridicule as children, which may make both of them develop a fear of, for example, public speaking. But I believe the intellectual barriers thrown in front of women are unique "in degree"—that is, they are much more difficult for women to overcome than they are for men. *Not* because women are less intelligent or less persistent than men, but because the barriers are higher.

As an example, I wrote that running away from home was the main reason I never went beyond high school. But even if I had stayed home, I would probably have taken a job right after graduating. I was raised in a lower-working-class environment—my father had only a sixth-grade education—and women were not expected to attend university or to pursue ambitious careers. Whether or not it was done consciously, women were discouraged from doing so. They were pushed instead into the traditional poses of mother, wife, and housekeeper. A college fund had been established, it is true, but the money was in my brother's name.

A certain school of thought will immediately and impatiently respond, "You didn't have to live up to those expectations, did you? It's a free country." Well, I didn't. And it may be. My purpose is not to complain about being a victim. When I mention the preference given to my brother, my purpose is not to create more gender hostility than already exists. I merely wish to observe that our culture makes it more difficult for women to achieve intellectual success and self-esteem than it does for men.

But in the final analysis, whatever your sex, age, or educational background, the healthy functioning of your mind is as much your responsibility as that of your body. The discussion that follows offers you a sense of the step-by-step psychological process I went through in order to get off the streets, both emotionally and intellectually.

STEREOTYPES

Women are unreasonable. Ask most men.

One of the things men mean by this statement is that women approach ideas and intellectual situations such as argumentation—more commonly called arguing—in a different manner than men do. What they really mean is that women approach these situations in a *less rational* manner. For example, women are more likely than men to burst into tears during a frustrating conversation. Of course, men are more likely to get into bar fights while disputing sports scores. But let's ignore that particular behavior for the moment and return to the accusation at hand: during arguments, women tend to employ emotional outbursts rather than reason. If this is true, it is learned behavior that can be unlearned.

Yet many men—and society in general—seem to consider learned behaviors such as being logical or reasonable as matters of biology. That is, men tend to have them, women do not.

There is some evidence that most women do take a different intellectual approach than most men. For example, on a strictly statistical basis, women tend to shy away from the hard sciences. Many of these rigorous realms might as well be posted with For Men Only signs. Within the boundaries of hard science, women often feel like second-class citizens who are attempting to emigrate.

Recently, a stream of books has investigated the possibility of genetic differences between men and women, and the possible consequences of any differences in terms of behavior. In her much-acclaimed book *Myths of Gender: Biological Theories About Women and Men,* biologist Anne Fausto-Sterling concludes that a great lack of substance underlies most claims regarding biologically based sex differences. I have not explored the claims on either side sufficiently to have an opinion.

Whether genetics contributes to behavioral differences between the sexes may be debatable, but it is undeniably true that our culture heavily influences sex-based behavior. After all, our culture deeply influences even so intimate a matter as how we view ourselves as individuals. Many of the societal cues aimed at women carry messages that, if taken to heart, naturally produce feelings of intellectual insecurity and inadequacy. The list is long. Women should not compete with men. Women become irrational when menstruating. Women do not argue fairly. Women—not men—must balance career and family. A wife should relocate to accommodate her husband's job transfer. A clean house is the woman's responsibility: a "good living" is the man's. A wife who earns more than her husband is looking for trouble. Women are bad at math. Girls take home economics while boys take car repair. If a man sexually strays, it's because his wife is no longer savvy enough to keep him satisfied. Women gossip; men discuss. The list scrolls on.

Women have a right to be outraged by the disrespect that society heaps on their intellectual abilities. The disrespect ranges from mild comments about "women drivers" and "isn't that just like a woman" to an explicit call to "keep 'em barefoot and pregnant." Whenever they stand up for themselves, women risk being labeled everything from "cute" to "a bitch." Often the only risk women *do not* seem to run is being taken seriously.

I felt a full stab of this anger at being dismissed several years ago. I had just delivered a lecture and was lingering by the podium, talking to people from the audience who drifted up with questions. A male friend stood beside me. Finally a middle-aged man made his way to the edge of the podium, waited patiently, then asked my friend, "What did Wendy mean when she said . . . ?" I was standing three feet away, no longer in conversation with anyone else, but the man chose to ask another man what I had meant when I said something. His actions were a complete dismissal of my intellectual existence. And, yet, the same man had cared enough about what I had to say to come out for my lecture and pay to hear my point of view. In short, I don't think the dismissal was a malicious one. I think he felt uncomfortable admitting confusion to a woman. Far better to admit it to a man.

Almost every woman I know feels some degree of intellectual inadequacy. This is true even of those who compensate by becoming superefficient, superinformed, and who can outcompete men as lawyers or professors. In fact, women who demand perfection of themselves may be the most intellectually vulnerable of all because they live in fear of error. This sort of insecurity can be acutely painful because there is no more intimate relationship in life than the one between you and your own mind.

The sense of inadequacy can be expressed in many ways. Wives defer to their husbands or to some other authority figure. Women do not stand up in classrooms to ask probing or confrontational questions. At parties, women stay to themselves and rarely argue aggressively about science or technical philosophy with men. Few of us pursue careers in physics or engineering. And if women do become part of the intellectual elite—part of academia or the diploma-professions—it is usually through the "soft sciences," the humanities such as literature or art or political science.

Every woman who backs away from the hard edges of her own intellect has her own motives, and expresses the decision in her own way. If that choice brings her satisfaction, it is not my place to quarrel with it. I am not among the feminists who believe it is wrong for women to chose domesticity and a family life. But, too often, women run from their own intellectual potential because they are afraid of failure: they are deeply afraid of appearing ignorant or stupid.

There is a psychological basis both to the process of reasoning (of being reasonable) and to the process of backing away from that capacity. Human beings express their emotions and their intellect in everything they do. Thus, overcoming feelings of intellectual inadequacy is as much a matter of psychology as overcoming negative feelings in any other area.

One of the most painful and frustrating things in life is to think of yourself as intellectually inadequate—as stupid or foolish. Yet nowhere in the shelves and shelves of self-help books aimed at women have I found a straightforward explanation from a woman's point of view of how to become more intellectually competent—on how to acquire the habit of being reasonable. A flood of books and videos teach us how to build leg muscles and slim down thighs, but next to nothing shows us how to flex our ability to argue and assume control of a conversation. Endless diets induce us to fast or to gorge on grapefruit, but no paperback offers us a scale on which we can weigh the reasonableness of our judgments. Nothing out there explains the psychology of reasoning within the current context of being a woman.

From personal experience, I know there are simple and commonsense steps women can take to overcome the psychological problems that are blocking them intellectually. In this volume I run through the techniques of reasoning and the skills of argumentation, but I present much more than purely practical information. I offer the basics by which you can acquire a benevolent attitude toward ideas and your own intellect, especially toward the errors that everyone makes at one point or another. And I offer a blueprint, not only for maximizing your individual potential, but also for establishing the sort of intellectual therapy group which proved so valuable to me years ago.

A simplistic sense—the vaguest taste—of what I hope is the book's nonpretentious and benevolent approach to intellectual psychology can be gleaned from the following list that spells out what I call *intellectual etiquette.* Just like good table manners, there are rules of etiquette that should guide intellectual encounters. You have a right to be treated with civility. And the following is a partial list of what you have a right to demand from others.

THE RULES OF INTELLECTUAL ETIQUETTE

A man's own good-breeding is his best security against other people's ill manners.

Lord Chesterfield, *Letters,* 15 January 1753

Everyone Has the Right to Be Uninterested

When you are trapped in an unpleasant or boring conversation, you are well within your rights to state, "I don't care to talk about this (or to you) further." Make the statement without hostility, as a matter of fact, then simply walk away.

No one has an unconditional claim on your time or on your attention. And the assumption that you should care about every issue and event in the world at all times is a ridiculous one. It leads to the intellectual equivalent of what the media has termed "compassion fatigue" —the emotional state of being overwhelmed and short-circuited by the demand that you care about every injustice committed on the planet. Don't allow yourself to be intellectually overwhelmed by the unrealistic demand that you find everything and everyone interesting.

Everyone Has the Right Not to Understand

Most of us spend a lot of time trying to avoid uttering the sentence, "I don't understand what you are saying." Too often, people see this statement as an admission of ignorance or inadequacy on their own part rather than considering the likelihood that the other person is either not explaining things well or holds a position that makes no sense.

Even if the intellectual ball is being dropped on your side of the discussion, what of it? No one understands everything, and it is folly to pretend you do. There is a vast difference between being confused about a line of argument and being stupid. The fear of appearing stupid frequently underlies our reluctance to admit that we simply do not understand what is being said.

Do not apologize. Just ask whoever is speaking to repeat or to rephrase what has been said. Ask them to clarify what they mean. Most people are more than happy to expound at length in front of an attentive audience.

Everyone Has the Right to Be Uninformed

This point of intellectual etiquette is closely related to, but distinct from, the preceding one. Rather than feeling unable to understand what is being said—either because the terminology is technical or the arguments are tangled—you are confronted with an issue you know nothing about.

Again, what of it? No one can know everything. In fact, in a world exploding with information, there are certain to be vast areas of human knowledge about which you are absolutely ignorant. There will always be books you have not read and events you have not heard about. The worst thing you can do is to become embarrassed and fake knowledge you do not possess. Instead, exercise the intellectual right to say "I am not familiar with that. Why don't you explain it to me?"

Everyone Has the Right to Make a Mistake

This is far more than a right. It is an inevitability. You will commit errors, and frequently. If this upsets you, then curse human nature. As a human being, you are a fallible creature without the godlike automatic knowledge of what is true and false, right and wrong. Yet many people will argue themselves (and everyone else) into the ground or into absurd intellectual corners rather than admit to the other person, "You're right. I'm obviously mistaken about that one point."

There is no shame in admitting "I made a mistake." Indeed, there is great strength in being willing to acknowledge your errors and to learn from them. This one trait alone, if developed as a habit, will give you an amazing advantage over most of the people you deal with intellectually.

Everyone Has the Right to Change Her Mind

Changing your mind or your stated position on an issue is not a sign of intellectual indecision or weakness. Changing your mind is part of the learning process by which you discover errors and correct them. Yet, like the person who will be reduced to absurdity before admitting a mistake, many of us will never admit to adopting a new position. The more publicly the former position has been stated, the more psychological resistance there is to retracting it.

Yet if someone convinces you on an issue, it is no more than a mark of intellectual honesty and courtesy to say "You've persuaded me to your point of view." After all, what is the alternative? Holding onto an untenable position just because that is what you believed yesterday? This would be childish behavior, like holding your breath until you get your own way.

Everyone has the right to say without shame, "Obviously I am wrong on that point," and not to feel diminished by this act of intellectual honesty.

Everyone Has the Right to Disagree

Whenever you hear a statement or argument with which you disagree, you have the right to say so. Often we are in situations where our opinion would be unpopular if stated. Perhaps a group of male co-workers are complaining about some unpleasant characteristic women are supposed to embody. Perhaps a family gathering has turned into a discussion of abortion, and you hold the only dissenting opinion. Your alternatives are wider than either stewing in silence or getting involved in an intellectual brawl. Simply, but firmly state, "I disagree." You don't need to justify yourself. You needn't become either hostile or apologetic. Simply state "I disagree" and walk away. Or stay and argue. The option is yours.

At this point, many people will ask themselves "Why bother? Why cause trouble?" In some cases—such as the family gathering—you may reasonably decide that speaking out is not worth the price you might pay for doing so. But showing discretion is different than allowing silence in the face of offensive opinions to become a habit. Such silence is destructive to the most important aspect of your intellectual life: your own self-esteem.

Breaking the silence and saying "I disagree" is important. If it were not, most people would not feel such resistance to making this statement.

Everyone Has a Right to Her Own Opinion

Everyone has the right to so weighty a thing as an opinion, and to express it. You do not need a diploma, permission from your spouse, a dispensation from the church: simply by being a human being, you have a right to reach your own conclusions and publicly state them.

It is true: the more you know about a situation, through reading or direct experience, the more likely your opinions are to be correct. But this does not mean that you should not reach a conclusion right now based on what you know about the situation. In fact, that is all anyone ever does: form opinions based on their current level of knowledge. After all, as noted above, you also have the right to change your mind if more or better information arises.

As a final note, books on reasoning can be intimidating. This one is precisely the opposite. For one thing, it assumes that you already know much more about reasoning than you realize. The philosopher Lionel Ruby opens his book *The Art of Making Sense: A Guide to Logical Thinking* with a charming excerpt from Molière's play *The Bourgeois Gentleman*. It is the passage where the hero, Monsieur Jourdain, asks a more educated man, a philosopher, to help him compose a love letter. The philosopher inquires whether the letter is to be in prose or verse. "I wish it written neither in prose nor verse," Jourdain replies. Upon learning that all writing is either one or the other, he inquires:

"And when one speaks, what is that?"

"That is prose, Monsieur."

"What! When I say, 'Nicole, bring me my slippers, and give me my nightcap'; is that prose?"

"Yes, Monsieur."

"Well, well, well! To think that for more than forty years I have been speaking prose, and didn't know a thing about it. I am very much obliged to you for having taught me this."

You almost certainly know more about reasoning than you realize. After all, reasoning is part of your nature as a human being. This is what Aristotle meant when he defined human beings as reasoning animals. The purpose of this book is to make your existing knowledge more explicit so that it can be available to enrich your life. To do so, the book approaches reasoning as a habit that can be developed step-by-step and, then, used to your advantage.

So . . . let's start by asking and answering:

What does reasonableness entail?
What is a reasonable woman?

1

What Is a Reasonable Woman?

That which has become habitual becomes, as it were, a part of
our nature; in fact, habit is something like nature, for the difference between "often" and "always" is not great, and nature
belongs to the idea of "always," habit to that of "often."

Aristotle, *Rhetorica* 1.11

Imagine two scenarios.

The first: A good friend named Anne is having brunch with you in
your upper-middle-class house one Sunday when she excuses herself
to use the washroom. As Anne is washing her hands, she glimpses
something that is lying in a small glittering pile in a corner of the tiled
floor. Stooping down, she realizes that the object is a very expensive
gold-and-diamond necklace for which you have been searching and
which you believe to be irretrievably lost.

Anne is nowhere near as affluent as you are, and she bitterly
resents this fact. Indeed, she is two months behind on her rent and the
landlord has threatened to turn her out of the apartment building. If she
pockets the necklace and takes it to a pawnshop, however, she will

have more than enough money to settle all her debts and start on a fresh financial footing.

Anne picks up the expensive jewelry and toys with the chain, examining it carefully while she considers various arguments concerning whether or not to steal it. She would almost certainly "get away" with the theft, and she knows you would recoup the cost of the necklace through filing an insurance claim. Anne begins to talk herself into committing the theft: You clearly do not need the money, whereas she is in extreme financial straits. Moreover, the two of you have spent the morning quarreling about a boyfriend Anne accused you of stealing from her years before. She is in no mood to be fair or considerate of your feelings.

On the other hand, you have been close friends for thirteen years now . . .

Finally, Anne emerges from the washroom with the necklace in her hand. "Look what I found," she announces.

The second scenario runs something like this: A good friend named Beth is having brunch with you in your upper-middle-class house one Sunday when she excuses herself to use the washroom. She sees the same necklace as Anne did. Like Anne, she knows you believe the necklace to be irrevocably lost. Beth is in precisely the same financial situation as Anne. Moreover, she, too, lost a boyfriend to you some years past and has never forgiven you for it.

Without giving the matter another thought, she scoops up the necklace and hurries to tell you the happy news.

The question is: Which one of these women displayed the most honesty? Anne, who was sorely tempted and actively debated the ethical and practical considerations of stealing from a friend? Or Beth, who is as intelligent as Anne, but to whom the possibility of theft never occurred?

I would answer that Beth was the more honest woman because honesty had become such an ingrained part of her approach to life that stealing no longer occurred to her as an option. Honesty had become an automatic response that required no thought. In short, honesty had become a habit.

THE ROLE OF HABIT

> We sow our thoughts, and we reap our actions;
> we sow our actions, and we reap our habits;
> we sow our habits, and we reap our characters;
> we sow our characters, and we reap our destiny.
> Charles Albert Hall

A habit is an ingrained pattern of behavior that leads you to act in a specific manner in virtually all situations. It is a disposition, a characteristic way of acting that results from having established an automatic response. A habit is a manner of acting that has become second nature to you. In other words, you act automatically without having to think.

In its most basic form then, a habit is simply an automatic behavior. You lock the front door as you leave the house, you turn the driver's wheel to the right onto your own street, you suds your armpits first in the shower, you turn the light in the garage off as you enter your home. In a more complex form, a general habit of behavior is a network of smaller habits that reinforce each other. For example, if you habitually defer to an authority figure like your father, you may have developed such supporting habits as lowering your voice in conversations with him, avoiding eye contact, or developing a headache whenever you visit your parents.

The specific habit we will address in this book is the complicated one of being reasonable. And, as the philosopher Brand Blanshard points out in his engaging work *The Uses of a Liberal Education,* "The end of education is reasonableness. The first point to note about such reasonableness is that it is a disposition or habit. Habit, not knowledge, is the main thing we take with us from a college education" (p. 74).* Blanshard expands on his theme by explaining that intelligence has little to do with the amount of information you have absorbed, and a great deal to do with how you process data: ". . . what is essential is not information at all, but the habit of reasonableness" (p. 75). Intelligence, in anything but its most

---

*The full citation for works quoted or recommended in the text may be found in the Recommended Readings at the end of this book.

raw sense, may reduce to nothing more than the pattern of how you deal with ideas. Intelligence may largely reduce to good intellectual habits.

Consider an example: Two of the most celebrated intellects of the nineteenth century were Lord Asquith and Lord Balfour who regularly sparred with each other in the British House of Commons. People were said to pack the galleries just to eavesdrop on their barbed exchanges, rather than wait to read them in the newspaper the next morning. Yet Balfour had such a poor memory that he had to write down in advance each and every word of anything he wished to quote. His genius—which was recognized throughout Europe—lay in his ability to perceive the fundamentals of arguments and to use logic in assailing them. What you know is usually less important than how you approach knowledge.

When the emphasis is placed on the "pattern" of a habit—on its repeated and prominent place in your life—a question arises regarding my analysis of the two opening scenarios. Namely, how can I judge whether Beth or Anne have the habit of honesty based on only one incident? The answer is: I can't. It is not possible to judge whether any action, taken in isolation, is part of a pattern of behavior: it is not possible to judge whether Beth has the habit of honesty. Perhaps Anne's contemplation of theft was an aberration, a once-in-a-lifetime occurrence sparked by her extreme upset at the preceding quarrel. Perhaps Beth's automatic honesty regarding the necklace came from the fact that she had taken a large sum of money from her friend's purse ten minutes before. In short, you can't judge whether or not someone is habitually honest, or reasonable, from examining an isolated event. You need to see the pattern.

Let me provide another illustration.

Suppose your neighbor is a meticulously neat man, whose public appearance over several years has always been polished and perfect. Even at casual events, his T-shirts are ironed, his blue jeans are perfectly cuffed, and his sneakers are spotlessly white. One particular morning, however, as you pass by him at his mailbox, you notice that his shirt is wrinkled and stained. He has not bothered to shave yet and you see, for the very first time, how dark his chin stubble is. From the top of his unbrushed hair to the tips of his scruffy shoes, the man is unwashed and unkempt. Does this one incident make him a slob? No, your neighbor is a neat man who happens to be wearing a wrinkled, stained shirt on this particular occasion. His unkempt appearance is out of character. It is an aberration within what is clearly habitual behavior.

Similarly, a sloppy man may decide to dress up for the evening in magnificently appointed attire: sparkling cuff links, matching tiepin, a dress shirt as white as a snowfall. This does not make him a neat person. It makes him inconsistent.

In order to judge whether a human being habitually embodies some trait—like neatness—you have to look beyond any one event to their pattern of responses. By this standard, your neighbor is a neat man because he displays the *habit* of neatness. It is a characteristic you expect from him on a day-to-day basis and an occasional wrinkled shirt doesn't change that. The same is true of the habitual slob.

To restate this key concept in other words: a habit is what you do without thinking about it. A good example is driving a car. Each time you slip behind the wheel, you don't have to puzzle out how to steer or when to engage the gears. These actions have become familiar to you; they have become habits, or second nature.

Or consider something you do every day, say, brushing your teeth in the morning. Even without coffee, most of us can stumble into the bathroom and perform this task automatically. It may seem to be so simple a task that it requires no attention whatsoever, but try changing the physical pattern of how you brush your teeth in the morning and you will discover how difficult it is to replace the old habit with a new one. And how awkward the new behavior feels.

These days, the word "habit" has fallen upon bad times. You hear about "drug habits," "nasty habits," "breaking bad habits," "overcoming habits." A great deal of negativity is attached to the word. But in classical Greek philosophy—especially in the works of Aristotle and of those, like Saint Thomas Aquinas, who developed the Aristotelian tradition—habits were viewed in a very different manner. The Greeks considered habits to be neither good nor bad in-and-of-themselves, but to be powerful tools that human beings could use to either good or bad ends. In answer to the question "How do human beings achieve happiness?" Aristotle replied that happiness was the by-product of good habits of choosing actions and things of real substance, in the right amount and in the right order.

In his extremely accessible book *Aristotle for Everyone: Difficult Thought Made Easy,* philosopher Mortimer Adler lays out the hierarchy of habits that goes from the simplest sort, e.g., brushing your teeth, to the most complicated ones, e.g., the habit of being reasonable. Adler writes: "Persons who have developed the skill of playing tennis well possess a good habit, one that enables them regularly to play well. Persons who have acquired the skill of solving problems in geometry or algebra have a good habit" (p. 98).

The first sort of habit, Adler terms "a good bodily habit." The second, he describes as "a good habit of mind." Such ingrained patterns of behavior allow human beings to perform specific actions with repeated excellence and without great effort. Yet another form of patterned behavior is "habits of action" by which people make choices regularly and easily, without having to go through the process of a long inward debate over alternatives each time. For example, you don't have to debate whether or not to get drunk every night because—as a habit of action—you have chosen moderation in drinking.

If these patterns of behavior—of playing tennis, doing math, embracing moderation—are habits that take your life in the direction you wish it to go, then they are good habits. The underlying assumption of our discussion is that reason and intellectual confidence both point to a direction in which you wish to go. Accordingly, whenever the word "good" appears, all that it refers to is a "useful" habit that is likely to produce the results you want. To a large extent, this is all the Greek philosophers meant when they used the word "virtue"—a useful habit.

And the most useful habits of all were termed "habits of pure virtue": that is, habits that settle into a person's character and become a tendency, or disposition, for her to make the choices that will benefit her life. These are the habits that become second nature, so that acting contrary to them feels like "not being yourself." One category of the habits of pure virtue is "intellectual virtues," including the virtue of reasonableness.

This book deals primarily with how to absorb and use the classical intellectual virtues that center around the activity of being reasonable, of being connected to the real world through a passionate desire to know and understand. The entire purpose of developing such intellectual habits is to increase your well-being as a reasoning woman. In this context, an intellectual vice, or bad intellectual habit, is merely a tendency to act in a manner that will decrease your well-being.

The important term here is "tendency." A dishonest person can perform isolated and honorable acts; that does not make her "honest," merely inconsistent. The word "honest" applies to a person's character, to her general pattern of behavior. The same is true of the habit of being reasonable. It does not mean you never act irrationally, but merely that such behavior is not characteristic of who you are.

WHY SHOULD YOU CARE ABOUT BEING REASONABLE?

> Reason, which ought always to direct mankind,
>   seldom does;
> but passions and weaknesses commonly usurp its seat,
>   and rule in its stead.
>
>   Lord Chesterfield, *Letters*

Before diving into what might seem to be a dry and intimidating topic —namely, the theory behind acquiring good intellectual habits—it's necessary to answer a question. I am often taken aback when someone asks me "What difference do ideas make?" "Why should I care about being reasonable?" "Why should the truth be important to me?"

On one level, this is a difficult question to answer. The person might as well be asking "Why should I care about being physically fit, rather than never exercising?" or "Why should I want to be sane, rather than psychologically unstable?" In questioning the value of her rational faculties—often considered to be the defining aspect of being human—this person makes as much sense to me as if she were asking "Why should I value my right arm?" It is difficult to respond to such questions because the answer seems so obvious: because you should value being as alive and aware as possible.

It is true that any one idea may not be important to your life. Quantum physics may never have any practical application to you personally or hold any interest for you. If so, it is quite reasonable for you to be absolutely indifferent to that whole field of human study. But a person who does not care about ideas at all—about the quality of what her mind consumes and how effectively she processes information—is like a person who does not care about nutrition or whether her body processes food well.

Yet people who are concerned about their physical health, who diet and exercise, will return with the query, "Why should I care about reason?"

The easiest way to answer is to point out that the questioner is already expressing respect for reason. Implicit in the request to produce proof that reason is valuable is a respect for evidence, as well as a willingness to entertain arguments on the subject. The skeptical questioner is like the student in Logic 101 who demands "Prove to me that logic works." Well, by asking for "proof," the person is demanding that you use logic to prove that logic works. Unless she already accepts that logic works, the question itself makes no sense. So, too, the person who asks for reasons to value reason is taking a position that reduces to absurdity. After all, if the person really does not give a damn about the truth, what is there to talk about? Why is she requesting evidence in the first place?

Another way to respond to the question, "Why should I care about reason?" is to observe that the answer lies in the realm of psychology, not within a book on reasoning. A cookbook cannot help a person who doesn't care about eating tasty or nutritious food. An exercise manual is irrelevant to someone who doesn't care about physical fitness. Equally, this book cannot convince you to care about reasoning or to prize the truth.

Too often, people treat such psychological questions as though they were philosophical ones: that is, they answer by trying to demonstrate the benefits of logic or reason to human beings when this is not actually what is in question.

The situation is analogous to one I experienced at a party some years ago. A fellow asked me why he should care that $2 + 2 = 4$. In response,

I took two match sticks and set them beside two that were already in front of me, then I counted out the total to arrive at the sum of four. After watching this process in silence, the skeptic responded, "This is all very well, but I must repeat my question. Why should I care?"

I argued that a respect for the facts of reality would allow him to act in such a manner as to achieve his goals. For example, accepting math would allow him to make correct change the next day. Or to count how many drinks he had had at the party.

"Yes, yes," the fellow answered impatiently. "Of course, I will use math when it is convenient. But, apart from when it is useful, why should I care that it is true?" This question is almost impossible to answer on an intellectual level. To reason with someone who doesn't care about truth is like singing to someone who blocks their ears. The question being asked is one of psychology and emotional motivation.

If the "argument" has deteriorated to this point, unless you are interested in moving the discussion from the realm of reasoning to that of psychology, you should walk away. Once you have demonstrated that a statement is true, your job is done. If someone comes back and asks you why he should be concerned with the facts of reality, then he is demonstrating a problem for a psychologist who is skilled at examining motivation. Do not walk away feeling like a failure because you cannot convince someone to care about the truth.

A chauvinist, for example, may acknowledge (or at least not dispute) the overwhelming evidence that women are intellectually the equals of men. Yet, when you finish your argument, he stands firm in his position: women are suited only to be barefoot and pregnant. You meticulously repeat your argument and ask him to point out the statements with which he disagrees. Waving his hand in blithe dismissal, he replies, "Those facts don't mean anything. I *know* that women are less intelligent than men, and nothing you say could make me believe otherwise."

Again walk away. And, no matter how much you have invested in this exchange, there is no need to feel like a failure when you do. In essence, the man has announced to you that he does not care for the facts of the matter, only for what he wishes to believe. He has been conducting a monologue under the guise of a conversation.

You cannot make someone care about what is true. You can only present the best arguments and evidence possible. Anyone who demands that you make them care about facts and evidence is asking far more than an intellectual exchange can provide. Moreover, they are the ones who are failing to uphold their end of the exchange, not you. Why are they talking, why should you listen, if they place no value on ideas?

A friend once expressed to me what he considered to be the difference between metaphysics (the theory of reality), epistemology (the theory of knowledge), and ethics (the theory of behavior). He expressed it through three questions: What exists? How do I know it? So what? In the final analysis, everyone has to answer "so what" for themselves.

WHAT IS REASON?

> To a rational being,
> to act according to nature and according to reason
> is the same thing.
> >   Marcus Aurelius, *Meditations* 7.11

The first step in answering the question "What is a reasonable woman?" is to ask a more fundamental one: "What is reason and what does being reasonable mean, without having a gender consideration attached to it?"

Reason is nothing more than an approach to knowledge that has been called an "impulse toward truth." For Brand Blanshard, the aim of education "is to produce reasonable minds. And by a reasonable mind I mean one which, in the varied situations of life, adapts its beliefs, attitudes, and actions to the facts of the case" (p. 74). Reasonableness is the intellectual tendency to base your conclusions and actions on evidence.

What else would they be based on, you might well ask. When dealing with ideas, some people seek approval, using only those arguments and reaching only those conclusions they know a particular audience wants to hear. For example, they might limit their political or religious expressions at the office to those with which their employer agrees, whatever their own beliefs. Their behavior might not spring from hypocrisy so much as from fear of being disliked by someone powerful.

Other people refuse to consider seriously any idea that would

threaten other more deeply held beliefs: for example, a white suprema-
cist might refuse to consider evidence that blacks have high IQs. Perhaps she desperately needs to feel self-esteem about something in her
life, and has attached exaggerated importance to her racial background
in order to do so. For her to dispassionately review studies that call her
racial views into question might make her sense of self-worth col-
lapse, and leave her with the realization that her life is a wasteland.

Other people choose to believe whatever constitutes the most popular cultural view because this approach involves the least conflict in
dealing with the world. They would be unquestioning agnostics during
the Age of Enlightenment, Protestants in the Reformation, and Cath-
olics during the Middle Ages. They view the analyzing of ideas as a
dubious luxury that endangers the far higher goal of "getting along."

The thinking of still others is based on expediency. They adopt
whatever view seems to be the most advantageous from moment to
moment. Like the lawyer whose only commitment is to win a case
quite apart from her client's innocence or guilt, such people will try on
arguments, like suits of clothing, with no commitment to underlying
beliefs or the possible consequences for others.

The foregoing are examples of unreasonable ways of approaching
ideas: that is, approaches that place a low priority on evidence stress-
ing instead emotional or strategic advantage. Reason leads you in a
different direction. Being reasonable means examining facts and
"arguments": it means basing your conclusions and actions on what
seems to be true. (By the word "argument" I mean an intellectual
exchange in which beliefs are supported by evidence, not the verbal
slugfests popularly referred to as "arguments.")

But the habit of being reasonable is much more than this, and far
less dry. It involves reveling in the enjoyment and power of your own
mind. It means surrendering to reflectiveness, which Blanshard considers to be a subhabit of reasonableness.

He comments, "Reflectiveness is just an extension of this habit.
The plain man is related to the reflective man as Dr. Watson was to
Sherlock Holmes" (p. 79). Holmes is well known for admonishing the
constantly amazed Watson, "You see but do not observe." Reflectiveness is the act of observing keenly and drawing inferences based on

those observations. To "the plain man," such inferences appear to be magic, but they are actually part of the enjoyment that accompanies reasoning. Where Watson would see a working man walking down the street, "Holmes would see a working man the color of whose hands indicated that he was a tanner of leather and whose cauliflower ear indicated a pugnacity that required strategic treatment" (p. 79).

In just such a manner, reason and reflectiveness can throw open windows of understanding onto the world.

When engaged in intelligent argument, reflectiveness is the abandonment of passivity in listening. Instead of standing in front of the speaker as you would sit in front of a television set, you actively though silently assess the meaning of her words, body language, and vocal intonation. The habit of being reasonable will show through in your willingness to listen to evidence that makes you uncomfortable and to viewpoints you don't share.

I once heard a wonderful analogy that epitomized the habit of reasonableness in approaching discussions and arguments. Imagine that you are the senior member of a team of two surgeons who are operating on a patient to replace a heart valve. As you scrub up for the surgery, an argument—an exchange of dissenting viewpoints—occurs between you and the other surgeon. Instead of operating on the heart valve as you had planned, the other surgeon says, "Look, I think we should make the incision in his stomach instead. I reviewed the x-rays and the test results and . . ." She goes on to argue (politely) that the patient's symptoms are due to a stomach tumor.

In other words, she seriously disputes your diagnosis and provides compelling evidence for her position. As the senior surgeon, the final word is yours. The patient lies unconscious, awaiting your decision.

Some doctors would react from their egos and immediately interpret the dissenting diagnosis as a personal attack. Refusing to consider the offending second opinion, they would insist on proceeding with heart surgery. Other surgeons, unwilling to admit their mistake in the face of compelling evidence, might save face by rescheduling the much-needed surgery for a later date. Then, with the patient absorbing the cost in money and health risk, more tests could be run. They could change their minds in a more graceful manner.

But a reasonable doctor, whose main concern is the health of her patient and with making the best diagnosis possible, would proceed to operate on the stomach if she were convinced that the second opinion was correct. No consideration would be more important to her than the best possible outcome for her patient.

Equally, the first concern of a reasonable person who is enmeshed in argumentation is to get closer to the truth of the issue under discussion. In an intellectual exchange, you and at least one other person are involved in dissecting the facts, theories, experiences, and arguments surrounding an issue. If you care more about what is true than you do about "being right" (even when you are not), you will base your conclusions and your actions on the evidence rather than having them dictated by your ego.

In essence, an intellectual exchange between two people can be viewed as having three participants: the two arguers and the truth— that is, the idea or issue that the two arguers are trying to clarify through discussion. If the other person persuasively counters your argument, you have a choice. You can hold fast to your position in the face of compelling evidence or you can say, "You are right, at least on that point, and I was wrong." If the purpose of the argument was to move closer to the truth—just as the point of surgery is to promote the life of the patient—then you won't have lost anything by making the admission of error. In fact, you would gain because you would move closer to your goal: understanding the issue.

It seems odd that society views whoever makes such an admission to be "the loser" in an argument when, in fact, whoever discovers an error in her beliefs is the one who benefits most. The other person may have gained nothing whatsoever from the discussion.

THE HABIT OF BEING REASONABLE

Virtue consists, not in abstaining from vice, but in not desiring it.
George Bernard Shaw, *Maxims for Revolutionists*

The habit of reasonableness is the ingrained habit of acting according to reason. It means that your disposition, your natural way of behavior, is reasonable: you manifest a basic concern with holding correct beliefs, that is, with holding reasonable beliefs that are based on evidence rather than on emotion, on popularity, or some other factor.

There is one thing that the habit of reasonableness does *not* mean: that you behave in a reasonable manner in all situations. Again, remember the neat neighbor. Perhaps you regularly seek out one of your girlfriends for advice on relationships and career choices because she has a very practical, commonsense approach to both. But this afternoon, when you met her for a complaint-fest about your ex-boyfriend, she responds with a long blast of rage at the man. Nothing you say can stem the flow of hostility. Even the tried-and-true approach of telling her how much you value her advice cannot get her into counseling-mode.

Were you wrong to have considered your friend to be a practical woman who gives good advice? No. Practicality is her general disposition, the tirade was an exception. When you judge a person to be reasonable or not, you are talking about a habit. Your friend is a reasonable woman who, on this one occasion, is acting unreasonably. Perhaps she just had a wretched scene with her own boyfriend. Perhaps when you repeated one of your boyfriend's comments, the phrasing sparked a painful memory within her. Perhaps she had a headache. The outburst was an exception.

In short, reasonableness does not live or die on the basis of an isolated act. It is a pattern of behavior that is acquired through practice and discipline.

Developing the Habit of Being Reasonable

> Habit becomes a sort of second nature, which supplies a motive for many actions.
>
> Cicero, *De Finibus,* 5.25.74

In his book *Talks to Teachers,* William James wrote:
"The hell to be endured hereafter . . . is no worse than the hell we make for ourselves in this world by habitually fashioning our characters in the wrong way. Could the young but realize how soon they will

become mere walking bundles of habits, they would give more heed to their conduct while in the plastic state. We are spinning our own fates, good or evil, and never to be undone. The drunken Rip van Winkle in Jefferson's play excuses himself for every fresh dereliction by saying, 'I won't count this time!' Well, he may not count it, and a kind Heaven may not count it, but it is being counted none the less. Down among his nerve-ends and fibers the molecules are counting it, registering it, and storing it up to be used against him when the next temptation comes" (p. 77).

Although I fully endorse James's recognition of the powerful role habit plays in human behavior, I take a much more optimistic view of changing bad habits even in adulthood. I tend to agree more with Adler's less dramatic and more useful assessment, "To form the habit of being on time for appointment, you have to try to be punctual over and over again. . . . When you have formed a habit and it is well developed, you take pleasure in doing [it] . . . because you do it with ease" (p. 102).

To say something is habitual is very different from saying you have no control over it. It is true that you may not have—or you may feel that you do not have—a great deal of immediate or direct control over a particular habit. After all, it may have taken a long time to develop and it may be reinforced by other behaviors in a manner you are not aware of. But there is no mystery to changing deep-seated habits. Even the strongest conceivable habits, called addictions, yield to sincere and persistent efforts to chip away at their bases.

In working on any sort of long-term problem, the key to grabbing control of it is to exercise as much choice as you have whenever you can. You may not presently have the psychological flexibility to do something that intellectually frightens you. For example, you may be physically unable to make your mouth form the words "I disagree" when speaking to an authority figure. But many aspects of your fear of authority *are* within your control right now. You always have the ability to analyze your behavior in safe privacy. You can close your eyes and imagine what it would feel like to speak out. (Chapter 3 addresses an invaluable technique known as systematic desensitization, which aids in overcoming such fears.) In short, you do have the ability to start working toward changing it, bit by bit. In some sense, the largest step toward forming an intellectual habit is simply deciding that you want to.

Then, exercise as much choice as you can. Life confronts you with innumerable choices every day. There are millions of alternatives offered to you on a platter. Indeed, if you were to lie in bed each morning and contemplate your range of choices, you would never throw back the blankets.

There is only one thing about which you don't have any choice: and that is whether or not you are going to make decisions. Decision making is a part of life. And seemingly mundane choices can have important consequences and implications. For example, the choice to consume food is a decision to keep on living. Even inactivity, such as staying in bed to contemplate your alternatives, is a choice. If you refuse to think about something, your decision will have consequences as dramatic and real as if you acted. The problem won't go away because you ignore it. Thus, the most basic control you have is to make whatever good decisions are under your immediate control so that the range of your control gradually expands.

The question remains: how *specifically* do you acquire the habit of reasonableness? This question assumes two things. First, that you do not presently have this habit; second, that you have other habits which substitute for reasonableness in your intellectual life. Much of the remainder of this volume deals with undoing bad intellectual habits and cultivating good ones in their place.

In other words, it addresses the psychology of reasoning.

EMOTIONS VERSUS MIND

> Great thought, great feelings came to him,
> like instincts, unawares.
>
> R. M. Milnes, *The Men of Old*

The preceding section is *not* meant to argue that psychology and reasoning are entirely separate aspects of human beings, which are at war with each other. This state of affairs may be true within individual human beings, but the ideal and healthy situation is to achieve a harmony between your emotions and your ideas. Such a harmony may well be what is meant by the phrase "peace of mind."

To me, the most interesting aspect of psychology is how the emotions relate to the mind: it is what might be called the psychology of reasoning. For example, whenever an idea sparks anger or fear within you, what exactly is it that happens to your reasoning process, and how can you prevent it from happening again? There is an underlying psychology to reasoning, just as there is underlying logic to psychology. Indeed, it would be amazing if the two aspects of who you are—both a thinking and a feeling human being—did not intimately connect on all levels of your life.

Most books on psychology, however, are not helpful in discovering this relationship. The general approach of modern psychology seems to be profoundly anti-intellectual. People are told to be open, spontaneous, and natural. They are encouraged to accept their emotions and express them in raw, almost unprocessed form. Indeed, the goal of many psychotherapies is nothing more than to expose the "natural" human being, who is an unreflective person.

This advice can be invaluable, if put in its proper place. Your raw emotions are rich sources of information, and it is quite sensible to focus upon and examine one aspect of who you are in order to isolate certain problems. Sometimes the best way to get in touch with a psychological response is to temporarily shut off your critical faculties thus creating an unfiltered emotional outpouring—a stream of consciousness.

But doing so constitutes a therapeutic exercise to be done in a psychologist's office or for a specific psychological purpose. It is not a blueprint for successfully living your everyday life. Yet, too often, the anti-intellectual attitude of modern psychology expands beyond its proper bounds. Emotions and reason are blatantly declared to be antagonistic aspects of who you are. The mind, in and of itself, is said to block the healthy flow of emotions through repression or suppression, and to distort emotions into unhealthy mental states such as paranoia. Much of popular psychology does not seem to recognize the possibility of a healthy partnership between reason and emotion. Instead, reasoning is said to turn off the emotions, like a switch, and make you lose "touch" with yourself.

To stay in touch with your "natural" self, many psychologies encourage you to bypass the clutter and logic of your mind. And, to be honest, a cluttered mind will interfere with your emotional health just as "cluttered emotions" will interfere with the efficient functioning of your mind. Rather than bypass either half of your humanity, it would be best to deal with them as a partnership and to understand how they interact.

Thinkers like Freud have *not* shown us that human beings are unable to balance emotion with reason. They have merely demonstrated that it is difficult to do so. As Blanshard writes: "The explanation is, roughly, that we have very imperfectly emerged from the animal level and that reason is a sort of oil with which we have to control, as best we can, waves of impulse and feeling that come surging from immemorial deeps" (p. 82).

Since human beings acquired the ability to reason—an ability that has been called "the Promethean fire"—they have asked "How does my mind relate to my emotions?"; "Is my animal nature at war with my rational faculties?"; "Where is the balance between intellect and emotion?" There is an intellectual aspect to everything you feel, just as there is an emotional aspect to everything you think.

The Greek philosophers believed that human beings could use reason to nurture and shape their emotions. In searching for the balance between the two, they advanced "classical virtues," like self-discipline, honesty, persistence, and courage. These behaviors were nothing more than good emotional habits, which had become second nature through repetition.

Recently, such behaviors have fallen into disrepute. Classical virtues like reasonableness are commonly denounced as "anal-retentive." That is, intellectual traits are commonly viewed as emotional blocks. Self-restraint is seen to be repression. Discretion is considered to be emotional cowardice. Courage is often viewed as an unwillingness to confront your fear. Self-discipline is used as a synonym for obsessive-compulsiveness. The virtues, or habitual behaviors, that Greek philosophers considered so essential to the harmony of a human being are commonly seen as barriers to psychological health.

Yet, turning away from such habits does not seem to have made the world a healthier, safer, or more fulfilling place in which to live. Perhaps only a harmony between the mind and the emotions can achieve this goal.

"Yes," the response might well be, "but do we not run the risk of having our minds override our emotions?" Quite frankly, few of us are in danger of thinking too much. Most of us think too little and react too automatically from a visceral level. Nothing else can explain the brutally violent, impulse-driven world that surrounds us. Bishop Butler once remarked that the world would be a better place if men remained selfish but at least became reflective about it, rather than remaining stupid and impulsive at the same time. You have far more to fear from your emotions overriding your reason than vice versa.

For me, the key to a healthy balance between reason and emotion is knowing when to give priority to which, and how to make cooperation between the two become a habit.

And the first step in creating a new habit is to clear away the barriers that prevent it from forming.*

SUMMARY

The habit of being reasonable is the automatic tendency to accept beliefs based on evidence and to act according to what you believe is true. It means that reason has become second nature to you.

Psychologists often claim that the intellect can block the flow of

---

*For those who wish to pursue the ideas in this chapter more thoroughly, I recommend the following books in addition to those already cited in the text.

Although it is not written in as accessible a manner as many popular books on psychology, *The Psychology of Self-Esteem: A New Concept of Man's Psychological Nature* by psychologist Nathaniel Branden is actually more in line with the old classical conception of man. Also recommended is the delightful *The Difference of Man, and the Difference It Makes* by philosopher Mortimer Adler, whose *Aristotle for Everybody: Difficult Thought Made Easy* provides a sense of the classical approach to man and reason.

For an entertaining and insightful glimpse into the deep anti-intellectualism of much of modern psychology, Wendy Kaminer's *I'm Dysfunctional, You're Dysfunctional* is highly recommended.

emotion. Certainly the reverse is true: emotions can block the flow of reason. Ideally, there should be a harmony between your reason and your emotions. Just as there is an intellectual aspect to everything you feel, there is an emotional aspect to everything you think, and to the process of thought itself.

Having examined what the habit of being reasonable means and the relationship of emotions to reason, it is time to examine how emotions can act as barriers to forming that habit.

2

Barriers to Being Reasonable

Perseverance is more efficacious than violence; and many things which cannot be overcome when they stand together, yield themselves up when taken little by little.

Sertorius, *Plutarch's Lives*

I was once a committed Freudian. I viewed human beings as collections of instinct, urges, and childhood trauma. I analyzed everything from political beliefs to food preferences in terms of their hidden psychological implications. Sigmund Freud once declared that "sometimes a cigar is just a cigar," but I was a sounder Freudian than he. In my defense, I was also seventeen years old.

Finally, after being psychoanalyzed a bit too often, a friend did me the great favor of intellectually bludgeoning me into a corner where I had to admit that Freudianism was a closed system that could neither be falsified nor verified. (See chapter 11 for a discussion of the importance of falsification.) I walked away from strict Freudianism but I retained my fascination with psychology, especially with how the emotions relate to the mind, and with developing intellectual habits.

Modern psychology offers at least two major ways to view the role of habit in your life. Many "depth" psychologies—like Freudianism—contend that habits result from deep biological conflicts and childhood traumas. Habits are merely the surface manifestation of deep psychological forces. To approach these behavior patterns with any hope of changing them requires in-depth analysis and years of work.

By contrast, behavior modification considers habits to be learned responses. That is, human beings are conditioned by parents, society, and other environmental factors to be as they are: jealous, insecure, ambitious, outgoing, alcoholic, depressive, and so on. The approach to psychology known as behavior modification is based on the idea that, if habits (responses) are learned, then bad habits can be unlearned and desirable ones substituted in their place. Changing behaviors—particularly ones without immense emotional undercurrents—can be a relatively swift and painless process.

But even habits that involve deep-seated emotions can be successfully confronted through commonsense techniques. All human problems—even intellectual ones—have emotional aspects. Although it is important to acknowledge underlying emotions, it is more important to go beyond the emotional analysis. Go beyond your snap-response and assume control of circumstances.

I became optimistic about the possibility of achieving real change when I read Albert Ellis's *Handbook of Rational-Emotive Therapy*. Ellis writes: "Once you accept the fact that external events (including early conditioning) significantly contribute to but do not actually cause your feelings, and that you largely feel the way you think, you enormously increase your power over your own emotions. . . . [Y]ou can appreciably make them subject to your decision processes" (p. 8).

Ellis addresses traditional psychological problems by analyzing the irrational beliefs that spark undesirable emotional reactions. In essence I reverse this process and examine the irrational emotions that feed into undesirable intellectual reactions. Without question, the most common and intellectually destructive emotion is the fear of making an error. Fortunately, this, too, is susceptible to change.

FEAR OF ERROR

> If God should hold enclosed in his right hand all truth, and in his left hand only the ever-active impulse after truth, although with the condition that I must always and forever err, I would with humility turn to his left hand, and say, "Father, give me this . . ."
>
> Gotthold E. Lessing, *Anti-Götze*

In his book *To a Dancing God*, Sam Keen records a conversation he had with his own fear. "I wish I could begin by saying, 'Damn you fear. Leave me alone!' But honesty demands that I address you as 'Dear fear,' for you have been with me most of my life. Now I want to understand why I am attracted to you and did not banish you long ago" (p. 109).

Although our fears may be consciously experienced as burdens, most of us have made arrangements of convenience with them. They have become old friends, like a comfortable pair of slippers. As much as we may complain about the fear, accommodating it is preferable to the confrontation that would be necessary to overcome it. Fear guides our emotions and behavior as much as desire, ambition, or anger. Indeed, fear is so powerful a force within our lives that we sometimes come to an arrangement with the very "fear of fear."

By this I mean, many of us preemptively avoid situations in which the very possibility of feeling anxiety might arise, situations such as disagreeing with an authority figure or speaking out in public. Comedian Jerry Seinfeld once remarked that public speaking was the number-one fear consistently expressed by Americans: their second most frequently expressed fear was death. From this data he concluded that, at a funeral, most people would rather be in the coffin than delivering the eulogy. At the risk of overstretching a joke, many people prefer to exist in an intellectually confined and cramped space rather than to confront their fears.

The most powerful fear that stands as a barrier to thinking clearly is the fear of making a mistake. This is intimately connected to the fear of looking and feeling ridiculous or inadequate, especially in public. People express the fear of making a mistake in different ways. Some become perfectionists, or know-it-alls whose every word assumes the weight of an encyclopedia; others avoid ideas altogether and never express their inner thoughts to anyone. Some people turn intellectually mean and become bullies who delight in ridiculing anyone weaker than themselves; others withdraw into a purely academic realm and divorce their emotions entirely from their ideas, so that their writing is stripped of humor, compassion, and excitement.

Many bad intellectual habits spring up from the simple fear of being wrong. Yet making mistakes is an inevitable and healthy part of learning, and excellence cannot arise without errors. There is no way to learn anything new without being wrong at least as often as you are right. After all, learning itself is a process of moving from ignorance toward knowledge, and it assumes you don't already know what you are doing. To habitually avoid making a mistake—or, more accurately, to avoid the appearance of making a mistake—is to block the learning process altogether.

The best way to overcome a fear is to stand up close and stare it down. Before discussing the fear of error and the invaluable role that errors play in intellectual development, it is important to touch upon one element which is common to all forms of error: namely, frustration. Frustration is a natural emotional reaction to not getting what you want. And error can almost be defined as not achieving what you want. Thus, error and frustration go hand-in-hand.

THE VALUE OF FRUSTRATION

> I count him braver who overcomes his desires than him who conquers his enemies; for the hardest victory is the victory over self.
>
> Aristotle

Many people consider frustration to be incompatible with their view of happiness and psychological well-being. And, certainly, if life is nothing but a series of frustrations, then something is badly askew. But occasional frustration—like occasional error—serves a useful function.

Frustration is the emotional stage that sets in when you have expanded your energy to no avail. In angry despair, you abandon the struggle for a solution; you sit down to watch television or listen to music or read a novel; with your attention directed elsewhere, suddenly a solution occurs to you. Psychologists have speculated that this is one of the healthy functions of frustration. It is as though your mind rebels at being pushed too far and demands a vacation before it will produce again. In pursuing a rich intellectual life, frustration is not only unavoidable, it is also a necessary part of creative thinking. (See chapter 5 for more on the value of frustration.)

If all of your problems arose in convenient logical order like matched socks, life would be much easier. It would also be quite dull. But life doesn't present itself wrapped in a neat ribbon and bow. Sometimes you have to expend a great deal of mental energy to figure out solutions. Frustration is a natural element of the process and part of what spurs us on, just as the surge of satisfaction that results from coming up with an answer is the natural reward of persistence. Perhaps by viewing frustration and error as natural and healthy aspects of reasoning, you will have more motivation to carry on during times when you feel like giving up.

To state the issue of frustration in another way: it is impossible to avoid conflict, in life or in solving problems. Indeed, by having a problem you are already experiencing some form of conflict if only within your own mind: for example, a conflict of desire between two possible ways to spend a limited amount of money. Without a problem to solve, there probably would be no need to think. Unfulfilled goals and striving create an inevitable tension and an imbalance within you. The desire to resolve the imbalance prompts you to think and to act. If you were entirely satisfied you would probably never think or act at all.

Some of the most intellectually productive and original people are those who appear, from time to time, to be utterly dissatisfied. Writers throw uncompleted manuscripts against the wall, scientists become obsessed with running failed experiments again and again, artists rage about the inspiration that just won't come. Examine the lives of the world's geniuses through (auto)biographies, and many of them will seem to be bizarre eccentrics. And the hunger to know or create that drives such people also causes a high level of frustration in their lives. Yet such people accomplish a great deal and often win the applause of society. And the frustration seems to be a normal aspect of their creativity.

It is important, however, to distinguish between two types of frustration. The first is almost an anxiety that is neither good nor healthy. It accomplishes nothing. This is what we might call general or non-specific frustration. It floats around, almost like a background music in your life, but you can't give a name to the source of the tension. You can't name anything specific and say, "This is the cause" of my discomfort. From time to time, this free-floating frustration seems to attach itself to specific problems you are having, perhaps in your marriage or career. But once the specific problem is solved, the disquiet does not dissolve. It remains as an unarticulated undercurrent of your life. This sort of frustration belongs in the category of a psychological problem and it accomplishes nothing positive in your life.

The other kind of frustration—the type that is involved in intellectual pursuits, or in any endeavor with the risk of failure—is a natural and healthy reaction. This sort of psychological discomfort will be a temporary but recurring emotional state within any active, striving, and goal-oriented person. The discomfort comes from the frustration human beings naturally feel when their goals are not satisfied, and they do not know whether they will succeed or fail. Once success is achieved, the frustration disappears and is replaced by a sense of satisfaction. Indeed, the alleviation of disquiet and the warm glow of satisfaction that takes its place may well be the hallmark of healthy rather than destructive frustration.

Thus, frustration is a normal aspect of producing intellectual accomplishments, whether the accomplishment is writing a great novel, working a math equation, or thinking through a psychological problem. Much of your intellectual life will revolve around false-starts and the frustration these "failures" engender, just as much of your romantic life may revolve around relationships that go nowhere. Be easy on yourself when you make an honest mistake, because all the mistake means is that you are a fallible human being. Indeed, because of the mistake you understand more about the problem, and you are making progress toward solving it.

Try to view the process of acquiring information or learning to argue as you would the process of learning to play a musical instrument, or becoming proficient in a new language. Playing a sonata perfectly the first time or speaking German fluently in two days are results you would never demand from yourself. Yet many people refuse to learn because they know the process would involve errors. This reluctance seems to grow stronger as we grow older. A child has no difficulty in accepting that she cannot just sit down at a piano and play the instrument well. Instead of dwelling on errors, she is delighted with almost any sound that emerges and pounds away with pleasure until someone shouts for the cacophony to stop. Over and over, a child will practice the scales and not be discouraged by how often the notes come out wrong.

But the adult woman expects more of herself. She is often so intolerant of her own mistakes that she won't even try to learn a new musical instrument. And if she is willing to put in the practice that learning requires, she does so in private as though ashamed of the process.

In his book *How to Read a Book*, Mortimer Adler discusses the habit of reading and how many adults resist acquiring it out of sheer embarrassment. He likens the process to learning to ski past childhood. "After all, an adult has been walking for a long time; he knows where his feet are; he knows how to put one foot in front of the other in order to get somewhere. But as soon as he puts skis on his feet, it is as though he had to learn to walk all over again" (p. 54). As Adler correctly concludes, the person feels like an absolute fool.

The fear of intellectual embarrassment and unwillingness to accept frustration is at the root of much hesitation and many lost opportunities. Many people cannot tolerate their own mistakes, even privately behind closed doors. Yet mistakes are an integral, inescapable part of the learning process, and excellence cannot come without error paving the road. To habitually avoid making a mistake—or, more accurately, to avoid the appearance of having made a mistake—is to block the learning process altogether.

Reconsider the role of frustration in your life.

A NEW VIEW OF ERROR

It is an established maxim and moral that he who makes an assertion without knowing whether it is true or false is guilty of falsehood, and the accidental truth of the assertion does not justify or excuse him.

Abraham Lincoln

So . . . let's take a long realistic look at error.

Many of the most common intellectual mistakes you will make fall into two categories: errors of fact; and, errors of circumstance.

Errors of Fact

The first and simplest type of error involves getting the facts wrong. For example, the error of claiming $2 + 2 = 3$. Or of claiming that Charles Dickens wrote *Moby Dick*. Errors of this kind don't mean a great deal in and of themselves. At most, if they occur frequently they may be telling you to do a bit more research before jumping into a discussion, or that you need to be more careful before you speak. Such errors are easy to correct and easy to avoid.

More importantly, this sort of mistake has little lasting psychological consequence. That is, the consequences are minimal as long as you are willing to correct the error when it occurs and not defend it simply because you are not willing to "give in" and admit a mistake. Your response to someone who politely corrects you should be a simple "thank you."

Errors of Circumstances

Errors of circumstance are ones which occur largely due to the context of your knowledge or some other aspect of the situation in which you find yourself. For example, if you had been taught in school that $2 + 2 = 3$ or that Charles Dickens did write *Moby Dick*, then your statements would not only be errors of fact, but also errors of circumstance. That is, you had every reason to believe what you said was accurate, but something outside of your reasonable control rendered it inaccurate.

Errors of circumstance are those reasonable errors that only become apparent in retrospect. When I look back, the years sometimes seem to consist of an almost uninterrupted stream of errors—much like most people's lives probably seem to them. But calling something an error is often a judgment I can make only *now*, in retrospect with the keen benefit of hindsight. At the time I acted, I wasn't consciously making a mistake: I was taking what I believed to be the appropriate action under the circumstances. Certainly, some of the mistakes came from sloppy thinking or from just not caring enough to think something through. Most of the time, however, I was doing the best I could and the mistakes I made were reasonable ones.

A reasonable error is one that occurs when the actions you took were based on the knowledge you had at a particular moment, and on the choices that were available to you at that time. In other words, you acted in a reasonable manner and the mistake was not your fault.

Sometimes the error may have resulted from important information you did not have and could not have been expected to possess. For example, perhaps you go comparison shopping for a new VCR, after having purchased the latest consumer guide and asking pointed questions of various sales clerks. You settle on brand X, with which you have had luck in the form of an old TV that has lasted forever without repairs. The very next issue of the consumer guide has on its cover a warning against precisely the machine you purchased. If you had had the extra information, you would never have purchased that particular machine. The purchase was a mistake, but buying the VCR was a reasonable and reasoned act on your part.

On other occasions, you may have all the solid information you need about a situation, then the situation changes. For example, you might purchase a new house at a great price and an attractive mortgage rate only to learn the next month that your company has suddenly been acquired and your job has been downsized out of existence. In retrospect, the purchase may be viewed as a wretched mistake, but you acted appropriately. You cannot base your actions on unexpected events: you need to base them on what is real at the time, and what you realistically expect to happen in the future.

Another form of reasonable error occurs when you take a step you know is a bad one to make but which, nevertheless, is the very best choice available to you at that moment. For example, you are unemployed and the rent is due. Out of desperation, you sign a six-month contract to work at minimal wages at a job you hate. As you sign the contract, you repeat to yourself, "This is a mistake, this is a mistake." In the grand scheme of a universe replete with possibilities, maybe it is a mistake, but within the confines of your severely limited options —options that run from bad to worse—the contract may well be the least bad step you can take. Even if well-paying enjoyable work materializes the next day, signing the contract was an appropriate act.

All of the above are reasonable mistakes that occur due to problems with circumstance. In short, they are not your fault, but the result of your context. In the cases where your frame of knowledge or the situation changed, you should be tolerant of committing such errors. After all, you are not a god who can rely on omniscience to sort through the possibilities. You don't have a crystal ball or a magic mirror to warn you about changing circumstances. After examining the possibilities in a reasonable manner, you did the best you could . . . so give yourself a break.

And, when dealing with errors of circumstance, don't listen to other people who will always be there to criticize and tell you where you went wrong. Friends and family—who have the distinct advantage of standing outside of a situation—often think they know precisely what it is you have done or are doing wrong. They heap unsolicited advice and criticism on you. With all good intention, these people might say, "I know you'd be happier if you'd only do X" . . . get married, have children, go back to school, lose ten pounds, move back home, dump the current boyfriend . . . the list of errors you are making scrolls on. Sometimes the advice is good, as are the intentions.

But it is always important to stop the person who is offering advice and ask her, "How do you know that?" What makes her so sure that the particular action she is recommending is the best one for you to take, given your unique context? Consider what might seem to be an unassailable piece of advice: lose weight and you'll feel better. How does the other person know that? Perhaps you are in the middle of a work panic, and food is the only way you relax or reward yourself. Absorbing the extra pressure of dieting might be disastrous for you.

It is easy to give advice, and we all have a natural tendency to listen to those who sincerely want good things for us. But ask yourself: Do they know you so intimately that they can see your heart's desire? How do they know what it is you want out of the situation they are analyzing? Are they familiar with the actions you have already taken and found to be unsatisfactory? What about their state-of-knowledge on this matter: do they know more or less of the details surrounding the choice than you do? For example, do they know the limitations that constrain you at this moment, including money, time, energy, and emotional flexibility? On what scale of wisdom have they weighed your actions and found your decision wanting?

In short, have they considered your circumstances?

I am not trying to minimize the role that friends and family can play in providing you with valuable perspective. On occasion, this assistance is exactly what you need. But don't automatically accept their evaluations of your "error," especially when the evaluations feel wrong or conflict with your own instincts.

My point is this: there are obvious errors. The equation $2 + 2 = 4$ is a factual matter, and if you maintain that $2 + 2 =$ something other than 4, then you have fallen into an obvious error. Friends, or the world at large, are quite right to correct you and to expect you to accept their statement of the mathematical fact.

But personal matters—personal errors—always have a much more complicated context than factual ones, and whether or not any particular action on your part is or was an error may be so subtle a matter that only you can judge the truth of it. No personal decision is absolutely right or absolutely wrong in the same manner that $2 + 2 = 4$ is true or false. Indeed, you can't even evaluate whether any personal decision is an error without knowing the context in which it was made.

What was the person's goal in taking the action? Even actions that appear to be clearly wrong cannot be evaluated outside their own context. For example, throwing a temper tantrum during a business meeting might seem to be a hideous mistake, especially when it leads to the person being dismissed. But if her goal was to get fired and so be eligible to collect unemployment insurance, then the temper tantrum was a successful strategy.

Consider a personal example. Many well-intentioned people have commented sympathetically on my lack of formal education. It is a condition I could easily change by enrolling at a university, and friends sometimes urge me to do so. But a university diploma holds no appeal for me. Quite the contrary. I sincerely believe that whatever originality I may be capable of would be severely damaged by going through a system that seems to process minds like a grinder processes meat. My conviction has only grown stronger as I have watched my husband endure grad school over the past few years. Given my goals, avoiding a formal education ceases to be a mistake.

The goal of a behavior is only one factor in evaluating whether or not a particular act is/was an error. Another factor is the extent of your knowledge when you acted. Sometimes you have to make a snap decision without the luxury of seeking out and examining the facts or possible alternatives. On other occasions, you may have spent a reasonable amount of time analyzing the situation, but some of your information was wrong or otherwise inadequate. Or the situation shifted.

(Note: I am not saying that circumstances will make a mistake less disastrous. But circumstances may well determine whether it was reasonable or unreasonable for you to hold a certain belief or take a particular action. Certainly, circumstances should effect how tolerant you are of your own mistakes.)

Another crucial factor in evaluating your "errors" is the range of actions available to you. If you are riding your bicycle down the street and the only way to avoid an oncoming car is to take a tumble in the other direction into the cement sidewalk, then crashing your bike is the proper action to take. Even if you hurt yourself by doing so.

In short, you cannot talk about whether a choice is right or wrong without knowing the context in which it is being made. You cannot judge a choice without first knowing the goal the person is trying to reach. In looking back at your errors, it is useful to ask yourself the following questions:

- Did I give the problem serious consideration?
- Given my limitations—e.g., time, money, etc.—what other choices could I have made? Was my choice the best one available?
- What precisely was my goal in acting? State the goal as clearly and explicitly as possible.
- Is the problem one that can be solved? Or are my expectations unrealistic?
- Did I err because of a lack of knowledge, a lack of planning, or some other factor?
- What information am I not in possession of? What might make me act differently?
- Did the error have any benefits? For example, did I learn something? Did I take another, better course of action as a result of what I learned from the first one?

Try to understand why the error happened.

Then, give yourself a break. We all hold ourselves up to a standard of perfection when, in reality, the only sane standard is "What alternatives were available to you at that time?" Moreover, errors of circumstance can be extremely productive.

Consider two examples:

You approach a problem, fully aware of what you want from the resolution and with what seems like a reasonable amount of information about the situation. Later you discover that further information existed that you could not have reasonably been expected to know. If you had known of it, you would have changed your course of action. In other words, your decision did not have enough information behind it to take you where you wanted to go. But the error arose through no fault of your own.

Consider another situation.

You have investigated a problem that has many possible solutions. Several of these solutions appeal to you, for whatever reason. You act on the one that is easiest to implement, and it doesn't work out. Your error, or failure, resulted from the fact that human beings are fallible, and don't always choose the right course of action the first time. You now know that you should pursue another course.

Both of the above errors are useful, because neither one of them indicates that you have done anything wrong. Indeed, they indicate progress. In the first example, you discovered important information about your problem which allows you to make a more informed decision the next time around. In the second case, you eliminated a likely course of action which provides you with the time to pursue another path, one that may have a greater chance of succeeding. In each case, you are closer to your goals than you were before you made the "mistakes."

All of us make useful errors every day. For example, every time you date a man who is wrong for you, you move one step closer to knowing the type of man who might be right for your life. But there is a catch. You will move closer to your goals in life if and *only if* you are able to let yourself off the hook for having made a mistake in the first place. If you constantly berate yourself for being wrong about something—however reasonable the error might have been—then you will be unable to learn from the error and use it as valuable information for the future.

Most of the psychology involved in errors of circumstance has to do with acquiring the intellectual confidence and emotional flexibility to benefit from reasonable errors.

ERRORS OF HABIT OR APPROACH

> Truth, crushed to earth, shall rise again;
> Th' eternal years of god are hers;
> But Error, wounded, writhes in pain,
> And dies among his worshipers.
> William Cullen Bryant, *The Battlefield,* st. 9

There is a third type of mistake that is far more significant than the preceding two. It involves how you customarily approach ideas, and it could be called an error of habit. Errors of habit do not pertain to specific mistakes, but to procedural mistakes when dealing with the intellectual realm. They are methodological errors that usually result from a sense of inadequacy or fears of appearing stupid or weak. Unfortunately, through repetition, these procedural errors become the ingrained habits which define our relationship to ideas.

Many people have habitual and unproductive ways of approaching ideas that almost doom their intellectual attempts to failure. For example, in discussing a sensitive issue, you might be unable to deal with the anger it evokes in you, even if the discussion is a friendly one. This tendency to "lead with your emotions," so to speak, during intellectual exchanges is an error of habit. It is an error of approach.

An example of such an error of approach is to be less than honest with yourself about how you feel or what you think. Perhaps, in the heat of argument, you've made a statement that you know cannot be justified. Yet you stand stubbornly behind it and refuse to budge, because you have a policy of never backing down even when you are clearly wrong. Or you have developed the habit of going blank during arguments, so that you never have anything to say even on subjects with which you are quite familiar. Or, perhaps, whenever you feel threatened, you attack the other person on a personal level rather than dealing with the substance of her statements and arguments. Or you become flustered because you are afraid the other person will not like you if you express disagreement.

Errors of fact are usually trivial matters that require nothing so much as more research. Errors of circumstance are often errors only upon reflection and can provide valuable information. But errors of habit are purely and simply self-destructive ways of dealing with ideas.

Such errors of approach are destructive because they teach you nothing, and they form barriers against forming the habit of reasonableness. It takes more than an act of will to overcome such errors. It takes concerted, sincere effort. In the end, it takes the development of new and better habits which can take their place. The next few chapters deal directly with how to go through this process.

A Cautionary Tale

I am currently dealing with a dramatic example of how destructive habitual errors of approach can be. I am editing a collection of autobiographical essays entitled *Dancing on the Cliff* which were written by a good friend. John Dentinger died of AIDS at the age of thirty-nine. He was one of the best writers I have ever encountered, but he was encumbered by what should have been an incalculable advantage: John was one of those people to whom the best things in life flowed easily. I would work for days to produce an op-ed piece that was graceful and tight. John could achieve the same result in hours.

In going through the stacks of papers and disc-boxes full of computer files he left behind, I found an essay entitled "Lord Acton's Dictum." In its original form, this familiar political dictum is: power corrupts, absolute power corrupts absolutely. The essay was John's adaptation of this dictum and an analysis of his own intellectual downfall, his intellectual Achilles' heel.

John began the essay by explaining: it is not only political power that can corrupt, but *all* forms of power whether in the form of extreme physical beauty, intellectual genius, or personal charisma. John had the mixed blessing of possessing a generous portion of all three. He wrote: "The point is: all these attributes represented a kind of power. And that power corrupted me. A few hours a week allowed me to produce prodigies of political writing and scientific consulting that others couldn't produce in a month. For years I fooled people into thinking I was doing my best, although I knew better."

John skated on the surface of what he could have produced, and developed such bad work habits that his writing was confined almost entirely to bursts that resulted in articles. Not in the book he truly wanted to write, but which would have required sustained effort. By the time John started to mend his ways, he had full-blown AIDS and he was finding it difficult to climb the single flight of stairs from his bedroom to his study. Nevertheless, he attempted to achieve the one goal that meant everything to him: to leave behind a book. Even in the hospital, with IVs and powerful painkillers hindering him, a laptop computer was constantly propped up so that he could squeeze out a few more paragraphs.

John died abruptly, and did not complete his book.

Among the last words John wrote were:

"I managed to prove . . . that I was able to do absolutely anything, including getting out of work. . . . And you know, for years, I somehow figured this proved I was smart.

"So now I've become smart or lucky enough to be unable to do anything but write. I face no choice but to make a success of it or die and be forgotten like last year's used-book drive. Or tomorrow's fishwrap."

Few of us face such a dramatic and pressing need to change our approach to ideas. But all of us should worry about it. All of us can learn from what John called his "cautionary tale."

In psychology, there is a saying: "Pain lets you know you're alive." The same thing is true of error: the discomfort caused by acknowledging and tackling your mistakes allows you to know that your mind is alive and that you are intellectually out there trying. A person who never makes mistakes is not a cautious thinker; he is probably not thinking at all. Just as the person who never feels pain is probably dead.

SUMMARY

The fear of error is a common and very intellectually destructive emotion. That is, the fear of looking and feeling ridiculous or stupid. Yet error is an inevitable and generally healthy aspect of pursuing ideas. Even the frustration of failure is a natural component of—and often a prelude to—intellectual achievement.

By examining the benign role that errors of fact and errors of circumstance play in your intellectual life, this emotional barrier to reasoning is lowered. By understanding the disastrous impact of errors of habit, you begin to identify how you are sabotaging your intellect. An error of habit is a habitually mistaken approach to ideas that usually results from a sense of inadequacy, or of fear.

Fortunately, there are practical and immediate steps you can take to unblock the power of reasoning.

3

Overcoming Bad Habits

Lord! how they chided with themselves,
That they had let him in;
To see him grow so monstrous now,
That came so small and thin.
Thomas Hood, *The Wee Man*

Habits are powerful tools, for good or bad. And they rule more of our lives than most of us are comfortable admitting. Mental habits are like physical reflexes. Just as a doctor can "make" your knee jerk by tapping on the proper nerve, it seems that other people can "make" you furious or intimidated or excited by tapping on the proper ideas. Yet intellectual reactions are neither automatic nor reflexive. They are learned behaviors that can be unlearned.

If you don't have the habit of being reasonable, you probably have intellectual habits that are substituting for it. Chances are they are bad habits, and until you eliminate them they will block the formation of good intellectual habits. Perhaps you get defensive when someone questions anything you say. Or, maybe a low sense of self-esteem makes you unwilling to say anything at all. The first step in ridding yourself of such negative habits is to identify them.

HABITS AND PSYCHOLOGY

> For the ordinary business of life, an ounce of habit is worth a
> pound of intellect.
>   Thomas B. Reed (from W. A. Robinson, *Life*)

There is no mystery to breaking habits—only hard work. Most bad habits have been cultivated over a number of years and you can't expect to change them in a matter of weeks or even months. But there is no need to get discouraged. Some habits will change easily, especially the ones without deep emotional roots.

Some bad intellectual habits may come from nothing more than mimicking the behavior of your family or social circle. If you don't know how to hold a civilized discussion about ideas, it may be because you never heard such a discussion take place between your parents while you were growing up. Acquiring this skill may be nothing more than a straightforward matter of exposing yourself to a more intellectual environment and mimicking the behavior you see there. Cue into the minutiae: How do intelligent people phrase questions? What is the length of their pauses? How do they express themselves physically and in the intonation of their words? Constructing arguments may be nothing more than a learning process—pure and simple —with little emotional content.

At other times, habits seem to be accompanied by deep emotional problems—yet they can be dealt with in isolation, without making the habits an integral part of a larger picture. If people can stop smoking— perhaps the most addictive habit I know of—they can deal with bad intellectual habits. For example, even if speaking in a low voice is a symptom of a deep-seated fear of authority, you can work on speaking more audibly without first resolving the psychological problems.

For example, a few years ago a close friend went through a painful breakup with a long-term lover. During this period, she developed some strange and destructive habits. One of the worst was a consuming doubt about whether or not she had locked her front door. All of us have this concern from time to time, but her doubts defied all reason. She became chronically late for work because she would turn around in traffic in order to go back and check the locks. This happened day after day, and it started causing real tension at work.

A Freudian would have explained to her that houses—at least, in dreams—symbolize one's life. The break-up made her feel that the structure of her life was under attack. In turn, this made her panic. And the panic was being translated into the nagging fear that her house (her life) was not safe: it needed to be secured.

Would such an analysis have done her any good?

Instead of a Freudian approach, I used behavior modification. I assumed her habit was a temporary reaction to a distressing situation. Once the crisis was over, I assumed it would go away as mysteriously as it had developed. The important thing was to minimize the damage it was inflicting. I made a suggestion: when she locked the front door, while the key was still in the lock, she should mark the back of her hand with a felt-tip pen. "X" would mark the spot. That way, when she was behind the wheel of her car and starting to be overwhelmed by doubts about whether she had locked the door, she could look down at her hand. The black mark would provide real-world verification that the door was locked. Whatever her doubts were screaming out, the X would let her know the truth of the matter. It was a small stop-gap solution, but it worked. And the behavior disappeared after about six weeks.

Not all habits have deep emotional roots. But some *do*. Take, for example, a woman who is too intimidated to ask questions at a lecture or other public gathering. This usually comes from deep insecurities and an abiding fear of appearing stupid. This sort of fear does not develop overnight. It comes from a lifetime of being made to feel inadequate, of being made to feel stupid.

This chapter, as well as the next two, are directly aimed at breaking such bad habits.

BREAKING A BAD INTELLECTUAL HABIT

> Plato did once chide a child for playing with nuts, who answered him, "Thou chidest me for a small matter."
> "Habit" (replied Plato) "is no small matter."
>
> Montaigne, *Essays* 1.22

Where do we start in breaking bad intellectual habits?

As simplistic as it may sound, the first step is to discover what your bad habits are. Some of them will be obvious to you: the stab of fear you feel at raising your hand in class or making a suggestion to your boss will be a sure giveaway. But some bad habits are far more subtle. For example, you did not receive a promotion because you failed a qualifying exam. You conclude, "I will never move ahead in this corporation. I just don't have what it takes." This conclusion is not absurd: it is simply not justified by the facts and, so, is unrealistic.

If you reach this sort of conclusion over and over again—if you take every small failure at work as an indication that your career is doomed—then you have formed a bad habit which may be difficult to detect. For one thing, it is based on *some* evidence. You *are* failing.

In *Handbook of Rational-Emotive Therapy*, Albert Ellis provides four useful guidelines for detecting irrational beliefs which can be adapted to detect bad intellectual habits. All of them involve experiencing extreme emotional reactions to relatively innocuous events. Such reactions are a litmus test for where bad habits are lurking.

1. "Look for awfulizing." What intellectual behaviors on your part or responses from others cause what seems like an exaggerated backlash of fear or otherwise painful emotions? If you brood for days about a small matter, such as a cutting remark from a co-worker, your inflated response probably indicates a fruitful area to explore.

2. "Look for something you can't stand." What sorts of intellectual actions or interactions do you systematically avoid, not because they bore you, but because you cannot stand to experience them? If you never, ever speak out at a public event because saying so much as "Can you repeat that?" terrifies you, try to verbalize exactly what is happening.

3. "Look for your damning of yourself or others." Do you feel the

urge to blame someone endlessly—even yourself—for an intellectual trait or situation? For example, do you constantly blame your failings on a poor education, or on your boss's attitude toward you?

4. "Look for your *must*urbating." By musturbating (an unfortunate term), Ellis refers to the statements/commands you make to yourself that contain strong emotional "musts" and "shoulds." If it is absolutely imperative to you to perform some minor intellectual task, such as reading a book from cover to cover, you probably have a deep emotional investment in the task that may be telling you something.

OUT WITH THE OLD . . .

A nail is driven out by another nail, habit is overcome by habit.

Erasmus, *Diluculum*

Once you get a sense of what your bad intellectual habits might be—or, at least, what one of them is—try to understand how it is functioning in your life. Ask yourself:

1. What am I doing to sabotage my reasoning?

For example, if you freeze mentally whenever you are confronted by a certain sort of problem—a math problem, or one requiring you to question an authority figure—you should ask yourself "What *specifically* am I doing?" Do you let your mind wander? Do you become dazed? Do you begin to giggle? Do you change the subject? Don't try to change anything yet. Just get a sense of the specific behavior that keeps you from focusing on the problem, or the conversation.

2. What purpose is my behavior serving?

For example, if you fall asleep whenever you have to read a book for school, ask yourself "Why am I doing this?" What are you getting out of your behavior? What are you avoiding? One possible benefit, for example, is not having to confront the fact that the material confuses you. It may be easier to simply consider it too boring.

3. Reflect on the history of the problem.

When did you start having this problem? How long has it gone on? Try to get some perspective on where it comes from.

One of my worst intellectual habits comes from insecurity. Whenever I think something is true, I rush to find quotes from prominent thinkers who agree with me on the issue. Then I heavily salt any writing I do on the subject with these supporting quotes. In conversation, instead of just stating my position and my reasons for believing it's true, I trot out the fact that Thomas Jefferson or Noam Chomsky or Margaret Atwood agrees with my conclusions.

This is a bad habit for a number of reasons. It allows me to avoid taking the intellectual risks that would help to overcome my underlying insecurities. Until I stand for what I believe—all by myself—I will never be intellectually independent. Moreover, relying on authority figures rather than on my own conclusion is what a Logic 101 professor might call a "fallacy"—that is, an error of logic, an error of approach. It is the fallacy of appealing to authority.

It is also poor intellectual etiquette. By bombarding other people with quotations, I make them argue, not only against me but also against Jefferson, Chomsky, and Atwood. My presentation may come from insecurity, but it is, nonetheless, a form of intimidation when directed at other people. It is not fair play.

Bad intellectual habits are strong barriers to reasonableness. The habits may feel like part of who you are, like an arm or a leg, because they are automatic responses that have become second nature. But just as you developed them somewhere along the line you can dispose of them right now and develop new ones.

SYSTEMATIC DESENSITIZING

Having identified at least one bad intellectual habit on which you'd like to work, the most practical method I have found to alter even deeply ingrained habits was developed by a psychiatrist named Dr. Joseph Wolpe who called his technique "systematic desensitization." This standard technique of behavior modification is based on the theory that many, if not most, of the anxieties you experience are "conditioned responses." According to this theory, things that often occur together in your experience become associated with each other in your mind. As those things recur, you tend to react to them in a manner conditioned, or learned, from your past reactions.

For example, if you were always ridiculed for asking questions as a child, you will associate the act of raising your hand and asking a question in class with a feeling of fear or intimidation. You may avoid asking questions of anyone and not even realize you are doing so. Your avoidance may not be in response to any current or real ridicule you encounter, but an automatic and conditioned response rooted in your childhood.

Systematic desensitization aims at "unconditioning" your behavior in four basic steps. The first step involves a stack of index cards and a pencil. Choose a specific anxiety-producing experience. Let's consider the most common intellectual fear—speaking in public. On each card, write down various situations in which you might find yourself at a podium. The cards might read:

- to give a toast at my niece's upcoming wedding, where there will be only family and friends;
- to deliver a successful quarterly status report in front of co-workers at the office;
- to deliver an abysmal quarterly status report in front of co-workers at the office;
- to deliver an abysmal quarterly status report in front of my employer at the office;
- to give a brief talk to a room full of strangers who are reacting with interest and approval;
- to give a brief talk to a room full of strangers who heckle me;
- to give a toast in front of strangers;
- to give a toast in front of strangers who are ignoring me;
- to deliver a eulogy at the funeral of someone I care for deeply;
- to stand and answer my boss's questions after my status report— that is, to think on my feet without notes.

Sort the cards so that the least anxiety-provoking one is at the top of the stack and the most anxiety-producing one is at the bottom. Then proceed to the next step . . . learning how to relax. Rather than dwell upon standard relaxation techniques, almost all of which involve consciously relaxing various parts of your body in turn, let me recommend C. Eugene Walker's *Learn to Relax: 13 Ways to Reduce Tension.* Or browse a good bookstore for the many similar books and cassettes that teach this rather simple skill.

Usually, the book or tape will teach a traditional relaxation technique that begins with you sitting in a comfortable chair, or reclining on a comfortable bed. Then, you focus on relaxing every part of your body in sequence. Tell yourself: "The muscles of my scalp and forehead are beginning to feel relaxed and peaceful." Repeat the sentence to yourself, all the while imagining the tension falling from your muscles like drops of water rolling off your skin. If you experience difficulty in relaxing, begin by tensing your scalp and forehead as tightly as you can. Then consciously release the tension while repeating the sentence. Follow this procedure to relax your face, your jaw, your neck . . . and so forth all the way down your body until you are as limp as possible from head to toe.

Remember the feeling. It is one you will want to be able to invoke at will. Again, the best method to achieve this feeling is through a good book or a cassette tape on relaxation.

After a few days, when you have trained yourself to relax, take the first card—the least anxiety-provoking situation—off the stack and read it aloud. Let us say, for example, you chose "To propose a toast at my niece's upcoming wedding, where there will be only family and friends." Close your eyes and envision this scene in as much detail as you can. What are you wearing? Who is sitting where? What's the noise level of the room? . . . Imagine standing at the podium, clinking a knife against the wineglass to catch the crowd's attention. Continue until you feel a pang of anxiety. Then stop immediately.

The goal is not to push your limits or to prove anything. It is to reverse a conditioned response, and frightening yourself only reinforces the conditioning. When you are completely relaxed, go back to the first card and envision it once more up to the point of discomfort. You might go straight through the bridal toast the second time around, or it might take you twenty tries before you are ready for the second card. But don't push yourself beyond fifteen minutes to a half-hour for each session. (Note: if you are anxiety-ridden from the instant you read the card, then you are starting with too difficult a scene. You need to begin with only a mildly frightening scenario.)

When you have worked your way through the stack of cards so that the anxiety they once produced has been severely muted, go through them again with a different purpose in mind. Ask yourself, "How do I want to act?" Hold up the first card and envision the toast you would want to make, the sort of toast you admire when others make them. Perhaps it will include an affectionate joke, or an expression of genuine love for your niece. Each time you feel anxiety stir, stop immediately and relax.

Then, make a real effort to deliver precisely *that* toast at the upcoming wedding.

BRAINSTORMING

> We may take Fancy for a companion, but must follow Reason
> as our guide.
>
> Samuel Johnson, *Letter to Boswell*

Besides conquering anxiety, one of the most commonly reported stumbling blocks to systematic desensitization is the person's inability to come up with scenes to list on index cards, or her inability to envision them in the required detail. Often, this inability is not due to emotional blocks, but to mental ones.

Brainstorming is a commonly used technique in both psychology and creative thinking to overcome such a block. Brainstorming consists simply of this: when considering a problem or trying to envision a situation, you should write down every thought that occurs to you about it, without censoring anything. Write *all* your ideas down, no matter how wild they seem. Instead of racking your mind to be brilliant or correct, try only for speed in writing.

Walker presents several rules governing this process, including the all-important "Free-wheeling is encouraged" (p. 68). In short, be as freewheeling and noncritical with your ideas as possible. If you are evaluating what you write down as you write it, you are absolutely defeating the exercise. The most basic rule of brainstorming is: no evaluation, the wilder the idea or its expression the better. It is easy to tame down, to edit your ideas when you go through them later on; it is much more difficult to come up with them in the first place. Remember, criticizing yourself intellectually is not a problem—it is your area of expertise. Allowing yourself to play with ideas, like a child playing with crayons on a blank wall, is far more difficult and an artform that most of us have lost.

State the intellectual goal "I want to be more self-confident" and—later on—its inverse "I appear insecure because . . ." Then, turn off your critical faculties. Do not analyze. Do not think things out. In brainstorming, there are no right or wrong responses. There are only approaches that will or will not work. And you can sort which is which later on. As another of Walker's rules espouses, "Quantity is what is wanted" (p. 68). Quantity, not quality, is the goal of brainstorming.

With these two rules in mind, try a simple exercise. Write down a general statement at the top of a fresh sheet of paper. Put your mind into gear and jot down whatever comes to you as you look at the two statements, no matter how strange or unrelated the thought may seem. Censor nothing. Write the same sentence over and over again if you need to. But keep writing.

Under the general statement "I do not appear self-confident because . . . ," you might write "because I eat chocolate. I am fat. The sky is falling. Mother hasn't called. I whisper, not talk. I forgot to pick up the dry cleaning. Arguing confuses me. Hostility frightens me. Green is my favorite color." Whatever comes into your mind when you look at the general statement is the proper response. Later on, you can sift through the mass of information that your subconscious has dumped onto the sheets of paper and permit yourself to wonder "Why on earth did *this* occur to me?" In some sense, the very purpose of the exercise is to give you material about which to wonder at a later date.

Try a variant on the above exercise. Write down the general statement "I do not appear self-confident because . . ." at the top of a blank sheet, then write the worst possible conclusion you can reach at the bottom of the sheet. For example, "I do not appear self-confident because . . . I am stupid and a coward and no one likes me." Between those two statements, write down everything that occurs to you and compare the results to the first brainstorming session that included only a header.

The beauty of brainstorming is that there is no way you can fail at it. The statements you write down are stupid? Great. The sentences make no sense? Wonderful. Creativity-in-the-raw often looks like non-sense. Are you doing it right? Since there is virtually no standard of "wrong" (other than asking that question in the first place), the answer is yes: everything you put down on paper is right. If you want to try for excellence in anything, try to write ideas down as fast as you can.

Brainstorming is a technique that is sometimes suggested to writers who are trying to overcome a block, which simply means their minds refuse to deal with their writing. Trying to force your mind to think is like pressing down on a coiled spring: the more you press it, the stronger its force becomes. In a sense, your mind is doing the same thing regarding some aspect of intellectualizing. It is refusing to deal with ideas. Brainstorming provides a detour around your intellectual defenses, those bad habits you've set up over the years.

By not censoring yourself, you end up with an accurate picture of what your thought processes are when you approach an intellectual problem. You glimpse the psychology underlying your thinking. Strengths and weaknesses will be highlighted. In other words, you'll gain perspective.

Evaluation, like spontaneity, has its time and place. After you have filled up as many pages as you can by brainstorming, then, and only then, click on your critical faculties. These sheets of paper represent your stream of consciousness regarding the general statement at the top of the paper. Be critical of the flow, but do so in a manner that is sympathetic and constructive to yourself. What do the pages tell you? What are you trying to tell yourself?

Don't pass judgment. Learn instead.

Fortunately, there are rules to guide the learning process of brain-storming as well. One of them is that you should give priority to insights about which you can do something easily, over which you have great control.

For example, in considering the material you've written under the heading "I do not appear self-confident because . . . ," you may come across the two statements "because my mother ridiculed everything I ever said" and "because I dress so shabbily." Both statements may be true. Of the statements, the insight about your mother's sabotage might be the most significant and the one upon which to focus in the long-term. In the short-term, however, you should focus upon the information you can actually and immediately use to advantage in your life. Do what is easy first.

Also consider the plausibility of accomplishing certain goals. There is no question that you can go out and buy yourself a new dress. There may be considerable question about whether you will ever get your mother to acknowledge her role in crippling your self-confidence. Do what is plausible first.

Another rule of thumb is to give priority to information that does not lead you to take irreversible actions. Consider the above two statements about your self-confidence. If you decide to go out and buy a new wardrobe or to consult a makeover artist, every action you take is reversible. In other words, the damage you might do to yourself is extremely limited. However if you call your mother and read her the riot act, thus causing a bitter family breach which ripples out to aunts, grandmothers, and cousins, the damage is nowhere near so reversible and very difficult to control. Always act on the safer insights first. That way, as you acquire confidence and perspective, you will be better able to judge whether or not you wish to pay the price of taking certain irreversible steps toward your own mental well-being.

As a final filtering measure, ask yourself "How much will I benefit by taking this action?" If you work at home and rarely go out in public, buying an extensive new wardrobe might be far less important than if you work at a "people-intensive" job where the feedback on your appearance is constant and overwhelming. In this circumstance, you might want to consider another statement you wrote during the brainstorming session: "I do not appear self-confident because I constantly apologize." You might want to focus on eliminating this pattern of behavior rather than color coordinating your closet. In short, ask yourself "What is the payoff versus the effort?"

Finally, with all the rules in place, cut yourself some slack. Again, the important element of brainstorming is not success or failure. The process is bound to be a combination of both. The key element is that you are now monitoring your thought process and how it affects your behavior. You are becoming a self-aware, self-possessed human being who assumes control and responsibility of her own intellectual behavior. Give yourself some credit for doing so.

LINEAR AND LATERAL THINKING

> We cannot carry on inspiration and make it consecutive. One day there is no electricity in the air, and the next the air bristles with sparks like a cat's back.
>
> Ralph Waldo Emerson,
> *Uncollected Lectures: Resources*

The purpose of brainstorming is to bypass linear thought. Some people view computer programs as ideal examples of linear thinking because they assign two possible outcomes to any situation: 0 = false, 1 = true. Most of Western philosophy is based on this approach to thought. For example, the law of identity states that A and non-A cannot be true in the same respect and at the same time. Something cannot at the same time be both all black and white, A and non-A, 0 and 1, true and false. The laws of logic—of which I am a great fan—are based on this binary approach.

Lateral thinking is more creative. It aims at solving problems by developing new approaches. Ideas are neither right nor wrong; they are useful or not, and this becomes apparent only later. Lateral thinking is a way of breaking through the binary box of logic and into the realm of speculation.

There is an old and classic problem that illustrates the difference between a linear and a lateral approach to problem solving. Nine dots are arranged as shown below and you are asked to connect them by using only four straight lines. You are given only one constraint: you are not allowed to raise your pencil from the paper.

The problem is not solvable so long as you accept the unstated, but almost always assumed limitation that the lines should not extend beyond the boundaries established by the outer dots. Once you break through this assumption, the problem is easily solved. Because of this solution, lateral thinking is sometimes called "thinking outside the box."

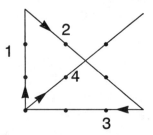

Often a tangled problem that resists the onslaught of linear thinking will loosen for a less analytical approach. Often, while engaging in ordinary daily activities—taking a walk, showering, or digesting a meal—a solution will rise to the surface of your mind. Or someone will make an offhand comment that will spark an association or trigger a train of thought. This is the sort of lateral process that brainstorming will nurture.

I hope you will achieve a balance between linear and lateral thinking, between logical and more intuitive thought.*

---

*Two books that provide excellent overviews of how to arrive at such a balance are *Fuzzy Thinking,* by Bart Kosko, and two books by Edward de Bono, *Lateral Thinking: Creativity Step by Step* as well as *New Think: The Use of Lateral Thinking in the Generation of New Ideas.*

CONCENTRATING ON CONCENTRATING

By perseverance the snail reached the ark.
S. H. Spurgeon, *Salt-Cellars*

The most common complaint that results from the process of brainstorming is "I couldn't concentrate on what I was supposed to think about." Although brainstorming may seem chaotic, it involves the odd combination of allowing your mind to wander, *but* on a specific topic. Many people lose track of the topic. For them even the focus of a statement written at the head of a page cannot keep their thoughts from straying down a dozen paths of random association that have nothing to do with the topic-statement. They view this wandering as failure.

While it is true that there are no performance standards attached to brainstorming, we cannot allow our minds to aimlessly wander without some focus, unless of course we intend to daydream. Accordingly, let's examine the subject of concentration.

Thought is nothing more than a train of previous connections between ideas in our mind. Much of it may seem random. You walk down the street. A strain of music wafts from a window and you remember the last time you heard that aria: you were in New York with free tickets to the Metropolitan Opera, one of which you offered to a business acquaintance. Afterward, he made a sloppy pass at you in a bar, a scene that set the emotional context for his behavior in the ensuing days at work. You now drift into contemplating the issue of sexual harassment and the possibility of filing an official complaint. Should you tell your mother about the problem? No, she thinks everything wrong in your life comes from your choice to be a single career woman. The last thing you need is another lecture, especially when she treats your brother like the heir apparent to a European throne.

From hearing a strain of delightful music, you have now arrived at anger toward your mother and resentment of your older brother, of whom you are actually very fond. This is a random train of thought. Without such associations, no thought is possible.

But how does the process of random association bear upon the subject of concentration? Concentration is generally defined as prolonged and sustained attention. It means keeping your mind trained upon one subject or, at least, having your mind return to the one subject whenever it wanders.

The first thing to realize is that the value of concentration lies entirely in the subject upon which your mind has fastened. Concentration has no value in and of itself. Many times, the problem people have with concentrating is that the subject matter is of little interest or relevance to their lives. A college professor assigns a paper on "considering calculus as a second language." Of course the students' minds wander.

Random thought, on the other hand, has the virtue of only touching upon things that are of interest to you for as long as they remain of interest. But the value of the subjects—how productive they are to the thinker's life—will be accidental. It may be fun to think about the sex life of Wonder Woman, but it will not necessarily enhance your chances to get into graduate school or get a promotion. Indeed, concentrating on certain subjects can be a negative thing. For example, if you need to write a term paper, focusing instead upon a long-standing resentment against your brother is a negative.

Concentration often involves guiding your thoughts away from your natural interests toward more productive, though less fascinating, subjects. This is where self-discipline enters the picture.

The goal of concentration is to prolong your attention span on subjects upon which you consciously choose to focus. But at the beginning, in order to stack the odds in favor of developing this habit, it is necessary to choose a topic that has some importance to you. Having done so, the following tips may assist you in developing the habit of concentration.

1. Write down your thoughts.

As in brainstorming, state the topic upon which you wish to concentrate across the top of the page. Unlike with brainstorming, however, you should consciously attempt to guide your writing so that it bears only upon the stated topic. Don't worry if your mind wanders: pull it back over and over again to the stated topic.

2. If the above fails, forget writing and try another tactic.

Speak your thoughts out loud, making sure, of course, that no one is within hearing range. There is no need to alarm your neighbors with conjectures about your mental stability.

Although you may believe that your thoughts are merely unspoken words, many of your unexpressed thoughts are actually manifested in images and in vague concepts without the hard, defined edges that words provide. Clarifying thought requires the sound of a human voice.

3. Remove distractions.

The art of remaining interested in a subject—in other words, concentration—involves removing other, more compelling distractions. If music interferes with your concentration, turn it off. Don't sit in front of a window that will draw your attention to the outside. Switch the telephone off. Dim the lights. If necessary, shut your eyes. It is difficult, if not impossible, for most people to shut their ears. But human beings are far more distracted by sights than they are by sounds. Close off this source of distraction.

4. When you catch your mind wandering, stop.

Trace your thoughts back to the point at which the departure from the topic occurred. This will give you insight into why and how the wandering began. Then, step-by-step, go through the same train of thought, this time refusing to be derailed at the point at which the wandering previously occurred.

5. Stop concentrating.

As paradoxical as it may seem, leaving a subject for a period of time may be the best way to concentrate on it. If your mind is spinning wheels, it might be telling you something valuable: no progress can be made at this point. The subject needs time to stew. Leave it for two hours. Leave it for two weeks. See what the mellowing of time does for your ability to concentrate on a particular point.

6. Be comfortable.

Never try to concentrate when you are experiencing physical discomfort: for example, the pain of a headache, lack of sleep, or hunger. As a biological imperative, the body will and should override the mind, and you can only threaten your health by ignoring its demands. Besides which, any thought produced under such adverse conditions is likely to be flawed.

7. Don't try to concentrate too much or too often.

Your mind will always wander, and this may be a healthy—even necessary—part of the process of thought. Just as it is undeniably true that human beings require dream time during sleep in order to maintain their sanity, so, too, may they require mental "down-time" while awake. Nothing is more random or mentally out of control than a dream. And, for many people, that elusive mental state known as creativity may result almost entirely from loosening mental controls rather than tightening them. This is not to denigrate concentration: it is to put that intellectual process in its proper place—as a powerful tool to use when and if the occasion calls for it.

SUMMARY

If you do not have the habit of being reasonable, you probably have formed bad intellectual habits that substitute for it. The first step in removing such barriers is to identify what they are in detail.

Common guidelines, adapted from psychotherapy techniques, not only will help you to recognize the areas that need changing, but also will provide a blueprint for how to change. By using techniques such as systematic desensitization and brainstorming, you reduce anxiety and free up your thought processes.

It is now time to define clearly the direction in which you wish to change.

4

Taking Yourself Seriously

The ancients gave us the injunction, "Know thyself."

Epictetus, *Discourses*

You have evaluated your own bad intellectual habits and sketched a rough sense of where you want to go. It is now time to take a cold, clear look at who you are intellectually and what directions are possible for you.

SELF-EVALUATION

Oft times, nothing profits more than self-esteem, grounded on just and right.

John Milton, *Paradise Lost*

Imagine a close friend has come to you to discuss a painful problem she is experiencing. In the course of doing so, she rants and raves about her shortcomings and increasingly runs herself into the ground. She utterly ignores her many good qualities, which far outweigh the bad. How would you react to her tirade of brutal self-criticism? As a friend, you would be patient, understanding, and helpful. You would tell her not to be so hard on herself, that she has a great deal more to offer than she realizes. And, besides which, wallowing in an orgy of self-recrimination will do nothing to address the problems that she does have. In fact, indulging in such a display might well be a way of avoiding the problems. You would offer your friend comfort and provide her with a sense of perspective.

Right now, you need to demonstrate this level of understanding and benevolence toward yourself. You need to treat yourself like a close friend and not like an enemy. Right now you need to appraise, as calmly and accurately as you can, who you are intellectually.

A cautionary note in opening: any attempt to reduce intelligence to a single intellectual skill seems doomed to failure. Intelligence itself seems to be a complex network of many different skills. And people develop at markedly different rates and in different directions.

Consider my husband. Recently, for his doctoral dissertation, he created a computer program that automated certain functions of a particle accelerator. Yet one of the most popular "family" stories about Bradford involves the first words he ever spoke—at the age of three. By that time, his parents were deeply concerned that their youngest son was mentally retarded and not the mentally gifted child he turned out to be. His father spent night after night holding up cue cards inscribed with letters and words in an attempt to get his son to repeat the sounds after him. Imagine his surprise when Bradford, upon passing a gas station that was part of a then common chain in Illinois, piped up from the back seat of the car and perfectly pronounced the word "Conoco."

It is probably a mistake to compare the intelligence of one person to that of another, especially based upon a single arbitrary and culturally biased test, such as an IQ exam. A person who does not perform well on one set of tests may do very well on another.

Imagine how difficult, if not impossible, it would be to administer a test to children to establish how generally talented they are. The goal of the test is too broadly defined to be useful. The first question a neutral observer would ask should be: talented at what? If the answer is not talented at anything in particular, just talented in general, then you should become suspicious of the test. After all, such a test might well rank a child who scored below the norm for everything, higher in talent than a virtuoso violinist who scored well only in that tiny section devoted to music. It is no more possible to assess a person's intelligence without asking "with regard to what endeavor?" than it is to assess talent without asking "talented at what?"

Simplistic and culturally bound intelligence tests, which may or may not be poorly administered, are as misleading as they are informative. Forget whatever IQ tests have told you. They were meant to measure a mythical entity called "the norm," and to distill intelligence to a single number that was more convenient to chart so that you could be processed through the school system.

I believe more people have been harmed than helped by having an almost arbitrary evaluation of their intelligence assigned to them as young children, to follow them throughout their academic careers. At formative ages, children already class themselves (and they are classed by others in positions of authority) as more intelligent than X, and less intelligent than Y. But this is like saying you are a better athlete than X. What if you are a runner and X is a weight lifter? What do the words "better" or "worse" mean in making a comparison between the two of you? Comparisons of intelligence are far from simple, and they are usually conducted in a destructive manner.*

Another manner of comparing yourself with others is to hold yourself up against cultural images, especially those provided through movies and television. But media images of intelligence no more apply to common life than do its images of beauty. No working woman, with or without children, can live up to the coiffed, perfumed, perfectly groomed and tailored vision of "woman" offered by commercials, news broadcasters, and sitcoms.

Equally, no one can live up to the witty repartee, the perfect sentences and delivery that pass for ordinary conversation on television.

---

*For a deeper appreciation of how foolish it is to judge yourself against statistical norms, graphs of intelligence, and allegedly random samplings, I highly recommend Darrell Huff's excellent little book *How to Lie with Statistics*.

TV actors do not mutter, lose their train of thought, or find themselves at a loss for words. They do not repeat themselves. Given that they are following a well-rehearsed script from a highly paid writer, their polish is not surprising. Nor is the fact that you, as an unscripted individual, sometimes stumble over words, forget your point, and tell jokes no one laughs at.

No wonder most people have a problem with performing a realistic self-appraisal of themselves, especially in emotionally sensitive areas such as intelligence or sexuality. They tend either to be overly optimistic or to be overly critical. Most women are overly critical of themselves, and seem to lack the braggadocio that many men possess in abundance. But just as there is no virtue in praising yourself beyond the point where anyone could recognize you, neither is there virtue in similarly demeaning yourself.

And there are at least two dangers.

First, as suggested above, underrating yourself can be a way of avoiding a real-life confrontation with the issues you face. By calling yourself "stupid," you escape the necessity of putting your intellect to the test. By preemptively declaring yourself to be a failure, you avoid having to confront your fears. There is no need to test a foregone conclusion. If you are too ugly for anyone to find attractive, there is no need to take the truly frightening risk of inviting someone you're interested in out to coffee. If you are too stupid to achieve anything worthwhile, there is no need to try to write a short story, to take an evening class, or to work toward the promotion you long for.

How do you know if you are being overly critical of yourself? A key may lie in the sort of language you use in the self-evaluation. For example, if you have a problem with mathematics, do you describe yourself as "confused," or as "stupid"? Do you use descriptive words like "I need a calculator," or emotional ones like "I am hopeless"? It is possible that you are hopeless at math, just as some people seem to be congenitally unable to carry a tune. But if such emotional descriptions occur over and over again in your self-evaluation, you are being too hard on yourself. Strong and self-denigrating language is often a sign that you have trouble coming to grips with an issue. The same can be true of moral judgments along the lines of "I'm just no good, and I never will be." Such judgments give you a reason to dismiss the problem without addressing it. Try to avoid self-flagellation and aim for accuracy instead.

The second danger of overcritical evaluations is that they can become self-fulfilling prophesies. Because you expect others to look down on you, you take preemptive action. You condemn yourself before they can and, to be safe, you condemn yourself more than they would. A certain circular pattern is set in motion: because you are afraid of failure you excoriate yourself; your lack of self-confidence keeps you from acting; without the confidence to make an effort you certainly fail, thus confirming your poor self-opinion.

Be as realistic about yourself as possible, but don't fret about the accuracy of your assessment. Nothing you write down is carved in stone. And your self-appraisal is bound to change during the ongoing process of reevaluation, in which you rethink and change your habits. As you get past your fears, you'll get a clearer view of your abilities and limitations.

AIDS TO SELF-EVALUATION

Men who know themselves are no longer fools; they stand on the threshold of the Door of Wisdom.

Havelock Ellis, *Impressions and Comments*

The following guidelines may help you edge closer to a realistic self-appraisal:

1. Avoid evaluative labels with emotional impact, like "good" or "bad."

Such critical terms tend to short-circuit change, rather than encourage it.

Try to think of your characteristics in terms of being either useful or counterproductive. Ask yourself: does this habit or trait get me to the goals I want to achieve? If it does, then it's a useful habit, which you should leave alone or simply polish up. If the behavior doesn't get you where you want to go, then it's not useful, and you should consider jettisoning it. Since the main point of reference here is the goals you want to achieve, it might be useful to keep a list of specific goals in front of you.

2. Don't include harmless intellectual eccentricities in your list of flaws.

All of us have quirky little behaviors, ones that "respectable" society doesn't consider quite normal. Most of these behaviors—if measured against the standard of whether they help you achieve your goals—are neither flaws nor virtues. Perhaps you like to read comic books: unless comics absorb so much of your time that they interfere with other pursuits, don't list this activity as a flaw. It is the intellectual equivalent of eating a Big Mac every once in a while. As long as comics are not a constant diet and source of nutrition, cut yourself some slack.

Perhaps you enjoy romance novels, horror movies, sharing gossip with friends, or playing hand after hand of solitaire. Be tolerant not only of your behaviors, but even of how you approach thinking about your behaviors. Perhaps you pace the floor like a trapped cat while you are trying to analyze your strengths and weaknesses. Perhaps you eat ice cream or tap dance in the bathroom or stand on your head or do somersaults on the front lawn. We all solve problems and work things out in unique ways. The biographies of great thinkers sometimes resemble the diaries of mad people.

Remember: there are more than enough people in the world to tell you that everything you do is wrong. You don't need to add to their number by joining their ranks. As long as your strange behavior is not destructive of your goals, be tolerant of it for now. You never know what function that behavior is serving in your life. Besides, what harm is it doing?

3. Don't go to friends.

Later on, when you are trying to reinforce specific behaviors, friends may play an invaluable role in providing feedback. What you are dealing with right now is your basic sense of self, which should be established as firmly as possible before you go to others for their input. Your sense of self is too important to become part of a democratic process.

When you eventually go to friends for feedback, don't automatically take everything they say seriously. Many of them will have no real concept of themselves intellectually, let alone a valuable perspective on who you are. Even well-meaning friends may serve up nothing more than a display of their own hopes, doubts, and fears. Many heads are not necessarily better than one.

Moreover, consulting friends before you have conducted a self-appraisal can be just another way of shifting responsibility for your life onto the shoulders of others. There will be a time later on in the process when feedback from friends may become invaluable. But right now, concerning the fundamental question of who you are and what you think of yourself, assume the responsibility yourself.

Now, for the actual process of self-appraisal.

The evaluation should occur on three different levels.

1. Your general capacities

Capabilities are the innate abilities and tendencies with which you are born. Some people are clearly born with the potential of being more physically capable of playing basketball than others. Since I am less than five feet two inches, I plead diminished capacity. Many biologists believe that at least some intellectual capacities are inherited, like physical ones. For example, everyone knows that certain people have "an ear for music" which predisposes them toward playing an instrument. Something similar may be true of other intellectual bents, such as a disposition to be good at verbal skills as opposed to visual pattern recognition. Neither capacity is superior to the other. Passing a judgment on your capacities is beside the point: right now, you just want to assess what they are realistically.

A cautionary note: do not become discouraged if you seem to have no traditionally recognized outstanding natural abilities. Among the capacities that cannot be measured easily are intellectual drive, curiosity, a sense of humor, and imagination. These capacities are invaluable, though you may have never given yourself credit for possessing them.

2. Your general skills

Although you are born with capacities, skills are acquired abilities. True, someone with "an ear for music" may find it easier to acquire the skill of playing the violin. But the capacity means nothing without the drive and the patience to learn and diligently practice. When Thomas Edison claimed that genius was 1 percent inspiration and 99 percent perspiration, he probably got the ratio right.

If someone is a skilled writer, it means that the person has taken the time to learn the basics and practice them. Perhaps few of us have the capacity for language to become another Eugene O'Neill, but almost all of us can acquire the skill of expressing ourselves clearly in writing. If you have never diligently pursued a particular skill, such as writing, don't jump to any conclusions about whether you are good at it, or not. These skills are learned habits.

Also, when you evaluate yourself as not having skill A, at that same moment ask yourself "why should I want to have skill A?" Perhaps, because you cannot draw a straight line and have no sense of color, you are unable to become a skilled artist. Why should you want to acquire this skill? How would it contribute to your goals and well-being? If you don't have a skill, it might be because you don't need or want it. Don't punish yourself for not being a good singer when a singing career doesn't interest you.

3. Specific accomplishments

These are the specific things you have done, like getting a degree, painting a picture, or reading a particular book. This is often the most productive area on which you can focus. For one thing, your accomplishments are more obvious and easier to chart than either your capacities or your skills. They are also easier to control.

When you have evaluated all three aspects of your intellectual self—capacities, skills, and accomplishments—spread the resulting sheets of paper around you and take stock for a moment or two.

Now, fresh from this self-appraisal, draw a line down a blank sheet of paper, dividing it in half. Label one side "Limitations"; label the other side "Strengths." On one side, list what you perceive to be your limitations. Make it a recitation of the capacities and skills you lack, and of the accomplishments you wish but which you have yet to actualize. On the other side of the sheet list what you perceive to be your strengths. These are your capacities, skills, and accomplishments.

Under limitations, for example, you might list capacities you lack, like a reliable memory; skills you haven't acquired, like computer literacy; and accomplishments at which you failed, like never finishing up that Bachelor of Arts degree. Under the strengths, you might list capacities you possess, like good concentration; skills, like speaking French; and accomplishments, like having redecorated the inside of your home.

The following is an extremely abbreviated example of what such a chart might look like—indeed, it's an early chart I drew up. (Note: sometimes the same capacity can be listed as both a limitation *and* a strength—the difference being a matter of circumstance. For example, being "extraordinarily stubborn" is a limitation if it prevents you from admitting a mistake. It is a strength if it prompts you to persist in your attempts to change habits.)

Limitations	Strengths
Capacities	
Slightly dyslexic	Excellent memory
Awkward with numbers	Good pattern recognition
Little artistic ability	Good ear for music
Given to frustration	Learn quickly
Extraordinarily stubborn	Extraordinarily stubborn
	Extreme curiosity

Skills

Little knowledge of math	Excellent verbal skills
Not sports oriented	Good at relationships
Weak in science	Writing/editing

Achievements

No novels written	Books/articles/scripts
A black thumb with plants	A very good cook

(Note: It is useful to file away the sheets of paper that constitute your initial evaluation of yourself, if only to pull them out several months [or years] from now and see the point from which you started.)

Again, the cardinal rule: don't be overly critical of yourself. Your intellectual limitations have nothing whatsoever to do with whether or not you are an intelligent human being. Intelligence refers to your ability to learn, not to your current level of skill or knowledge. If you lack a certain intellectual skill—like the ability to argue effectively—be candid about it. Not knowing how to argue is no cause for shame.

Arguing is a learned behavior and such behaviors are usually acquired on a "need to know" basis. Perhaps you simply haven't needed to argue as yet. Perhaps your childhood training in a verbally violent family has resulted in your learning another behavior: namely, you can detect when an intellectual brawl is about to erupt and you are an expert at circumventing it. If you always defer to others, you will have never had the occasion to develop the skill of arguing.

SETTING GOALS

> Men would be Angels, Angels would be Gods.
> Alexander Pope, *Essay on Man*

Just as it is difficult to understand what being self-confident means without breaking it down into specific behaviors, it is difficult to make any progress in changing your habits without having explicit goals. These goals provide you with a standard against which to measure how close you are to success. Indeed, without clearly formulated and specific goals you don't even know what constitutes success.

Break your goals down into bite-sized parts.

Consider the statement: "I would like to become an intellectual." This is a laudable goal, but not a very useful one. What does it mean to be an intellectual? You cannot simply step out of bed one morning and be an intellectual because that characteristic is expressed only through specific behavior. The question becomes: which specific behaviors embody for you the act of being an intellectual? These are useful questions because they pinpoint what, for you and for your purposes, constitutes achieving this particular goal.

For example, you might write down: I want to read one nonfiction book a week; I want to stop watching TV; I want to take a class on screen writing; I want to develop a correspondence on current events with a pen pal in another country; I want to stop my mind from wandering; in arguments, I want to speak more to the point, rather than rambling. Even these more specific goals can be further broken down into more manageable units. For example, corresponding on current events with a pen pal may require reading the newspaper every day, and subscribing to newsmagazines.

By breaking down your original goal—"I want to be an intellectual"—into successive subcategories, the goal becomes not only manageable, but also intelligible. You now know what being an intellectual looks and feels like.

Making proximate, or short-term, goals is as important as making explicit ones. These are goals you can achieve within a reasonable amount of time, with a reasonable amount of effort. Proximate goals are particularly important to people like me, who work on long-term projects which have no short-term rewards.

If your goal is to write a book, you should be prepared for months and months of unrelenting effort. In long-term goals, the effort can be overwhelming and the day-to-day frustrations may be difficult to endure: the rewards are at the end of a long journey.

This doesn't mean you should abandon your "big dreams"—the

dream of writing a novel, for example. But understand that it may take years. During this time, there may be little feedback and few satisfactions. Proximate goals—like coming up with a title, or taking a class on how to write dialogue—will give you a much-needed sense of progress.

Be very careful to set explicit and proximate goals—ones you can achieve—because they will become how you judge your success or failure.*

Get several sheets of paper, a pencil, and a watch with a second hand. Give yourself two minutes to list the main intellectual goals you want to achieve in life. Leave a lot of space after each item. For the moment, don't worry about being specific. Don't censor yourself. Don't be critical of what you write. This is just an exercise; you can always do it again. It is just a piece of paper; you can always tear it up.

Now go through the list and start filling in the space you've left under each general goal. For example, on the first pass you may have written "I want to be more confident" or "I want to write a book." The second time through, be more specific. For example, under "I want to be more confident," one of the things you might write is "I want to be able to speak in public." Under "I want to write a book," you might say "I want to write a science-fiction novel by the end of this year."

The third and final pass is to prioritize the goals, using what Alan Lakein calls the "ABC Priority System." Put an A beside those you value most highly; a B beside those of medium value; a C beside the lesser ones.

This prioritized list serves as a game plan.

Remember: your goals are written on paper, not carved in stone. Their purpose is to make your life easier and more enjoyable. They are not obligations or burdens. They should not be a source of guilt or ulcers. They will change and evolve over time. This change will be a sign of progress, not failure.

It is a good idea to reassess your game plan every month or so. As you get a better sense of who you are and what you want intellectually, your goals are bound to change.

---

*The best book I have found on setting goals is Alan Lakein's *How to Get Control of Your Time and Life.*

TAKING A CHANCE

> The terror we fear is often empty, but nevertheless it causes real misery.
>
> Johann Schiller, *Piccolomini,* act 5

Seeing your goals in front of you in black and white may cause anxiety. Pursuing them will probably cause even more anxiety, because the pursuit will entail taking emotional and intellectual risks. The process of changing your intellectual habits is becoming real. And the next step is to start reaching out aggressively for what you want from the intellectual realm. Anxiety, like frustration, is a natural response.

Life is a series of decisions and, where there are actions, there is always the possibility of falling flat on your face. This is especially true when you are trying to overcome old habits and to achieve something new. Most of our activities are done habitually—that is, without conscious thought. When you set a new goal, however, you must frequently redirect your habits, and the possibility of failure looms ever closer. It is precisely this fear of failure that condemns many people to a life of dreary routine devoid of significant risks, but also devoid of significant challenges and rewards.

Whenever the idea of making a mistake or being embarrassed holds you back, keep this in mind: If it were not for the possibility of failure, success would not be an accomplishment. If it were not for the possibility of error, truth would not be an achievement.

Life can be a banquet, but you have to pay its price. You have to take a chance. The best way to get comfortable with the risks involved in becoming intellectually alive is to take at least one chance every day. You'll find that risks add up over a period of time, and become major achievements.

If you have trouble remembering to take a risk each day—if you conveniently forget—write notes to yourself. Stick them where you can't help but see them. On your bathroom mirror. On the toilet lid. On the refrigerator. On your coffee mug.

What constitutes a risk? A risk is any conscious activity that is emotionally difficult for you to perform and which involves the real possibility of failure. The risk need not involve cataclysmic changes to your lifestyle. A risk can be something minor, even trivial. This is fine—in fact, it might be a good way to start. You are not trying to impress anyone; you are trying to break old habits and form new ones, which can be a private process. Most habits consist of a network of activities; each activity, considered by itself, is usually mundane. But they add up to a strong pattern that can be unraveled one string at a time.

The risks you take might include committing twenty minutes a day toward thinking about a particular issue, or reading a book. You might decide to speak up for yourself once a day in a conversation. You might look for an opening in order to make the statement to someone, "I think you are mistaken about that."

The content of the risk is entirely subjective. For some people, speaking up is a risk; for others, staying quiet and listening is much harder. As a rule of thumb, if you feel great resistance to an activity— especially a minor one—it is probably good risk material.

For example, if you are intellectually shy around strangers, make a point of addressing a comment or question to someone you don't know, and do it every day. Buy a newspaper from a vendor and ask him "How's business?" Ask someone on the subway what they think about a headline in the newspaper. If the prospect of doing this is too unsettling, reduce the level of your daily risk to thinking for twenty minutes about "why" this is so difficult.

What constitutes a risk? A risk is any activity that:

(a) is not done habitually,

(b) will put you closer to some goal you have established,

(c) entails the possibility of failure, and,

(d) requires you to overcome emotional resistance to taking action.

Two other conditions must be met:

(1) The risk must result from a conscious decision to take an action, and the action must be perceived as a risk at the time. You must think to yourself, in effect: "I am about to take a risk." Then, do it. There are no "risks in retrospect." You cannot reflect at the end of your day and select an action as a risk unless you viewed it as one before you took it.

(2) The risk must be recorded in writing. You must make a brief

note each day stating—at bare minimum—what the risk was and how you did with it.

Habits change slowly. They respond best to a persistent, sincere effort over time. You don't need to impress anyone but yourself.

PUT IT IN WRITING

One risk deserves particular emphasis. And that is taking the risk of putting your thoughts down in writing, even if the record is for your eyes only.

Writing improves thinking. By and large, you are fooling yourself if you tell yourself that you think very well but you—somehow—can't seem to write your thoughts down. Writing down your ideas is a process of clarifying them. It also makes them real. The most irrational conclusions you can imagine can be honestly held as long as you do not put them down in words, where their absurdity becomes apparent.

Such beliefs are often the result of associational thinking by which emotions and images are stored away in your mind and unconsciously form the basis of your conclusions, rather than the result of evidence and logic. For example, if you had a happy childhood on a family farm in Ohio and someone argues that it is all for the best—at least, economically—that small farming is disappearing in America, you might react through association. In lashing back, you might be protecting the memory of your childhood, and not dealing with the content of the speaker's ideas at all. Emotional reactions substitute for reasoned ones. This sort of inward sleight of hand only can go on, and honestly so, as long as you do not express your thought processes in explicit terms.

In fact, evasion can almost be defined as the refusal to translate sub-verbal thoughts into fully verbal form. Evasion often involves one of two processes: obfuscation, and equivocation. Obfuscation (to be discussed in chapter 10 dealing with definition) is the tendency to use loose, or flowery, or metaphorical words that confuse meaning even as they appear to advance it. For example, a friend for whom you are arranging a blind date asks you, "What does he look like?" You answer, "When his sense of humor ignites and flashes out through those eyes, he'll dazzle you." You really mean, "He's not good-looking." Through obfuscation, your words are robbed of literal meaning, and no one—including you, perhaps—is quite sure what you are talking about.

Equivocation is the act of using a word in two different ways without specifying the differences. For example, you may use the word "freedom" to mean "lack of restraint" in one sentence, then speak of "economic freedom" meaning "a guaranteed minimum income" in another. If you constantly shift the meaning of your words, no one knows what any particular statement means.

There are three stages in processing ideas, each one of which is a step toward reality.

The first step is simply thinking something to yourself. The second step is stating something to another person. Step three is putting it in writing.

You will never find people claiming that they can clearly write an idea down on paper, but cannot think it through clearly in their own minds. Nor do they claim that they can explain it to another person but not to themselves. It is always stated the other way around. Namely, that the thought is clear in their minds, but the expression of it—whether verbal or written—gets muddled. Each of these stages of stating an idea is also a stage of clarifying it.

What is different between these three steps? One difference is the degree of objectivity involved. By putting your thoughts into words and then onto paper, you are making them explicit. With each step, you are sticking your neck out a little bit farther. Why is this the case?

If you think about something, but you never express those thoughts, there is no risk of being criticized. Let's say you have a deeply held and emotionally charged belief that you have never expressed to anyone who might challenge you. For example, a position on abortion. Even if someone you are talking with goes on a rant about abortion, you can silently find reasons why her analysis simply doesn't apply to your position. After all, because you've never stated your position, the other person hasn't addressed its specifics.

People make excuses of this kind all the time. But what happens if you express your thoughts publicly? Your thoughts have become more tangible and more vulnerable to attack. You've opened yourself to criticism from the people who've heard you. If you openly state "x, y, and z," someone may well come back with "maybe x and y but never z." You have made yourself open to public criticism, and this often entails having to deal with your emotional reactions to confrontation and possible error.

Yet even with a clearly stated position, you still have two escape routes to avoid any criticism. First, you can convince yourself (and others) that you have been misinterpreted and, so, shift the intellectual blame away from yourself. Second, unless the conversation is on tape, it will be quickly forgotten and, in a short while, you can always claim that the other person misremembers what you said.

But what happens when you put your thoughts into writing? What if they are published and available for third parties to consult? You have just closed off your escape routes. Your thoughts are in black and white, with far less likelihood of being misinterpreted or forgotten. In other words, if you write "x, y, and z" and people say you're wrong, you cannot claim they have misunderstood your argument. They can point directly to your statement and you will be unable to retreat gracefully. People could point out your mistakes for years.

Each of these stages—from thinking to speaking to writing—involves increasing your intellectual risk. This is precisely why you should pick up a pen and start writing. (Chapter 7 addresses in detail the process of keeping an Intellectual Diary.)*

A QUICK FIX—THE COSMETICS OF BEING AN INTELLECTUAL

> The magic of a face.
> Thomas Carew, *Epitaph on the Lady S——*

---

*Although style can be an important aspect of writing, it is like the icing on a cake; it is applied only as a finishing touch. According to the eminently reliable Henry Hazlitt, you should have four style books on your desk as you write: "*The King's English*, by H. W. Fowler and F. G. Fowler, *A Dictionary of Modern English Usage*, by H. W. Fowler, *Usage and Abusage*, by Eric Partridge, and *Modern American Usage*, by Wilson Follett."

Precisely because changing your habits can be a long process, it is important to avail yourself of any quick and relatively easy gains along the way. Just as repackaging your exterior can induce men to give you serious sexual attention, so, too, does creating the proper impression help you in being taken seriously on an intellectual level.

In the best of all possible worlds, your words and ideas would be judged according to their inherent worth, according to the principles laid out in chapter 9, "The Tools of Reasoning." In the real world, many people will judge your intellect, at least initially and to some degree, on more cosmetic grounds: is your accent British or Brooklynese? Do you make eye contact or stare at the ground as you speak? Is your body language submissive? Your ideas may be less vulnerable to the tyranny of superficial judgments than many other aspects of your life are. People may consider you to be intelligent and take you seriously no matter how you appear. Intelligence is often judged by other independent standards. But repackaging yourself may bring unexpected benefits. Diamonds in the rough are often valued less than zircons in fabulous settings.

Fortunately, self-help books that detail how to improve every aspect of your exterior self seem to be a cottage industry in the United States. And, although there are useful guidelines presented below, personal style is so individual that I encourage you to browse the self-help shelves of bookstores for what feels right to you.

Having offered this advice, there is one invaluable book by the "wardrobe engineer" John T. Molloy, *The Woman's Dress for Success Book.* If you take Molloy's advice for businesswomen, you will have a formula for "intellectual power dressing."

The following guidelines—presented briefly—have been useful to me:

Dress

Having recommended *The Woman's Dress for Success Book* so highly, let me add a caveat. The best strategy might well be for you to look at the women who are taken seriously in your intellectual field. The proper dress code for a biologist or an aspiring advertising executive is not likely to be the proper dress code for a political radical or feminist. The former are likely to favor rather conservative business outfits, the latter may consider blue jeans to be *de rigeur.* What is considered to be appropriate dress may also be determined by geography—that is, by the cultural differences between various regions, or cities. A lawyer in Los Angeles may dress casually, preferring not to wear a jacket over her blouse. The same lawyer might always wear a tailored suit when on business in New York City.

Mimic how successful women around you dress. Over time, you may develop your own style. For now, play it safe and go with something that's been proven to work.

Voice

Women tend to speak softly and with more emotional intonation than men. Both tendencies can strip your voice of power and authority. Moreover, a soft, high voice can easily be drowned out by any man who speaks in a normal manner. As a remedy such a woman should:

- drop your voice by half an octave,
- increase your volume, and
- cultivate a matter-of-fact tone.

An effective method of practicing is to read a book or magazine aloud into a tape recorder and, then, listen critically to how your voice sounds. This is how it sounds to other people. As you practice your vocal range in daily conversation, keep a weekly appointment with your tape recorder in order to monitor how your voice is changing. If you need encouragement, compare the old tapes with the new ones.

Gestures

As a general rule, anything that distracts from the literal content of your argument is negative. This is especially true when you are repackaging and, perhaps, redefining yourself intellectually. Later on, when you are more experienced and confident, gestures may well add emphasis and color to your arguments. At that point, you may want to cultivate them as effective means of nonverbal communication—that is, body language—or they may develop naturally.

Right now, your gestures are probably expressing your self-doubts rather than your self-confidence. Your hands are more likely to be making conciliatory motions than aggressive ones. In the beginning, aim at making a neutral but confident impression: feet firmly on the floor, body erect, arms comfortably by your side, a minimum of hand waving.

Hair and Makeup

In arguing for medium-length hair, Molloy writes, "When Delilah cut Samson's hair, he lost his power. If women cut their hair too short, they do the same thing to themselves. Women with very short hair and with very long hair can be very feminine, very sexy, very appealing—and very nonauthoritative" (p. 84).

Just as you apply makeup and style your hair differently for a night out than you do for housework or to have lunch with a girlfriend, so, too, should the goal of being taken seriously determine your appearance in this regard. Do not wear colorful or shimmering eyeshadow that draws attention away from your words. Do not style your hair so that locks keep falling across your eyes, or need to be frequently tossed over your shoulder. These are unnecessary and negative distractions.

Again, hair and makeup are so personal that the final word must be yours, it must come from what feels right to you. But the same principle that applies to gestures is at work here: whatever distracts from the content of your words is probably working against you.

Quick Intellectual Fixes

Apart from quick physical fixes, such as putting power behind your vocal cords, there are intellectual pitfalls that women can easily avoid in order to be taken more seriously.

- Avoid traditional "women's topics," such as cooking, child rearing, boyfriends, or gardening.
- If you wish to speak of, e.g., cooking, do so in an intellectual manner. For example, explain how the rituals of serving food and communal eating have different meanings in China than in the West.
- Do not criticize yourself, as in "I am *so* forgetful," or "I can never get this straight." Some men will be looking for reasons to dismiss you intellectually. Make them work hard.
- Don't flirt.

Now, pushing cosmetics aside, let's return to issues of inherent worth.

SUMMARY

To change your intellectual habits, it is necessary to take a cold, clear look at who you are intellectually and at which directions are possible to you. By following the road map laid out in this chapter, you will arrive at a realistic and productive self-evaluation. The next step is to set explicit goals and to put them in writing. This process, in and of itself, can cause anxiety because the prospect of action is becoming more real. And action involves risk. It is important to take bite-sized risks, and to avail yourself first of all the comparatively easy changes that are within your control.

You are now psychologically prepared to begin forming new intellectual habits.

5

Forming New Habits

Every man has at times in his mind the ideal of what he should
be, but is not. . . . Man never falls so low that he can see
nothing higher than himself.

Theodore Parker, *A Lesson for the Day*

GETTING SPECIFIC

If you do not feel intellectually competent or assertive, what can you
do to change the situation? One of the keys to changing habits is to
be as specific as possible. This step is where a lot of well-intentioned
people stumble. You cannot get past the starting point unless you
become as specific as possible in stating your goal. Try not to think in
generalities. For one thing, you can't work well with a vague and general statement such as "I want to change, or I want to be self-
assertive." What precisely does that statement mean to you?

It is rather like waking up one morning and commanding yourself,
"Be happy!" The goal is admirable, but precisely how do you go about
being happy? Contrary to the popular conception, happiness is not

101

merely a state of mind. Happiness is embodied and embedded within specific actions, and has no sustained existence outside of those behaviors. If, instead of issuing the command "Be happy!" you had ordered yourself to listen to music you enjoy, have lunch with a close friend, plan a much-anticipated outing, or play with your children, then you would have had a useful game plan for pursuing happiness. You would know what to *do* to be happy.

Even when you deal with happiness as an attitude in and of itself, rather than as a by-product of behavior, the command "Be happy!" is not very useful. You need to know specifically what that attitude looks like, what it feels like, what it sounds like. How specifically do you express happiness? How do you walk when you feel buoyant about the world? Do you stride, or take a leisurely pace that permits you to enjoy the landscape? How does your voice sound? What colors and style of dress do you wear? Only by knowing—which means, possessing a clearly visualized picture—how you express happiness can you manifest that attitude on command.

Returning to the self-command, "I want to be more self-assertive," the question becomes "How do you translate this order into terms that are useful to you?" The answer is, again, to become as specific as possible. Instead of saying "I want to be more self-assertive," visualize what behaviors embody self-assertiveness to you. Then give yourself specific commands such as "I want to stand up straight on both feet while talking," or "I want to maintain eye contact in my next conversation," or "I want to speak in a clear, medium-volume tone."

By breaking down your goals into explicit, bite-sized bits, you can grab onto something concrete and work on it. And as you achieve these "stepping-stone" goals—as you are able to attend parties and stand up straight, maintain eye contact, and speak in an even tone—your sense of self-confidence will increase. This circle of reinforcement will begin to establish assertiveness as a habit.

To restate this key step in other terms: changing a habit involves breaking it down into little, manageable components—into the isolated units of behavior that all go together to form the habit you wish to develop.

It is also useful to break down the isolated units of behavior that form the interfering habit you wish to discard. Remember, if you are not being assertive, this usually means that some other pattern of behavior is substituting for self-confidence and blocking the path to change. For example, you may have developed the interfering habit of being socially anxious. Break down that habit into its specific strands of behavior. During conversations, your voice may sink to almost inaudible levels in terms of both volume and energy. To increase your self-confidence, you can concentrate on this one manageable component of social anxiety. You can focus on keeping up the level and energy behind your voice so that you are audible throughout the discussion.

The more specific you can become in breaking a habit down into its components, and in visualizing the circumstances that bring the habit to the surface, the better your chances of success.

Try an exercise that draws upon the systematic desensitization discussed in chapter 3. Visualize a conversation in which you begin to feel anxiety. Imagine the details: To whom are you speaking? On what subject? Where are you—at a party, in the office? Is anyone else standing by, listening? Are you talking, arguing, or listening? What do you feel? What specifically is the person saying or doing to make you feel this? How are you reacting in terms of your body language? How does your voice sound when you reply? What do you say? What would you like to say? Ask yourself these and dozens of other questions, until the situation is absolutely clear in your mind.

This is what I mean by breaking down an interfering habit into little units. Each question gives you something manageable to deal with. You can work on a seemingly huge intellectual problem by confronting controllable aspects of it. Over a period of time, the interfering habit will recede. The old habit is being nibbled away at the corners. And as you acquire confidence from these changes and practice new behavior, the habit of self-confidence becomes second nature.

An extremely useful technique in speeding along this process is to uncover, to verbalize as explicitly as possible, the exact wording that goes through your mind when you begin to feel uncomfortable. What statements supporting the old habit have you internalized?

SELF-DESTRUCTIVE STATEMENTS

One of the strongest intellectual barriers you are likely to discover is what I call "unstated and self-destructive assumptions," an area psychologist Albert Ellis has dealt with extensively. These are the silent statements you make to yourself—the unstated evaluations you make of yourself—that shut off the reasoning process and encourage an emotional response to flare instead.

In general, the unstated assumptions held by men and those held by women seem to differ in at least one important manner. The intellectual barriers that many men erect seem to revolve around vigorously protecting their competitive egos. The blocks that women throw up usually spring not from bravado but from insecurity, or anxiety. Women's blocks usually revolve around protecting their poor self-images against a bruising exposure. Men's unstated assumptions more naturally result in aggressive behavior: women's tend to be expressed defensively.

The particular unspoken evaluations that silence you may be difficult for you to enunciate at first, but keep listening to the feedback your emotions are providing. When someone asks for your opinion and, instead of giving it, you freeze or your mind goes blank, try to verbalize "why." What particular assumption caused the reaction that short-circuited your mind? Try to state it in the form of a sentence.

In *A Guide to Rational Living* Dr. Albert Ellis describes his intriguing philosophy of rational-emotive therapy, which details how human beings create for themselves most of their pain and fear, rather than having pain and fear inflicted upon them. Ellis identifies irrational assumptions that interfere with reasoning. The following list is based upon Ellis's insights but diverges considerably in order to emphasize the impact such assumptions have upon women.

1. You must be loved by everyone and everyone must approve of everything you do.

Women, in particular, want love and approval: they are culturally trained to do so. Women have an exaggerated fear of other people's anger, especially anger expressed by a man or an authority figure. For the many women (like me) who have experienced real violence in their lives, an almost animal instinct for survival can take over. The urge to back away from hostile situations can be an extremely difficult barrier to overcome. Unfortunately, there are people who will manipulate your fear to intimidate you into silence or bully you into agreement. Such people convert your natural desire for approval into an extremely self-destructive emotion.

Under the best of circumstances, however, trying to win the approval or love of everyone is folly. Some people will love you for the same characteristic that inspires hatred in another. It is impossible to be constantly loved by any network of people, and it is tremendously self-destructive to require this of yourself. You not only doom yourself to failure, you also slowly become an uninteresting human being with no distinct identity. Whenever an unpopular idea or desire arises within you, you will naturally cloud your mind or otherwise veer away from it. It is far more intellectually productive and healthy for you to learn how to disagree without giving offense.

Whenever you verbalize an unstated assumption that is silencing you, you should immediately and silently repeat to yourself a countersentence that you have formulated beforehand. Try to capture what feels to you to be the emotional opposite of the negative assumption. For example, in response to the demand that everyone like you, you might repeat the countersentence, "Standing up for myself is what will make people respect and approve of me as a human being." Use whatever sentence is most effective for you.

2. You must be thoroughly competent, adequate, intelligent, and achieving in all possible respects.

Our culture expects women to be consummate professionals for eight hours a day, and caring mothers and wives for the remainder—except, of course, for when the lights go out and we throw a switch and become sexual dynamos. Yet every woman I know feels nothing but lucky if she even gets one of these roles right during the course of a day. Demanding intellectual perfection of yourself is no less ridiculous than the foregoing.

No one—not even Da Vinci, the paradigm of a Renaissance man —had the wealth of knowledge to draw on to be competent at every endeavor and familiar with every field of human study. No one you will meet in your lifetime will have such a reservoir of information as to make them thoroughly competent across a broad spectrum of knowledge. Even people who are acclaimed as the best in their areas do not expect themselves to excel in other fields. If such a standard of competence were imposed upon the world, no one would ever voice an opinion on any subject. There is not an iota of shame involved in saying, "I'm not familiar with that issue. Can you explain it to me?"

A countersentence to the internal demand for absolute competence might be: "All that is necessary is to do the best I can—that's all anyone ever does."

3. Certain thoughts are wrong or wicked, and people who think them should be severely punished.

This is the intellectual equivalent of sinning in your heart, and it makes no sense. Although many things are wrong to do, nothing is wrong to think about. Indeed, it is one of the ironies of thinking that the more you attempt to suppress a thought, the stronger it becomes. Like a spring against which you press, the coils return the pressure in equal measure. The best way to defuse an uncomfortable thought is to expose it to the light of day and to careful scrutiny.

Yet many women judge their thoughts as pure or wicked, when they are actually a mishmash of everything in between. Perhaps we have been culturally conditioned to do so. Is there a parallel in the male world to the whore/madonna phenomenon—viewing women as either sluts or saints? Are there situations in which men have to face anything similar to being defined only by the extreme positions possible with nothing considered in between? Yet, for centuries, women have been defined by the two extreme positions possible to them. Many women still accept—at least on some vague emotional level— that either you are a good woman (a virgin, or monogamously married) or a slut. Many of them have difficulty thinking even to themselves about wicked things, such as sex or being angry at someone.

A countersentence might be: "There are no good or bad thoughts, only good or bad actions." Or, "It is important for me to think about *everything*."

4. It is catastrophic if intellectual exchanges are not as you would like them to be, e.g., if you appear to be stupid.

I think this irrational assumption crosses the gender line, affecting both men and women equally.

Allowing the fear of appearing stupid (or of any other intellectual "failure") to silence you is extremely self-destructive. It usually involves confusing ignorance with stupidity. Ignorance is a common and natural human state, from which there is no escape—at least in a broad general sense. You are born ignorant of everything and you will die ignorant of most things. There is quite simply not enough hours in a lifetime for you to master more than a sliver of the collective human knowledge. Moreover, it is an absolute certainty that you will appear stupid from time to time, if only because this experience happens to everyone, and often. Trust me, I know.

Often the fear of appearing stupid is an emotional excuse that people hide behind rather than face the strenuous changes they would have to make to cure the problems. It is easier for them to curse the injustice of their own nature, of their own genetics or upbringing, than to do the brow-breaking work that might be necessary to remedy the situation.

A countersentence might be: "So you might make a mistake. . . . Nothing ventured, nothing gained."

5. Intellectual success is the result of external events and happenings that are forced on you and that you have no control over.

Women are dealt a bad cultural hand when it comes to their intellectual potential. The lower-working-class family into which I was born made great sacrifices to ensure a college fund was established—for my brother who would, after all, have to support a family one day—who was, after all, the male offspring. Nothing similar was done on my behalf. I don't believe my parents loved me less, but they valued and believed in my mind less. Rather than offer assistance, they threw up a hurdle.

Yet the ultimate responsibility for my education—by which I do not mean a university degree—was and is mine. The ultimate responsibility for my own mind rests with me. It cannot be otherwise, as no one but me can actually control my mind.

A countersentence to this unstated assumption might be, "No one else can control my mind. Only me. My mind is my own responsibility."

6. There is one perfect solution to every problem, and if it is not found, the result will be terrible.

On issues of logic and fact, there may indeed be "proper" answers. The fact that Paris is a city in France is a fairly clear and undebated point. But on a great many issues—indeed, most of the moral and intellectual issues that will confront you on a daily basis—there are as many answers as there are human beings, because such issues usually involve contextual considerations which revolve on circumstance.

For example, consider these common ethical questions: Is late-term abortion proper? or Is euthanasia moral? or Should taxes on middle-income families be increased? Since these are questions that either do or can affect your life in a dramatic manner, you not only have a right to an opinion, you may have a responsibility to formulate one. If you believe something is wrong, you have a responsibility to say so, even if your opinion may prove to be wrong.

Besides which, even if there were such an absurdity as one and only one "right" approach to a specific ethical matter, that doesn't mean you shouldn't express intellectual curiosity by asking questions.

A countersentence might be: "This approach to the issue is interesting to consider in-and-of-itself, whether or not it is the *proper* one."

7. It is easier to avoid intellectual difficulties and responsibilities in life than to face them.

How can you avoid your own mind? All you can do is wage a civil war of sorts, shutting off undesired thoughts or pushing them away, till you resemble a person who deliberately learns to limp through life rather than test her leg muscles. If you do not face fundamental problems, your entire life will revolve around and be defined by the process of avoiding them.

For example, sidestepping intellectual insecurity by keeping silent or never stating a disagreement is almost a blueprint for converting the fear of confrontation into a habit. The fear becomes an ingrained and automatic aspect of your personality. Rather than avoiding insecurity, this process makes insecurity a defining part of who you are. The only way to become intellectually self-confident is to confront your fears and take responsibility for them.

An effective countersentence might be, "Expressing my opinion is not a matter of life and death. Speaking up will not kill me."

8. "If I can't think well on my feet, I must be stupid."

People seem to believe that ideas either flow into their minds naturally or they don't: people are either naturally smart or stupid. In the literary world, I constantly encounter a parallel to this belief. It is that if you are talented, words should fill the page naturally in a flow of exquisite and inspired prose. If they do not, you have no talent. In reality, every good writer I know is actually a talented editor who labors over the screen of a PC, polishing and repolishing words until they appear to be seamlessly natural. In other words, thinking and creativity are hard work. If these activities come naturally to you, then you are beloved by the gods. But if it requires incredible effort for you to appear intelligent and talented, then you are in the same intellectual soup as the rest of us.

If you read the biographies of renowned writers and scientists, you will know how hard some of them had to work to understand ideas and to form clear thoughts. The most brilliant minds—from Charles Darwin to Albert Einstein—expressed severe doubts about their abilities even to understand the books they read. They downplayed their intellectual prowess in almost embarrassing displays of modesty and self-doubt. Thinking is hard work. Reasoning is a skill, like playing the piano, and needs the same level of discipline. With practice, reasoning comes more easily, but it is not an automatic process.

Don't worry if you feel stupid or slow. The only important thing is to maintain your curiosity about the world and to have the courage to pursue ideas for the fun of it. In the course of life, many things will go wrong, and anyone who takes the risk of living fully is sure to fall flat on her face on a regular basis.

An effective counterresponse might be: "This is just a conversation, an intellectual exercise. Nothing crucial is at stake here."

9. "I should be certain I am not making a mistake before I open my mouth."

Although being careful about your facts and how you construct arguments is laudable, you can *never* be certain that you have not made or will not make a mistake. For one thing, it is always possible that there is information of which you are unaware. Or that the information you have, however carefully researched, is inaccurate. To demand absolute certainty of yourself is to aspire to become a deity, a goddess. As attractive as I know this goal can be, you should remember a rule set out under the section on brainstorming: namely, prefer goals that are plausible.

Discussing ideas should not be an egotistical "game of checkers," in which honest errors accrue on a score pad against you. Ideas should be discussed for the joy of understanding them, just as games should be played for the joy of the sport.

The countersentence to this particular obstacle might be: "Errors are not important as long as I learn from them."

10. "If I am assertive, I will look like a bitch."

This is a peculiarly female concern, and a popular one. Men do not seem to worry about being assertive in arguments. Quite the contrary. I wish I could tell women to dismiss this internalized sentence as wholeheartedly as the foregoing ones, but there is more than a grain of truth to it. Many people in our society will consider an assertive woman to be a bitchy one and, in some circumstances, an assertive woman may pay a high price for standing up for herself intellectually. Yet I encourage every woman to do so for the simple reason that speaking out is immensely better than living in silence, even if your voice annoys some people.

A common assumption behind the fear of appearing to be a bitch is that people like you because you are timid and sweet. And, perhaps, some people do. Are these the people you wish to cultivate as intimates?

In general, however, timidity usually inspires contempt and opportunism in others. Unconditional sweetness is usually considered to be an invitation to walk over someone as though she were a doormat. Those you associate with on such terms will tend to take intellectual advantage of you simply because they can.

The truth is that being assertive has no necessary connection with being bitchy, insulting, or offensive. It merely means you are a vital, strong human being who stands up for herself. The important thing is to do so with class.

The countersentence for this fear might be: "I can be assertive without being hostile: I can be aggressive in a classy manner."

11. "It is important that everyone agrees with my opinions, and that they acknowledge I am right."

The bottom line is that what other people choose to believe and acknowledge is no more any of your business than are their emotional reactions or their religious convictions. If they decide to maintain a clearly false position, that's their problem and not your concern. In a perfect world, people would immediately acknowledge your intellectual virtues and be converted by a reasonable argument, but it can come as no surprise to anyone that this is not a perfect world.

Instead of judging yourself by something you could never control—that is, other people's reactions—use the countersentence, "My only responsibility is to argue my position as clearly and respectfully as I can."

12. "I am responsible for other people's feelings, which I must not hurt."

Women are taught to put other people's feelings above their own. But since you can never really know what other people's feelings are, this is a losing game. Being honest with people and intellectually respectful of them is the very best you can do. If you hurt someone's feelings by mistake, nevertheless, it is always possible to say sincerely: "I'm sorry."

But don't retract your statement unless it was purposefully hurtful. No one is responsible for the life and well-being of another adult human being. Assuming responsibility for the actions and the soul of another human being is putting yourself in the role of God. And God, unfortunately, is silent.

A countersentence might be: "I should be as honest as I can and always be prepared to say 'I'm sorry.' "

A KEY QUESTION

> Circumstances are beyond the control of man; but his conduct
> is in his own power.
>
> Benjamin Disraeli

After analyzing in detail everything you are doing to thwart your own intellectual abilities, consider the possibility of altering not only yourself but your circumstances.

Earlier on, you envisioned an intellectual scene that made you uncomfortable. Perhaps you envisioned standing up in a particular classroom to ask a question, or arguing with someone who intimidates you. Analyze the situation(s) again, but this time concentrate on the elements outside of yourself and your attitudes that might be improved.

For example, consider that your intellectual discomfort may be partly due to the professor, who could be boorish to women. If you visualized arguing with an acquaintance who always leaves you feeling frustrated or inadequate, consider the possibility that the situation might not be your fault. This person may not be intellectually honest or secure enough herself to give you the feedback you deserve.

All of us react to our circumstances. We're all sculpted by our experiences. In fact, your past experiences are probably the reason you formed bad intellectual habits in the first place. To break these habits, it is not enough to change yourself; you need to change the circumstances that are reinforcing them.

Instead of condemning yourself for not handling some situations well, you should wonder if those situations are abusive and should not be tolerated. Some situations are like abusive people: you should avoid them. We have all had the experience of having an endless argument that goes nowhere, and eventually we walk away with a headache and a wasted evening. It would have been much better for us to have avoided the conversation in the first place.

The key is knowing when to walk away from a situation. Just as you would not willingly let people physically abuse your body, you should not let anyone mentally abuse you. If you can, avoid classes in which you are treated as subhuman. Back off from conversations with anyone who uses ridicule and sarcasm instead of arguments. Make the choice to seek out positive, rather than negative reinforcement. In short, start controlling your circumstances.

The first step in doing so is to ask a key question: *What do I want out of this situation?*

It is important for you to know what you want out of an intellectual situation before you walk into it. It is important to pin down exactly what you are trying to accomplish by continuing to be in that situation.

Suppose you are trying to get over being intimidated in a classroom. Be realistic about what you can accomplish from week to week. During your visualization of this, it is fine to fantasize about an entire classroom bursting into applause at the astuteness of a question you have just asked the boorish professor. Fantasies are useful. They give you emotional fuel and a sense of the direction in which you wish to head. But such situations are not real, and pursuing them in reality is not productive.

So, realistically, ask yourself what is possible for you to achieve in the situation you are entering. Perhaps a realistic scenario includes no more than forcing yourself onto your two feet, asking a well-rehearsed question, and sitting back down. If you do this, reward yourself by realizing you have fully accomplished a difficult goal and nothing more is expected of you. It doesn't matter if your knees trembled, if your face flushed, or if your grammar slipped. Merely getting to your feet and speaking makes you an intellectual success who stands head and shoulders above those who are not willing to take such a risk.

The professor may well respond with biting sarcasm or an otherwise belittling remark. Do not take his response seriously. Do not evaluate yourself by the class's reaction. Neither of these responses are part of the goal you have set yourself. If the responses are positive, this is a bonus. If they are negative, they don't affect your success. You cannot control other people's actions or emotions, and it is foolish to let something as important as your intellectual self-esteem ride on uncontrollable factors. Don't let other people define how you feel about yourself intellectually.

Do not accept intellectual abuse from anyone. Do not take it inside yourself and allow it to become part of your intellectual self-image. I learned this from one of my best friends, an eighty-six-year-old lady whose faculties are still sharp enough to run rings around just about everyone. As a devoted union activist, she has lectured for decades before hostile crowds. And, for years, she has been my ideal of intellectual aplomb.

She handles those who wish to abuse her better than anyone else I've seen. Not with hostility, which would make her lose control and seem ruffled. Not with embarrassment, which would give her critics the response they want. She completely and calmly dismisses them, and then moves on.

I remember how she handled one situation in particular. After giving a lecture, she entertained questions from the audience. A middle-aged woman stood up and asked: "My husband boycotted your talk but he told me to come here and find out how many lovers you've had." To me, the husband's motivation seemed clear: he wanted to embarrass or degrade an intellectual woman by whom he was probably intimidated. The wife's motivation escapes me to this day.

My friend did not miss a beat. Nor did she give much of a reaction. She simply stated, "That's classified information" and immediately took the next question. If I had been in her place, I would have become angry . . . which is another form of being rattled . . . which is what the questioner probably intended to provoke.

My friend explained her aplomb to me afterward. Her unshakable stage presence was the result of over sixty years of experience. During these decades, she had encountered many such insults which were masked as innocent questions. After being badly thrown by the first few, she had sat down and worked out several standard responses. One of which was "That is classified information."

I've learned a lot from this woman, especially how to prepare for abuse so that it doesn't fluster me when it comes.

Every woman is well-advised to do the same.

And in doing so—in handling abusive situations—one of the emotional responses you will confront is frustration, and your need to deal with it.

AGAIN, DEALING WITH FRUSTRATION

> To go into the water and grasp the foam.
> Chinese proverb

One of the most important circumstances you can control is your attitude toward the intellectual process you are undertaking. This is true not only of the abusive situations you will occasionally encounter, but also of the commonplace intellectual occurrences such as errors. A common and natural emotional response to such situations is frustration.

To many people, frustration is an internal indication that something is going wrong. Frustration can almost be defined as the emotional response that indicates you are not achieving or getting what you want out of a situation. If your intellectual life is nothing but a string of one frustration after another, then something certainly needs to be remedied in your approach to ideas. But *occasional* frustration—even deep frustration—is a natural part of dealing with errors and with taking risks, and it serves a useful function.

To state this in other terms: if people take risks, they cannot avoid conflict. Indeed, the very act of thinking can be considered a form of conflict by which you perceive a problem (a lack of knowledge) and begin to process information. If there were no problem or unknown, there would be no need to do any thinking at all. Equally, unfulfilled desires create conflict that drives people to act—physically or mentally. If you had no unfulfilled desires and were entirely satisfied, it is unlikely that you would ever act at all, or think.

Psychiatrist Viktor Frankl, whose compelling book *Man's Search for Meaning* cannot be too highly recommended, used to ask a key question of severely depressed patients. It is a question that can be easily adapted to intellectual concerns. Frankl asked "What is it that keeps you from committing suicide?" The patient's answer gave him a clue as to what gave emotional meaning to that person's life. Sometimes it was family or religious belief, other times it was a book or other project that the person longed to complete.

In a similar vein, readers of this book who are intellectually frustrated and think so badly of themselves should ask, "What is it that keeps me returning to the intellectual world?" After all, if you are reading this book, you have not given up on the intellectual realm. What is it that keeps your mind alive and keeps you interested, despite the frustration?

And is frustration necessarily a bad thing? Many psychologists believe that frustration actually plays a valuable role in the creative process and in creative thinking. Frustration is the stage of creation at which your brain has been working furiously to no avail and, now, it demands a vacation. Your mental faculties seem to shut down. You switch on the television or take a nap or listen to music or read a trashy novel. Suddenly, perhaps an hour or a week later, a flash of insight occurs and the problem you've been dealing with has a solution.

Before this flash, however, the problem remains unresolved and stirs up tension within you. You might pace the floor, snap at your husband, and appear to be in a state of general dissatisfaction. Your frustration is a natural and healthy response to the fact that the problems you are trying to solve are not presenting themselves in a logical order to be sorted out easily and solved. Some of the most productive and creative people also seem to be often dissatisfied, despite their accomplishments and success. Indeed, frustration seems to be an integral part of their drive to create.

My purpose here is to put in a good word for occasional frustration and conflict as being natural aspects of human striving and creativity so that you will not be discouraged when these reactions arise within you. Anyone who wishes to enjoy a rich intellectual life will probably have to learn how to handle the frustration and internal conflict that comes with the flow and occasional blockage of ideas.

> When I am, as it were, completely myself, entirely alone . . . say, traveling in a carriage, or walking after a good meal, or during the night when I cannot sleep; it is on such occasions that my ideas flow best and most abundantly. *Whence* and *how* they come I know not nor can I force them.
>
> Mozart

TOLERATING YOUR OWN ECCENTRICITIES

> There was never a great genius without a tincture of madness.
>
> Aristotle

Another circumstance under your control is how you view your own intellectual eccentricities. Everyone has them. The brilliant classical pianist and wit Oscar Levant—the man who once remarked that he had known Doris Day before she had become a virgin—was pathologically afraid of lemons and Sara Lee cake. Yet his eccentricities are considered colorful because, at some point, the world chose to recognize his genius. In the words of Elizabeth Taylor, "Success is a great deodorant." But what of the rest of us ordinary working women who may also fear lemons?

Many people consider such reactions within themselves to be aberrant and outright embarrassing. These people automatically assume that if they had spent the morning pacing the bedroom floor, their time has been wasted. They tend to suppress their own eccentricities, rather than to view the behavior as basically harmless and quite possibly productive.

As long as it is not obsessive, try to tolerate such behavior within yourself instead of passing judgment on it. If you like to read German philosophy or Dilbert cartoons while taking a bubble bath, allow yourself to revel in the experience. If dancing naked around the bedroom while watching Fred Astaire movies helps you to write your novel, dance away. If running through the sprinkler on the front lawn loosens up a math equation on which you are stuck, get wet. Even if it is not ultimately productive, what harm are you doing to anyone on earth?

And given that no harm is being inflicted, don't let other people censure your behavior. As long as the behavior is not self-destructive or hurtful to innocent bystanders, there is no right or wrong in the strategy you use to spark the creative and intellectual flow within yourself. Or, more precisely stated, the right or wrong of the behavior lies in whether or not it produces the result you wish. Do the ideas flow? It is folly to judge the right or wrong of your behavior against some arbitrary standard of normality. If it works for you, it is a "correct" strategy.

A friend has a clever name for one such strategy, a pattern of behavior for which many people have criticized him. He terms it "creative evasion." Whenever he faces a deadline on an article, he ostentatiously fritters away his time by going to movies, watching Bugs Bunny cartoons, or oversleeping. His actions are deliberate. There is no question that he is evading the task and the responsibility before him and that he is doing so because the task intimidates him. He freely admits this. *But* he insists that the frittering of time is a necessary prelude to the creative stage of utter panic from which he derives the push to meet his deadline. Often he does so in one concerted work session.

Is he correct about this being a successful strategy? If he immediately sat down and turned his hand to writing, could he reach his deadlines without the angst and panic? Is his movie-going and wandering about merely a form of procrastination that borders on self-destructive behavior? I don't know, and it is not possible for me to judge. Perhaps the best test of this question would be for him to sit down and honestly try to write without his customary evasions. What I do know is that he always meets his deadlines and he seems generally content with life. Whether or not his strategy is the best possible one, it seems to be one that works for him.

Until you show some sympathy toward your own eccentricities you will never be able to view them objectively. You will never be able to assess whether they are a benefit to you intellectually. You may discover that your eccentricities are among the most interesting aspects of who you are.

SUMMARY

Forming new intellectual habits requires you to be as specific as possible about the behavior you wish to make second nature. If you wish to become self-confident, you must know what confidence looks, sounds, and feels like.

As you begin to adopt the desired behavior, you are likely to encounter the internalized and self-destructive statements that have hindered you in the past. There are practical methods of sweeping away these negative self-evaluations, thus clearing the path for new habits.

After considering how to arrange circumstances so as to maximize the likelihood of success, it is time to reach outside of yourself into the real world.

6

Books and Other Good Friends

Thus we can roughly define what we mean by the art of reading as follows: the process whereby a mind, with nothing to operate on but the symbols of the readable matter . . . elevates itself by the power of its own operations. The mind passes from understanding less to understanding more.

Mortimer Alder, *How to Read a Book*

In *How to Read a Book*, an excellent overview of the art and habit of reading, Mortimer Adler identifies four levels at which people read. The first is the *elementary* level, during which a person passes from illiteracy into mastering the literal meaning of the written word. Instead of words remaining black marks on white paper, they become symbols of real things in the world. Instead of seeing the word *horse* as an unintelligible arrangement of lines, it becomes a symbol that evokes the picture of a real horse in our minds.

As adults we have all had the experience of being thrown abruptly back into the elementary level when confronted by a foreign language. On such occasion, we have to revert to the habits of childhood: we

121

squint and puzzle out "What does this word mean, how about that one, and how do the two words relate to each other to make any sense?"

The second level of reading is the *inspectional* one. Having mastered rudimentary reading skills, the reader now begins to skim and scan material for items of specific interest. Typically, inspectional reading occurs when time is limited. An example is when you scan the newspaper, skipping the boring bits and zeroing in only on the relevant ones. The goal is to get the most value out of your reading for the time you invest: the goal is information or entertainment. Instead of asking yourself "What does this word/sentence mean?" you ask "What is this article/book about?"

Whenever you glance at a book's preface, noting subtitles or the author's expression of a goal, whenever you study a table of contents or check out its index, you are reading on the inspectional level. So, too, when you peruse the blurbs on the book's dust jacket.

The third level is *analytical* reading. The goal is to understand not merely the information of the material but also to analyze and digest the author's perspective or arguments. Analytical reading is thorough and complete, without the time pressure involved in skimming. Unlike inspectional reading, this level is rarely directed at acquiring information or being entertained. It is directed at understanding the meaning and purpose of the book, of grasping the author's view of an issue.

The fourth level of reading is the *syntopical* one, which might be called comparative reading. During this process, the reader actively places the book in the context of and in relationship to other works. Yet, as Adler observes, "Syntopical reading involves more. . . . [T]he syntopical reader is able to construct an analysis of the subject that may not be in any of the books . . . it is the most active . . . kind of reading" (p. 20).

The ensuing discussion bears upon all four levels of reading, but the focus is upon the psychology of reading rather than the art of it. For my money, there is no better overview on the art than the extensive *How to Read a Book*. Of course, as the fellow philosopher Lionel Ruby remarked in *The Art of Making Sense: A Guide to Logical Thinking*, "If you didn't already know how to read a book, you couldn't have read Mr. Adler's book" (p. 9). All wry comments aside, Adler's work is an excellent guide for increasing the value you receive from opening the covers of a book. Rather than summarize its insights, I will take note of Montaigne's pointed remark in his *Essays*: "Every summary of a good book is a stupid summary" (p. iii, ch. 8). So admonished, I will merely urge you to seek out Adler's book on your own. His style is both accessible and entertaining.

THE BENEVOLENCE OF BOOKS

> Books are the most mannerly of companions, accessible at all times, in all moods, frankly declaring the author's mind, without offense.
>
> Amos Bronson Alcott, *Concord Days*

The most important single tool you have in pursuing ideas are books. The following tips on how to use books are not set in stone. They are techniques that have been productive for me. Before launching into the list, however, I want to pause to offer, albeit briefly, my psychology of reading, if you will.

It is not possible to say enough about the benevolence of books, and the psychological safety they offer to people who are hungry to learn, yet insecure about doing so. Displaying ignorance in front of another human being can be an acutely distressing experience that leaves you vulnerable to whatever comments she chooses to throw back at you. The very fact that you are asking a question is an admission of ignorance and of a desire to understand. To take advantage of this is more than intellectual discourtesy on anyone's part: it is intellectual cruelty.

Yet it happens so often that people take the cruelty for granted, and do not even recognize it as such. Innocent remarks are ridiculed. Honest questions receive sarcasm or other abuse in response. Even good questions or arguments occasion vicious attacks on the speaker: sometimes the attacks are prompted by the fact that the question *is* good, and difficult to answer in any other manner. With each buffet that results from asking a question, an insecure person becomes a little less likely to ask another. A person whose only sin was intellectual curiosity learns to stifle that impulse behind a wall of silence. Soon silence becomes a habit.

Guard your curiosity and your intellectual innocence. For example, never trust someone who assures you, "There are no stupid questions." There is a high probability that these words of encouragement are a setup and her response to your query will indicate—implicitly or explicitly—that, well, maybe there are stupid questions after all. Often the setup is a public one, such as a professor encouraging a student to voice her doubts or confusion in class only to score a cheap laugh from the other students at her expense. This is an inexcusable thing to do to another human being who is only trying to understand. Yet it is a common occurrence.

The best counter I know of to the above scenario occurred in my tenth-grade math class, and it remains an example to me of how a public display of ignorance on the part of a student can be handled with benevolence by a teacher. In high school, my personality—which was/is as shy as it is stubborn—generally made me hang back and eschew the limelight in any form, athletic or academic. During one geometry class, however, I quite simply lost my temper with a teacher who had made me comfortable enough to have that reaction.

The source of my temper was the fact that I could not understand the problem being presented, and not understanding something always makes me angry. In front of the entire class, I vigorously challenged her claim that the angles of all triangles, when added together, must add up to a certain number of degrees. She paused by the blackboard, then walked over and handed me a ruler with the words, "All right, then draw me one." The class resumed quite naturally around me as I futilely drew triangle after triangle trying to prove her wrong. By the end of class, I had wholeheartedly accepted her claim. She watched without comment as I returned the ruler to her desk and never brought the incident up again.

She was a good teacher and a benevolent one, but you cannot rely upon meeting her like upon turning every corner. Far more common was a history teacher who regularly humiliated his students, once because a ten-year-old used the term "et cetera" at the end of a list of historical examples. Perhaps the student *was* being a bit pretentious. Perhaps he just didn't know how to end the list gracefully. To the teacher, the term meant that the student had run out of examples and he was attempting to cover up the fact. Even if he was correct in this assumption, the student did not deserve to sit through the next twenty minutes with his face burning scarlet with humiliation from the public dressing-down he received because he had tried to use a grown-up word.

The world brutalizes people intellectually as surely as it batters them emotionally and sexually. This is particularly true of women who are not only perceived to be the weakest members of our society, but also the most undervalued intellectually.

Books cannot provide the gentle personal guidance displayed by my tenth-grade math teacher, but neither will they humiliate you for your use of words, for asking a stupid question, or asking a good one. Books will never criticize you for being slow to understand if you need to read a passage over and over again to get its gist. They never ridicule you for having a misconception, or for opening them to ask a stupid question. When you go to them for knowledge, they will either provide it or not. If they do have the knowledge you ask for, books will patiently explain the same material to you over and over again, offering information at exactly the rate you are best able to absorb it. Books, in and of themselves, are acts of kindness.

Moreover, they are fun. Books are true time machines that take you back in history and allow you to read the words of Thomas Paine—the very sentences that sparked a revolution when they were nailed up on fenceposts. Through Thomas Jefferson's voluminous correspondence, you can virtually eavesdrop as he describes the why and wherefore of revolution to friends in Europe. You can be in the audience as American patriots cry out eloquently for representation under taxation. You can read the heartbreak in the diaries of women whose husbands and sons were killed in battle.

Reading a book can be like holding a séance. You can receive messages from the dead, and you receive the best part of them, the part they once put on public display to their peers. Having said all this, however, I must rush forward to knock books off the altar on which I've placed them.

DEMYSTIFYING BOOKS

> To mind the inside of a book is to entertain one's self with the
> forced product of another man's brain.
>
> Sir John Vanbrugh, *The Relapse*

It is time to step back and place books—the physical object you hold in
your hand rather than their intellectual substance—in their proper place.
With the sole exception of collectors' editions, a book is not to be revered
and mystified, but to be used as a tool.

I remember how upset I became when I first saw a book being
mutilated. I was in a book-cluttered newspaper-stacked New York
apartment, sitting next to a man I still consider to be a mentor—an
economist and prodigiously productive writer named Murray. As
Murray explained something in his squeaky Brooklynese voice, he
ripped a page out of a paperback book we were discussing and handed
the paper over to me so I could take a particular passage home in my
purse to quote in an article.

It was a cheap, readily available paperback, of which he had duplicates. Nevertheless, my hand almost shot out to restrain him. Although
I controlled that gesture, I must not have controlled the horror on my
face, because Murray hastened to reassure me. "It's okay, sweetie. I've
got another book. Books are what we economists call a renewable
resource." Indeed, I could see another copy of the same paperback sitting safely on a bookshelf by his work desk to one side of us.

It became clear that Murray routinely bought duplicates of any
popular (read inexpensive) book he knew would be useful in his
research. Then, as he sat up writing late at night, he would tear out the
pages of duplicates on which there were quotes he wanted to use. The
disemboweled pages were stacked in a file folder awaiting the final
stage of his writing: namely, creating footnotes and checking quotes
for accuracy. The duplicate book was a renewable resource to be
chopped up in the process of being used, and then thrown into the
trash the moment that use was over. Meanwhile, the book's information resided within the original copy still safe and sound on the sprawl-
ing shelves of his personal library.

The system worked for him, which means that ripping out the pages of a book was a good use of that book for Murray. It took me years to become comfortable enough to perform such mutilation, even in a good cause.

On another occasion, I borrowed an obscure text from Murray's personal library because I couldn't find a copy in the public one. (His personal library literally coated the walls of his huge rent-controlled New York City apartment, extending even into the kitchen and bathrooms.) At home with the borrowed text, I spent more time puzzling over his copious marginalia than in reading the book. Across the bottom of one page, Murray had scrawled something that looked like "attabaye." I finally figured out what it was: "atta boy!" He had been enthusiastically expressing agreement with the author's point of view. And, if scribbling on the margins made reading the book more enjoyable for him, then this, too, was a good use of the book for Murray.

Indeed, committing the sin of marginalia is one of the methods of using books that I value as well. With the sole exception of collector's items—by which I mean rare, hard-to-find books, or ones with unique characteristics such as an autograph—I feel free to scrawl in the margins or to bend over the edge in a dog-ear that marks the place of a quote to which I wish to return. For some reason, this use does not seem like mutilation to me, perhaps because the book remains structurally intact.

Adler apparently agrees, as he provides a list of techniques to use in effectively marking up a book—a process he refers to as "how to make a book your own." The techniques are:

- underlining to note major points or particular forceful statements
- vertical lines at the margin to emphasize a major passage that is too long to underline
- a star or asterisk at the margin, used sparingly, to emphasize the ten or twelve most important points of the book
- numbers in the margin to indicate the sequence of points being made in an argument
- the symbol "Cf" (reference) in the margin with the number of other pages in the book that bear on a point

- circling key words or phrases for much the same purpose as underlining
- making notes at the top or bottom of the page to record questions or observations

Having answered the question "What do I mean by using books?" let me pose a question to you. What do you mean when you use a book?

After all, the word "use" presupposes a purpose. Without a purpose, nothing is useful. Even the necessities of life, such as food and shelter, are useful only if the purpose envisioned is to maintain life. A man who wishes to commit suicide may well view food as not only a useless but also a negative thing. So, rephrase my question and ask yourself, "When I pick up a particular book, what is my purpose in doing so?"

When I read a book, the purpose I have in mind generally dictates the manner in which I will use it. If I am reviewing the book for a newspaper, I will read to fill specific needs, e.g., to find a quotable passage that encapsulates the book's theme. The perusal will be a swift one, as book reviews do not pay well and, so, cannot occupy large blocks of my time. If I am reading for pleasure, I will often reread a favorite novel and linger over an especially well-written passage. If the book is part of academic research, I will take meticulous notes and carefully record all the publication data for inclusion in footnotes. The way you use a book cannot be divorced from the purpose for which you use it.

When you hold a book in your hand, ask yourself, "What reason do I have for opening it?" If the reason is for the pleasure that reading it will give, suspend all rules. Using that particular book well means nothing more than whatever use maximizes the pleasure. Who cares if it gets wet from falling into the bathtub? When the pages dry, the plot and characters will be waiting exactly where you left them.

If you are reading to conduct research, you will want to be more critical and systematic in your approach. All the different ways of reading a book are legitimate depending on the purpose you have. And, depending on the purpose, your attitude toward the book is likely to change as well. For example, you will not read your daughter's favorite fairy tale—which fills the purpose of lulling her to sleep—with the same critical eye as you would a political treatise. Yet you may be attentive to any hidden ideological messages being passed onto your child.

Books are tools. They are vehicles to transmit information, understanding, and pleasure, nothing more. The substance of the material may be worthy of reverence: graceful poetry, foundations of reality like the Pythagorean theorem, the genetic blueprint of man, all deserve intellectual respect. But there is nothing sacrosanct about ink on paper glued into a binding. Books are to be used. If you aren't using them in such a way as to extract the most information and pleasure you can get, then you are missing the full experience they have to offer.

GENERAL GUIDELINES TO USING A BOOK

What is the use of a book, thought Alice, without pictures or conversations.

Lewis Carroll, *Alice's Adventures in Wonderland*

Use every book that appeals to you, from romance novels to technical manuals and recipe books. Be aware of the purpose which specific books serve, but don't let that awareness make you shy away from letting your mind consume whatever appeals to it. Although some people might consider this advice to promote "poor intellectual nutrition," I think most women starve themselves intellectually and they need nothing so much as to binge on whatever they hunger for intellectually. Later, far down the road when reading has been firmly established as a habit and as a source of pleasure, there will be time to read works like Brand Blanshard's *The Uses of a Liberal Education* and become more discriminating. Or not.

For the moment, I am only concerned with how to establish good habits in using books. Part of this process involves cultivating commonsense attitudes toward books. These attitudes include the following:

- Mark books up if it helps you to learn from them or to increase your enjoyment of them. For example, if you are reading an investment book in order to discuss possible financial strategies with your husband, marking passages to read aloud to him over coffee in the morning is a good use of the book. Or, perhaps, you want to quote a particular paragraph in a term paper. Or maybe it just gives you pleasure to respond to the author with a bit of marginalia. The only reason to deny yourself this pleasure is if your book is a collector's item whose resale value will be diminished drastically by being marked.

- Put a book down if it doesn't interest you. Some women view reading a work from cover to cover almost as a moral duty. They waste hours which could have been spent on another book that was more worthwhile. But following your interests and developing the joy of reading means avoiding dull books through which you plod out of a sense of duty. Would you eat food that tasted bad? Or buy clothing that didn't fit? Why read a book that doesn't appeal to you?

- Skip around if you wish to—skim this chapter and hop over to the next one—in order to get the information you need. Although this may be bad advice in suspense novels or books that build a meticulous argument chapter-by-chapter, it applies to most of the books you will encounter. For example, when you use a recipe book to make beef stew, you don't feel obliged to read about desserts. You skip right to the section you need. When you do research, you go to the table of contents or the index and go to the references you require. Indeed, that is why indexes are provided. Get the information you value and don't squander your valuable time on the rest.

- Integrate books into your lifestyle. Cram them into your purse, stack them on the passenger seat of your car, keep some stuffed in a drawer at the office. That way you can read whenever you have time: in a doctor's office, at a gas station, during a coffee break. Brand Blanshard once said that if you spent something like thirty minutes a day reading in a certain area, within a very few years you would be a scholar on the level of a Ph.D. in that area. An amazing thing about the intellectual realm is how much you can accomplish in very little time.

- You may have a fair amount of intellectual dead time, by which I mean time occupied by tasks that require virtually no mental activity, e.g., ironing clothes, washing the car, exercising. Although these activities do not permit you to read effectively, they are almost tailor-made for listening to the flood of books now available on cassette tape. Indeed, original documentaries written for cassette are widely available in areas such as history and philosophy.

- Let some portion of the books you read be the intellectual equivalent of junk food, and do not feel embarrassed if you are thrilled by Gothic horror, romance novels, comic books, or science fiction. Reading a book doesn't have to be a ponderous matter, with your opinion of it hanging like a balanced sword. Sometimes you are looking for nothing more than an intellectual diversion. Not all books are full-course meals; some are snacks.

- Read in an area that doesn't interest you. For one thing, how do you know that biology, astronomy, or Talmudic philosophy offer nothing interesting if you haven't given those subjects even a cursory go? Even if you do nothing more than confirm your disinterest, the material will give you an entirely different perspective on an aspect of the world which had been hidden from you.

- Don't pick up the first book you see on a subject. You are as likely to get "a good read" through that tactic as you are to engage in a scintillating conversation by speaking to the first person you see. Ask a librarian or someone at a small bookstore to recommend a book that's considered definitive, or a "classic in the field."

- Occasionally read authors with whom you disagree for no other reason than that you disagree with them. After all, you can always throw the book against the wall in irritation, or tear out the pages and flush them down the toilet. Especially when you are brooding about an issue, books on the other side offer a new way to think about it. Even if you ultimately dismiss every aspect of a book's approach, merely having considered the issue from a different angle can shake loose your thought processes. Besides which, when an issue persists through time and attracts good minds who vigorously dispute with each other, there are almost certainly elements of truth on both sides. While you read the other side, ask yourself, "What is it about this position that makes it appeal to so many intelligent people?"

- Do not try to force yourself to read at an artificial speed. Although speed-reading courses may allow you to process information more quickly, the goal of reasoning is not quantity but quality. Allow yourself to dwell upon a provocative sentence and to follow its logic wherever it may lead. The book will still be in your hand when you wish to resume reading.

People have different rates of reading, just as they have different rates of learning. Brand Blanshard admits that he has always been a slow, plodding sort of reader. Yet a myth persists: thinkers of Blanshard's caliber are automatically assumed to read and write quickly.

The above guidelines will allow you to use books more productively than you realized was possible. Armed with a new attitude and a fresh sense of what books can offer you, try an experiment. Buy a cheap replaceable paperback and rip out the pages one by one. Do this exercise even if you never intend to destroy a book ever again. The purpose is to confirm that you have demystified the role of books in your life and assigned to them, instead, a proper role: they are invaluable intellectual tools that will educate and provide pleasure to you throughout a lifetime.

YES, BUT WHICH BOOKS SHOULD I READ?

No worse thief than a bad book.
Italian proverb

The homey American philosopher Ralph Waldo Emerson used three guidelines by which he selected books to read that would not waste the most valuable commodity he possessed, time.

1. Never read a book that is not at least a year old;
2. Never read a book that is not famous; and,
3. Never read anything but what you like.

The modern reader faces a more complicated choice than Emerson did. Information and areas of human study (e.g., genetic engineering, robotics, computer programming, aerodynamics) have exploded in the last few decades. More literature is available to people who seem to have less time to read anything. Women who have been caught in the pressure-trap of maintaining both jobs and families have to guard their leisure time, the time spent on their own needs. A book that wastes your time is, indeed, a thief.

Emerson is certainly not the first or only lover of books to suggest guidelines for how to choose what you read. Originally, I paid little attention to his rules as they seem antiquated and oddly worded. But I find them increasingly appealing.

Never Read a Book that Is Not One Year Old

If a book is worth reading, it will be waiting for you after a year has elapsed. What will have vanished are the advertisements, fanfare, and faddishness that surrounds something new simply because it is new. If you were to catalog the most popular books of the first several decades of the 1900s, you would be amazed at how few have survived even their own century. A more palatable phrasing of this advice would be "Find the books that have withstood the test of time."

Never Read Anything that Is Not Famous

I would change this advice to read "Never read anything that is not recommended by someone you respect." After all, great books are not necessarily famous books. Substance is not a characteristic a book can acquire through a popular vote.

Fortunately, book recommendations are easy to come by. Any

library should be able to provide you with several lists of the "Best Hundred Books," "The Classics," or "The Great Books" drawn up by scholars eager to share their enthusiasm. Moreover, the librarian or university professor should be able to point you to what is considered the "definitive" work in an area. Take the blurbs on the back of dust jackets seriously: look for recommendations by people or publications you respect. Buy a subscription to the *New York Times Book Review* section, or read the reviews of books that are available on the Internet at http://www.amazon.com.

Never Read Anything But What You Like

Although this guideline presupposes you are reading for pleasure or to pursue your own intellectual course—as opposed, for example, to the more mandatory reading of a college student—it contains real wisdom. Discover your own interests by allowing yourself to thoroughly browse a bookstore, picking up titles at random and returning them to the shelf after sampling their wares. Use books as a form of self-discovery.

And, again, don't censor your interests for not being cultured enough, or not showing serious intellectual intent. Read as though all ideas and areas of study were equal in the eyes of Aristotle. Blanshard offers a wonderful quote to describe the process of learning or reading anything. He likens the process to climbing a mountain whose summit is hidden by mist: "And if men can learn . . . that is a better thing to travel than to arrive, they will be prepared to face the secret hidden behind that mist. The secret is that there is no summit there at all. There is only an infinite slope that goes up and up till it is lost among the stars" (p. 407).

THE IMPORTANCE OF PERSONAL FEEDBACK

And now a good word for the benevolence of human beings. Books may be crucial to your intellectual well-being, but they have at least one important failing. They cannot give you real-world feedback. They cannot give you the visceral face-to-face sense that you are not alone on the planet. In short, a book can't hug you, laugh at a joke, commiserate over a failure, join you in scooping up chocolate-ripple ice cream while discussing a problem, or pick up the phone at three in the morning.

Forming friendships is an essential aspect of being human. At least, this appears to be true based on the fact that human beings are the only animals that have evolved to communicate their psychological reactions to each other with great subtlety. We spend hours in conversations that produce nothing more than camaraderie and the pleasure of having communicated who we are to a fellow human being. Part of the pleasure comes from clarifying our thoughts by putting them into words. But much of it seems to come from nothing more than sharing an experience—the bond that Aristotle called "a single soul dwelling in two bodies"—and from receiving good feedback.

In discussing how to sketch a realistic self-appraisal, I advised you to eschew the opinions of friends. The most basic conclusion a person can reach in life is the answer to the question "Who am I?" and most of us are in far more danger of having the small voice within drowned out by other people's input, rather than starved for the lack of it. But once your self-appraisal is completed and your goals are clear, it is time to turn to friends for all the encouragement and assistance you can get.

Please note, however, that seeking "encouragement and assistance" from others is very different than allowing them to play a major role in making your decisions. Most of the situations you face in life can only be handled by you, and you are the one who will live with the consequences of your choices, good or ill. Sometimes your perspective on an emotionally charged situation is so distorted that you will place a high value on a more objective opinion from a friend. But in the vast majority of cases, you have far more information than anyone else and the decision must be yours. The real role of friends will be to serve as sounding boards and psychological supports while you struggle along your own path, making your own choices.

The importance of good intellectual feedback should be obvious, but it is often overlooked. In dealing with emotional problems, people know that they need support from other human beings. They go to spouses and lovers, friends, family members, therapists, and priests. In the absence of those outlets, people in emotional turmoil will corner strangers on park benches and adjacent subway seats in order to pour out their troubles. Talking about problems seems to be a genetically human impulse and part of the healing process.

Yet our culture seems to be losing the social networks of support upon which our parents and grandparents relied. The close-knit system of extended family has slowly unraveled over the past decades to the point that many families stay in contact only through Christmas cards. Mobility, the generation gap caused by the technological revolution, and the frantic pace of life have taken a toll. With many people, family has been replaced with a sense of isolation. In *Learn to Relax*, C. Eugene Walker comments on the lost support system, "There was a security in knowing that one was not alone. There were people who cared and who could be called upon for help in times of crisis. . . . There were no questions asked. It was family. People did what had to be done to see each other through" (p. 88).

Today, friends often serve the traditional role of family. The hours we spend talking to friends usually have less to do with exchanging information than with reducing our anxiety by allowing us to connect to another human being. In making a productive connection, Walker emphasizes the importance of empathy over sympathy. "Empathy is the ability to understand and fully appreciate how a person feels while still remaining objective about it. . . . In sympathy you feel the same emotions as the person and become involved in the same experience as he. This reduces your ability to be objective and to effectively help him" (p. 92).

Thus, friends can provide invaluable emotional support. When dealing with ideas, however, people generally assume they are on their own. And, at least based on the evidence of the feedback they receive from the world, they may be right. How many priests would be sympathetic to a parishioner who was tormented by having unclear rather than unclean thoughts? How many friends would patiently listen if you are having difficulty with logic rather than love? We live in a profoundly anti-intellectual world which does not nurture young struggling minds. Instead, it laughs approvingly at sarcasm, ridicule, and all the forms of gratuitous cruelty that can be heaped upon someone who asks an honest question. This is precisely why the feedback from friends you can trust is essential.

Intellectual problems and insecurities can be as painful as emotional ones. Indeed, it is often difficult to draw a line separating the two areas. Try to remember the last time your intelligence was ridiculed in public, perhaps by a professor in the classroom or an employer in front of co-workers. Your response was not cerebral: it was intensely and painfully emotional. There is no need to go through such painful incidence and the process of changing your habits all by yourself.

But be selective. Other people are like mirrors, giving you back a sense of yourself. Be sure it is a sense of self that helps rather than harms you.

Reflect on how the individuals you know treat you intellectually. Many of them may be dismissive, not only of you but of any and all intellectual matters whatsoever. Often the dismissal will not be malicious, only uncomprehending. We have all been in frustrating situations in which it is clear no meaningful communication will take place. Perhaps you have returned to your hometown from university or a successful career in the city, and you no longer have anything in common with high-school friends. Or maybe you have tried to discuss a defining moment in your life (like falling in love) with someone who has not experienced anything similar, and the person could do nothing more than stare back at you in confusion. The more you attempted to describe how you felt, the less you seemed to be understood.

In such situations, no one is doing anything malicious or wrong, but there is also nothing to be gained from continuing the relationship. At least, not on an intellectual level. Many friendships are limited ones, based on shared hobbies or some other mutual interest. Don't try to expand a friendship beyond its natural borders. Don't expect more from such people than they have to offer. Become realistic and converse with them about the areas you do share.

Or spend your time elsewhere.

Seek out those with whom you enjoy discussing ideas, whether in the form of politics, religion, current events, literature, whatever. These people can give you what is called "visibility." They are like mirrors, reflecting your ideas and a positive intellectual image of yourself. More than this, they help to refine and to lift our intellectual sensibilities.

In short, feedback plays too important a role in your intellectual development to leave to chance. Analyze your family, friends, and acquaintances one by one. Listen to the quality of what they say to you. Try discussing intellectual issues with them and focus on their response, not only on their words but on their body language and the emotional messages in their voices. Are you satisfied with their reactions to you, and with how they deal with intellectual issues?

Some friends may hardly react at all to your attempts to open conversations about ideas or current events. They may give you a confused or blank stare, and return almost immediately to a more comfortable subject such as who is dating who, and what so-and-so said last Friday night. This reaction may stem from their own intellectual insecurities. If so, you should respect this reaction, while, at the same time, taking pains to gently point out that they are changing the subject. If they persist in doing so, encourage them to discuss "why" and take the risk of discussing your own feelings of intellectual insecurity. If they have similar problems, treat them with the same consideration you'd like to receive from the world at large. Just as an honest emotional exchange requires someone to open up first, the same is true of an open intellectual one.

On the other hand, some friends may change the subject, not as a matter of personal discomfort on their part, but as an act of dismissal because they are not interested in anything you have to offer intellectually. Associating with such "friends," at least on an intellectual level, can do you great harm. They are not giving a lack of feedback; they are giving you an abundance of bad feedback, which can only reinforce the negative images you already have of yourself.

For example, a friend may constantly put you down in some manner. Perhaps she ridicules your beliefs, or the way you express yourself, or expresses cynicism about anything you say.

Check out your response. You are probably adopting a defensive attitude, such as flippancy, silence, or counterhostility. Pause and consider that what you are being flippant or quiet about is your own ability to reason, about your own deeply held beliefs. In other words, this person is leading you to emotionally disavow one of the most important aspects of who you are: namely, what you believe to be true. Is this person really your friend?

Some years ago I had the occasion to ask myself this question. I had finally decided to tackle mathematics, a field of study that intimidated me. It never occurred to me to go to someone for help, although a physicist friend had persistently tried to interest me in the hard sciences for years. I bought several math-made-easy books, mostly in geometry and calculus, and settled down to decipher them myself.

Unfortunately, one of the first people to whom I mentioned my math aspirations was a lawyer, who probably had the same difficulties I did. After listening to me complain about how turgid one of the texts was, he asked, "Why bother?" and advised me not to use up all my brain cells on the venture. Fortunately, I also mentioned my studies to the physicist who immediately sent me two delightful cartoon-style books by Larry Gonick on physics and genetics: *The Cartoon Guide to Genetics* and *The Cartoon Guide to Physics*. Shortly afterward, two more books arrived in the mail, both by the charming and brilliant physicist Richard Feynman: *Surely You're Joking, Mr. Feynman!* and *What Do YOU Care What Other People Think?* I defy anyone to read the books listed above and remain indifferent to the hard sciences.

Friends like the physicist help to keep away the intellectual chill of the world, and should be held close. With friends like the historian, conversations should be relegated to the areas in which you relate well.

You cannot carry on a relationship over time without having it affect you. Avoid the wrong kind of feedback. Note however that this doesn't necessarily mean avoiding people who disagree with you. Indeed, such people can stimulate more thought and intellectual growth than those who share your convictions. Moreover, if someone's perspective differs from your own, they will be far more likely to point out gaps or weaknesses in your reasoning. As T. Sharper Knowlson observes of such conversation in *The Art of Thinking*, "[W]e drag our thoughts out of their hiding-places, naked as it were, and occasionally we are not a little startled at the exhibition. Unexpressed ideas are often carefully cherished until, placed before other eyes as well as our own, we see them as they really are."

There is no problem, and great advantage, to having someone disagree with you as long as the disagreement is a respectful one. Avoid people who treat you without respect—that is, people who dismiss your arguments or dismiss you intellectually.

Seek out at least one friend with whom you correspond, with whom you express your thoughts, for reasons that should become clear in the next chapter.

SUMMARY

One of the most fruitful and least threatening intellectual relationships you form with the outside world is to befriend books. This involves learning the down-to-earth rules of how to use a book, which depends in turn on your purpose in using it.

As you undergo the anxiety-provoking process of forming new habits, you will also need flesh-and-blood friends who can provide emotional and intellectual feedback. Choose your friends well, and avoid interacting intellectually with those people who reinforce your negative self-image and habits.

For me, the most valuable intellectual feedback I ever received came by way of an intellectual therapy group that was modeled after psychotherapy ones.

7

Intellectual Therapy

Health and intellect are the two blessings of life.
Menander, *Monostikoi*

Every emotional problem conceivable, from bulimia to paranoia to being addicted to shopping, seems to be addressed by shelves of books and hundreds of psychotherapists. There are discussion groups, twelve-step programs, chemical solutions, Betty Ford centers, support groups for the family. If you are in emotional distress, the world will overwhelm you with answers to your problem. But if you are in intellectual trouble, you're often on your own.

Don't expect universities to help you. They are not equipped to deal with intellectual problems; they exist to process people, who are already presumed to be functioning well intellectually, through an established program.

Books *can* help, especially (auto)biographies of creative people who have faced the same sort of intellectual problems you confront. Learning that Eleanor Roosevelt was so painfully shy that she had to force herself to speak in public can be encouraging to women plagued with intellectual doubt. In diaries, novelists describe how they ago-

141

nized over their writing, doing draft after draft and never being satisfied. Sometimes philosophers and others who write in the humanities discuss how they find reading books to be slow and difficult.

Reading, writing, and thinking can be lonely processes, with none of the flesh-and-blood solace that comes from being hugged or laughing at a joke with a friend. Developing the habit of being reasonable doesn't have to be a lonely journey. It can be done in the warm and sharing atmosphere created by a group of people with common concerns and sympathies.

The next two chapters are devoted to examining a unique intellectual therapy group created by the philosopher George Smith, in which I was fortunate enough to participate. I vividly remember some of the exercises the group members conducted to come to grips with their intellectual problems. To a large extent, these exercises were lifted and adapted from standard psychotherapy, especially from the biocentric therapy of Nathaniel Branden (as expressed in *Breaking Free* and *The Disowned Self*) and the rational-emotive therapy of Albert Ellis. Both psychologists place special stress upon the crucial role your irrational beliefs and ideas play in causing your own psychological problems.

In his anthology *Handbook of Rational-Emotive Therapy*, Ellis explains that Rational Emotive Therapy (RET) is a self-help tool aimed at discovering the ways in which people cause their own destructive emotional patterns by misinterpreting or misevaluating their own events and experiences. Ellis writes of RET, "This process includes the detection of irrational beliefs . . . and the heavy use of the logico-empirical methods of scientific inquiry: questioning, debating, challenging, and disputing of irrational beliefs" (p. 3).

Many of the techniques may seem almost banal, aimed only at loosening the group's mood and stirring up conversation, but they accomplished a great deal of good. If small groups of women are able to meet regularly, they might find the results to be surprisingly beneficial.

The situation is somewhat similar to the consciousness-raising groups of early feminism in the 1960s, which are sometimes credited with sparking the contemporary Women's Liberation movement.

INTELLECTUAL THERAPY: A PERSONAL JOURNEY

About fifteen years ago, I was intimately associated with a remarkable experiment in intellectual therapy, based largely on the work of Dr. Ellis and psychologist Branden. I attended and helped to organize a series of intellectual therapy groups aimed at reducing the psychological barriers to reasoning.

Years earlier I had entered psychotherapy to deal with the unresolved fears and anger that had resulted from an abusive past, including the time I spent living on the streets. For me, the most valuable part of the process had been group therapy, perhaps because so many of my psychological barriers revolved around a fear of people. The group dynamic forced me to confront both my fear and the flesh-and-blood people who caused it. Most intellectual problems involve the fear of other people, e.g., the fear of speaking in public, or of appearing foolish. And, for me, the group dynamic within the intellectual therapy group was as important in overcoming fears as it was in practicing skills publicly.

This chapter and the next one provide an all-too-sketchy blueprint for setting up an intellectual therapy group. During my stint as an assistant in such groups, I found my former exposure to psychology to be invaluable. Indeed, the group dynamics in both types of therapy were quite similar. I highly recommend that anyone who plans to establish an intellectual therapy group seek out popular paperbacks dealing with whatever school of therapy that appeals to them, and read the discussions of group dynamics.

As for the five intellectual groups with which I was involved, each one consisted of about eight people who met for two hours every week over a two-month period in order to work together. The group members came from all professions, including housewives and the unemployed. There were no special membership criteria, with the exception of one "advanced" group which required members to have "graduated" from the more basic group. No other level of education, professional status, or recommendation were required.

Chapter 8 presents about a dozen intellectual therapy techniques that spring from my experiences in such groups, but nothing there constitutes a direct report of what occurred in any particular session. As with psychotherapy groups, one of the entering rules was confidentiality: nothing that specifically happened within the group, especially the identity of members, was to be discussed on the outside. Everything, including exercises which seem to be reported in a documentary style, is merely a representation of the actual event.

None of the intellectual therapy techniques are carved in stone. Almost all of them have been adapted from exercises used by various schools of psychotherapy, most prominently Biocentric and Rational-Emotive Therapies. Other schools, such as Gestalt or Transactional Analysis, use provocative group exercises, and you should plunder their literature as rich resources. The only rule for adapting such exercises is to switch the focus from the purely emotional response to an intellectual/emotional one.

For example, in his book *Breaking Free*, Branden presents a list of questions which he discovered "elicited the most productive and revealing responses" in his clients (p. 12).

In abbreviated form, these twenty-two questions are:

1. Did your parents view the world as irrational?

2. Were you taught how to develop your mind?

3. Were you encouraged to think independently?

4. Were you free to express your opinions openly?

5. Did your parents ridicule your opinions?

6. Did your parents treat your thoughts with respect?

7. Were you psychologically visible to them?

8. Did you feel you were a source of pleasure to them?

9. Did your parents deal with you fairly and justly?

10. Did your parents physically punish you?

11. Did your parents believe in your basic goodness?

12. Did they believe in your intellectual potential?

13. Did they take cognizance of your knowledge and context?

14. Did your parents cultivate guilt within you?

15. Did they produce fear within you?

16. Did they respect intellectual and physical privacy?

17. Did they want you to have self-esteem?

18. Did they make you realize that what you made of your life was important?

19. Did your parents encourage a fear of the world?

20. Were you encouraged to openly express yourself?

21. Were you encouraged to like your body and sex?

22. Was your masculinity or femininity reinforced?

Interestingly, of the twenty-two questions offered by Branden as being psychologically productive, over half directly concern intellectual functioning. This is consistent with Branden's belief that "The primary task of parenthood is to equip a child for independent survival as an adult. That entails doing everything in the parent's power to encourage the child's development as a rational, thinking being" (p. 28).

The "intellectual/emotional" questions can be lifted and used wholesale. The purely emotional ones can be adapted as follows:

7. Were you intellectually invisible to your parents?

8. Did they enjoy talking to you?

9. Did your parents discuss issues with you fairly?

10. Did they intellectually punish you?

11. Did they believe in your intelligence?

14. Did they make you feel guilty for disagreeing?

15. Were you afraid to disagree?

16. Did they want you to be intellectually self-confident?

19. Did they encourage a fear of ideas, e.g., of math?

21. Were you encouraged to like the workings of your mind?

22. Were you intellectually treated differently than a sibling of the opposite sex?

As the first intellectual therapy "exercise" presented, type up the revised list of questions and have a copy ready to hand out to every member at the beginning of the first session. The purpose of the list is not as a springboard to conversation. Such a wide-ranging discussion would too easily become emotional and lose the focus of the group. Instead, have each member post the list somewhere prominent in the home—on a mirror, or the refrigerator, or a door. Over the eight weeks of sessions, and perhaps long beyond, each member can scan the questions and see what reactions percolate.

Before diving into a session-by-session blueprint for intellectual therapy, it is necessary to lay some groundwork to explain some of the techniques and the group function in a far more efficient manner.

GROUNDWORK FOR AN INTELLECTUAL THERAPY GROUP

> No rule so good as rule of thumb, if it hit.
> John Kelly, *Scottish Proverbs*

The following rules are actually guidelines, though I highly recommend each one.

Charge a Fee

The fee to join the group is not meant to be remuneration for the therapist, though I have no ideological or practical objection to people being paid for their labors. A modest fee is important for three reasons:

1. Handouts will be provided to members at the end of each therapy session, and modest refreshments will be served during the sessions' breaks. The cost of duplication and refreshments should not fall upon the shoulders of the therapist or facilitator.

2. More importantly, people value anything they pay for more than what they receive for free. Even a small fee will increase the members' tendency to do the assignments and attend regularly.

3. The fee is a filter. If someone balks at paying a modest amount of money for eight weeks' worth of therapy, then they are expressing a lack of commitment to the process and would probably not make a valuable contribution to the group.

Keep an Intellectual Diary

By my rambling digressions I perceive myself to be grown old. I used to write more methodically. But one does not dress for private company as for a public ball.

Benjamin Franklin, *Autobiography*

A recommendation adapted from Henry Hazlitt's excellent *Thinking as a Science* that the intellectual therapy groups vigorously incorporated was "to keep a notebook or a journal" (p. 145). It is important for the facilitator to be able to clearly communicate to the group why the diary is an essential aspect of the intellectual therapy process. For this reason, the facilitator should reread the section of chapter 4 entitled "Put It in Writing." Photocopy that section and distribute it to group members.

One of the least threatening methods of writing down your thoughts is to keep a diary, a private chronicle of your thoughts and your thought process. An intellectual journal is a combination of a notebook and a diary, to be kept on a daily basis. It is a record of what you have been thinking about, how you approached an idea or issue, and the emotional reactions invoked by the process.

Most young girls receive a diary at Christmas or on their birthdays. There they record their fantasies about boys and careers, their secret longings and fears. An intellectual diary can serve much the same purpose. It is a combination notebook and journal. It can chronicle the problems you have been thinking about, how you have approached them, and, especially, which emotions you experienced during the whole process. It can also serve as a record of your stream of consciousness on any topic you choose, so long as it is the topic of thought you write at the top of the page.

Here is a good strategy for maintaining your intellectual diary:

1. Get a loose-leaf binder and a stack of punched paper. Every week at some set time—perhaps Sunday night or Monday morning—date seven sheets of paper to correspond with the next seven days. Place these in your binder, with plenty of spare sheets to be inserted as required.

2. Commit at least fifteen minutes a day to writing down your thoughts and any intellectual problems or insights you have had in the last twenty-four hours. After getting started, you might want to write on and on. Do so. The fifteen minutes is meant to be a minimum, not a maximum.

3. Devote a specific time in the day to your diary. This can be a chronological time, like 7:30 A.M., or a slot in your schedule, like during a coffee break. Make a daily appointment with yourself to consider who you are and who you would like to be intellectually. Be selfish about it, because regularity is the key to establishing the diary as a habit. If you habitually feel the urge to write for a longer period than your daily slot allows (e.g., during a coffee break), consider switching to a more open-ended time, such as directly after dinner.

4. Don't censor what you write about. As long as the topic bears on your intellectual life, let yourself explore it. The topic of the day's diary can be quite abstract, like the purpose of religion in your life, or very concrete, like the merits of switching to one newspaper from another. The important thing is to think about things in terms of principles. Don't slip into simply venting your emotional reactions to the issue on paper.

5. If you wish to write about emotions, do so, but not as a way of venting them on paper. Try to *analyze* them instead. For example, instead of brooding on a remark that hurt your feelings, try to write down every possible interpretation of the remark and every possible

motivation a person would have for making that statement. Try to *analyze* whatever you are thinking about. For example, suppose you want to write about becoming more assertive. Instead of merely recording how bad you feel about being unassertive, ask yourself "What does it mean to be assertive?" Is it the same as being aggressive? Is assertiveness always desirable? Can assertiveness be learned?

6. Describe how you feel toward yourself intellectually and what emotions are being stirred up by the risks you are taking in your daily life or, perhaps, by merely recording your thoughts. Be honest. If you feel optimistic, say so. Your emotions provide fuel and feedback for your mind, and you cannot expect your mind to function well without motivation. If you are on an emotional downswing, writing about it, particularly in this analytic manner, may do much to dissipate it. Your emotions provide the fuel and feedback that your intellect requires to function well.

7. If you fail to keep your daily appointment with the diary, make sure to jot down the reason why. That page of the diary may read "I forgot," "I lost the notebook," "My daughter was ill." This is important because, over time, you may see a pattern emerge from the excuses you record. When you review the diary at the end of the month, you may find that several entries claimed "I was too intimidated," or "I was too tired," or "I cannot remember." This may mean that you should reschedule your appointments with your notebook for a better time in the day, or it may give you insight into how you approach ideas, even those with relatively little risk attached to them.

8. If your mind switches off when you sit down in front of a blank sheet of paper, note this reaction. Try to break through this barrier to thought by speculating about it. Does the blankness happen often? Have you ever been able to get past it? Can you describe what it feels like? Does it make you sleepy, or dazed, or irritable?

Then, at the end of every month, review the preceding month's entries. Look for patterns. Look for problem areas.

As a fall-back position to writing down your thoughts in a journal, if this is too difficult a regime for you, write letters to friends and family in which you discuss ideas. Having a practical goal of keeping in touch with people and the feedback they can provide may ease the process of writing ideas down. Knowing that someone is going to read your thoughts can motivate you to express them.

Just be sure to keep copies of both sides of the correspondence.

Reading Assignments

The reading assignments that are handed out at the end of one session and discussed at the beginning of the next are not randomly chosen, but reflect the sentiment of a chapter heading in Henry Hazlitt's *Thinking as a Science*: "Things Worth Thinking About." Hazlitt concludes that one of the areas most worthy of thought—at least, the one that most provokes thought—is ethics. What actions are good or bad? How is "good" to be defined? Perhaps "good" is an end in and of itself, or perhaps it is defined in reference to whether or not it produces another end such as happiness or health. Ethical debate is a rich and deep source of human thought.

It also has the extreme advantage of requiring no specialized knowledge. Unlike physics or biology, ethics is based on experience, intuition, and the sort of observations that are open to all human beings on an equal basis. Although philosophers may well have given more thought to questions of ethics, they have no knowledge of goodness that is not available to the average human being. Thus, readings in ethics will allow group members to understand the material and discuss it on an equal footing even if their educational backgrounds are widely divergent.

The more basic the ethical question, the better. "What is the good life?" "Is virtue its own reward?" Any good introductory university text on ethics should be a fruitful place to find such material.

Another rich source of reading material that does not require specialized knowledge and provokes thought is the political issues that impact everyone's lives. The more philosophically phrased the issue is—phrased in fundamental terms—the more likely it is to provoke debate. For example, rather than assign an article critiquing the Vietnam War, assign one that examines the conditions under which making a declaration of war can be justified. To find such articles, browse the "politics" section of a bookstore or library until you find several books on provocative topics. The prefaces are likely to be a good source of handouts.

Or simply fall back on the tried-and-true questions over which human beings have argued for centuries. These include: Is there a God? Whether or not there is a God, is there some form of afterlife such as reincarnation? Can anything be objectively true? Do humans have free will?*

The group leader should copy a sufficient number of articles from useful texts to allow each member to take one home for analysis. Each member should preserve these handouts, and any others, in a binder or file folder.

Taking a Chance

> Nature magically suits a man to his fortunes, by making them the fruit of his character.
>
> Ralph Waldo Emerson, *Conduct of Life*

The facilitator should refer to the section in chapter 4 of the present volume entitled "Taking a Chance" in order to establish a broader context for the risk taking that will be part of the group's "homework." Copy that section and distribute it to group members. Every week, each member will be asked to take at least one intellectual risk, though taking daily risks is far more effective.

What constitutes a risk? To quote what I said earlier: "A risk is any conscious activity that is emotionally difficult for you to perform and which involves the real possibility of failure. . . . A risk can be something minor, even trivial." Specific examples of minor risks that people commonly have difficulty taking are:

---

*Three valuable sources for such general philosophical questions are John Hospers's two overviews *Human Conduct: An Introduction to the Problems of Ethics* and *Introduction to Philosophical Analysis*, and Bertrand Russell's classic *History of Western Philosophy*. Also valuable as a resource is *Great Treasury of Western Thought: A Compendium of Important Statements on Man and His Institutions by the Great Thinkers of Western History* edited by Mortimer Adler and Charles Van Doren.

- striking up a conversation with someone you've dealt with anonymously;
- reading a book with which you strongly disagree;
- asking a question in a public forum;
- complaining to a waiter about inadequate food or service;
- writing a letter to the editor;
- thinking about an issue for X number of minutes; and
- standing up for yourself when someone criticizes you.

The content and the emotional level of the risk will vary widely from person to person. Any of the above-listed minor risks might well be a major one for a particular person. Work up to major risks cautiously. Each member should tackle whatever level of risk she can emotionally handle. The purpose is *not* to cause trauma but to increase confidence and intellectual flexibility. Your goal is to grind away at fears in order to establish better intellectual habits: don't be so heroic as to scare yourself into giving up on the spot.

So, to reiterate: what constitutes an intellectual risk? A risk:

(a) is not done habitually;
(b) moves you closer to a goal;
(c) entails the possibility of failure;
(d) stimulates emotional resistance to acting;
(e) is a conscious decision; and,
(f) is recorded in writing.

If you have trouble remembering to take a risk, then write notes to yourself and put them where you can't help but see them every day, even if that means posting them on the toilet basin.

A Tape Recorder

Every member should bring a tape recorder and a cassette to the sessions. The purpose is to record their own participation in specific exercises, *not* to record the entire session. Under no circumstances should a member record the comments, exercises, or conversation of any other member even if that member gives her consent. After all, people often have second thoughts. From time to time, however, it will be valuable for individuals to have their own group work on tape to review during the week.

One cassette is probably all that will be necessary. After the material has been recorded in a session, the member should turn off the machine, leaving the cassette in place. New material should be recorded at the end of the prior one so that each member has a good record of her own participation to review when the group process has ended.

SUMMARY

Emotional problems can be alleviated by the support and dynamic of group therapy: the same is true of intellectual problems. Setting up an intellectual therapy group is similar in many ways to establishing a psychotherapy one. This is especially true because the goal of the group is to deal with the emotions that underlie and accompany intellectual problems. Indeed, many psychotherapy techniques can be used with very little modification.

The ground rules of forming an intellectual therapy group are explained, along with the three forms of "homework" that continue throughout the group experience. Ideally, they will continue afterward.

Explanations can not offer a real-world sense of an intellectual therapy group, however. The following chapter is meant to provide that.

8

Forming an
Intellectual Therapy Group

Reason's whole pleasure, all the joys of sense,
Lie in three words—Health, Peace, and Competence.
                        Alexander Pope, *Essays on Man*

In a society that prized intellectual matters as highly as emotional ones, it would be an easy matter to find therapy groups to help correct problems with reasoning. Some people assume that such correction is a function of Logic 101 classes at universities and colleges, but logic courses no more address your personal intellectual problems than psychology courses solve your emotional ones. Fortunately, it is always possible to establish an intellectual therapy group of your own.

In a chapter entitled "Teaching Unconditional Self-Acceptance," Windy Dryden's book *Inquiries in Rational Emotive Behavior Therapy* offers a virtual blueprint for establishing what she terms a "Self-Acceptance Group" which is organized along Rational-Emotive Therapy (RET) principles. The RET groups are remarkably similar to the intellectual therapy (IT) ones with which I was involved years ago: indeed, the IT groups in which I assisted may well have been originally modeled upon them.

Dryden's groups involve seven to nine people, with the expectation that at least one member will drop out along the way. They run for eight weeks and use a "cognitive-emotive" approach that acknowledges the psychology of reasoning. Other than a commitment to participate fully, the only rules for membership are a promise to respect confidentiality and to avoid any negative criticism within the sessions. Constructive criticism, that suggests changes and avoids attacks, is encouraged at various points.

The following formula for forming such a group is an integration of my earlier experiences and of Dryden's blueprint for RET groups. Many of RET's techniques and much of its structure can be lifted wholesale and used to good purpose in forming a group to explore the psychology of reasoning.

FORMING AN INTELLECTUAL THERAPY GROUP

> Surely every medicine is an innovation; and he that will not apply new remedies, must expect new evils.
>
> Francis Bacon, *Essays: Of Innovations*

One of the few advantages of creating an intellectual therapy group virtually out of thin air is that you can sculpt it to meet special needs or goals. The ensuing formula for conducting an IT group is nothing more than a suggestion, perhaps more to be honored in the breach than in the observance. From my experience, however, I suspect that five rules are important to observe in organizing the group.

1. There should be no more than eight members in the group. This limitation not only ensures a certain intimacy, it allows time for each member to participate in the various therapy exercises without rushing.

2. The sessions should be two hours long, with a break of ten minutes, and be held on a weekly basis.

3. Confidentiality must be observed in order to allow each member to expose vulnerabilities without fear of any consequences occurring outside of the group.

4. The leader, or facilitator, should enforce a policy of tolerating only constructive criticism among the members.

5. Homework should be included as a regular feature, to be discussed at the beginning of each session and assigned at the end. If a member refuses to do homework—as opposed to merely having trouble with it—the facilitator should exclude her from the group.

The week-to-week sequence of the specific therapy exercises—some of which are detailed below—is arbitrary. You will need to use your own judgment to employ whichever one seems correct at the moment.

The general structure of the sessions I experienced followed a well-remembered and set pattern. The members reported on their homework assignments (except for Session One, of course), the readings were discussed, the facilitator explained one aspect of what the group hoped to accomplish through the general IT process (in the ensuing descriptions, this portion of the imaginary sessions revolve around material from *The Reasonable Woman*), one or two exercises occurred, and homework was assigned. Homework consisted of three elements: keeping an intellectual diary through the week as previously discussed, reading assigned material, and taking one intellectual risk, such as speaking in public or striking up a conversation with a total stranger. Somewhere in the two-hour session, a ten-minute break occurred during which refreshments were served.

Session One

The group members, who are seated in a loose circle on the floor or in chairs, introduce themselves to each other by giving their names and briefly stating the reasons they joined the group. The facilitator explains the general purpose of the meetings, as well as the rules: all group interactions are absolutely confidential and—except if a specific therapy exercise calls for a show of anger—all interactions are to be respectful. She hands out the list of questions adapted from Branden's *Breaking Free* (in the preceding chapter).

In her book, Dryden describes how she begins the first session. She asks the group, "Who wants high self-esteem?" After a show of hands, she asks each member to respond individually with a sentence or so to the question, "What would raise your self-esteem?"

The groups in which I participated began with a sentence fragment thrown out by the facilitator. They began with a variation on an exercise called "sentence completion." This technique, perfected by Branden, involves the facilitator throwing out the first words of a sentence which dangles, and which is meant to provoke a probing response from the group member(s) who complete(s) it.

In the IT groups, the sentence fragments were meant to elicit both emotional and intellectual responses. In this particular variation, the facilitator threw out the fragment for each member of the circle to answer in turn, as quickly as they could. (More traditionally, sentence completion is a one-on-one rapid-fire process, rather like word association, during which the member has little chance to think about her responses. With each new sentence fragment, the IT facilitator should begin with a new member and move clockwise.)

The first opening sentence fragment was "I am a person who . . ." Moving around the circle, the following responses would be typical, though they are not the actual responses of any session:

—likes to think
—thinks she stinks
—is angry
—is scared
—likes music
—feels like a failure
—sleeps too much
—fidgets

At this point, the session paused so that each person could pay attention to her physical posture. Had it changed from when she sat down? If so, how? The purpose of checking yourself over was to become as self-aware as possible of any emotional reactions such as anxiety or anger that the questions elicited. Was your jaw clenched? Or your fists? Did you feel flushed and sweaty?

Then, the second sentence fragment was thrown out: "Intellectually, I am a person who . . ."

—reads a lot
—knows nothing at this point
—puts on acts
—makes excuses for myself
—makes things up
—is easily confused
—is having a problem with the question
—wants to feel more confident

Again, each member took a moment to note any change in posture or emotional response. Then, the third sentence fragment: "Being intellectual to me means . . ."

—having intellectual achievements
—being right
—feeling a great deal better
—being a good bullshitter
—thinking about things
—having a very broad perspective
—being smart
—having as much information as possible

Again, posture and reactions were noted.

For the remainder of the first hour of the two-hour session, the facilitator outlined the classical view of what habits were and the role they played in people's lives (see chapter 1). She sketched what was meant by the habit of reasonableness.

After the ten-minute break, she summarized her earlier presentation and answered any questions group members had. Then, the homework assignment was explained in detail. The homework consisted of three elements: keeping a daily intellectual diary, as detailed in the preceding chapter; reading the material that was handed out at the end of each session; and, taking an intellectual risk.

As the members left the session, they passed by a huge empty pickle jar which was labeled "pizza fund." If a member did not take her weekly risk, or if she did not make entries in her diary each day, she owed a dollar to the jar. It was not uncommon for every member to have missed at least one day in the diary and for two or three to have not taken a risk. On average, the pizza fund seemed to grow by about 15 to 30 dollars a week.

Session Two

(The session, like all subsequent ones, started precisely on time, with no catch-up offered to those who arrived late.)

The first order of business was to review the homework, beginning with how successful the members had been in maintaining their daily intellectual journals. Each member, in turn, gave a brief report. The report did not include the substance of what had been written in the diary, nor did it address the actual content of the diary. Instead, the report dwelled upon any problems the member experienced in writing down her thoughts and upon any emotional reactions the diary had elicited.

Had the diary been maintained each day? If not, why not? The following are typical—though again not actual—responses:

• I wrote every day, but only for a few minutes. I sat behind my desk and turned on the computer, and decided to write about the question of how people know anything. I asked questions like "How do I know there is a desk here?" Then I said to myself, "Well, I know there is a desk here." I didn't do an analysis. I just defend a position. Which probably means I don't have an open mind.

• I was a failure. When I tried to think about something, my mind would immediately wander. I couldn't focus. When I tried to focus, I got a headache and gave up. Every day the same thing happened.

• We had some company over the other night and someone made a comment that made me think. But, before that, I didn't know what to think about so I only wrote for the last three days. I would think about something in snatches, but not really in what I consider to be a train of thought. And maybe I misidentified the process of thought. I think of thought as being the same way you construct a sentence. I had more success at writing than at just sitting and thinking. I didn't keep it in a diary but I wrote a letter to a friend.

• Pass. (This is always accepted as a valid response as long as it doesn't become habitual.)

• I missed two days because I forgot. On the other days, I just started a stream of consciousness in writing, figuring that some other time I would organize the thoughts. I tended to think of a subject in terms of all the other people who have said something about it. I wasn't aware of the extent to which I substituted all that I had heard about something for my own thoughts about it. I don't know if I am appealing to authority or whether it is just laziness.

• I enjoyed the assignment.

• I got in three sessions, because it was hard to write down my thoughts. I think best when I am walking. I started out thinking about some of the things that have meant a lot to me in my intellectual life— projects. The books I'd like to write some day. I wrote some things down, but I found it hard to concentrate and to follow subjects through to their logical conclusions. I tended to sort of drift along.

• I have to write as part of my job, so I am totally resistant to sitting down in my spare time and dealing with abstract matters.

As each member reported on her intellectual diary, the facilitator asked a few questions and made suggestions about how to improve the process. Then, the topic of risks was addressed. Each member reported on the risk taken (or not). Typical risks included: reading a particular book, asking a question in class, trying to convince an employer to give you a raise, browsing through a night-school brochure for the next semester, speaking to a stranger, bringing up a political disagreement with a parent, joining Toastmasters to learn public speaking, writing a letter to the editor.

Next, and for the remainder of the first hour, the group discussed the content of the reading assignment in an open forum structure, which allowed every one to participate but did not demand that anyone do so. The facilitator did take note, however, of the members who spoke and of those who hung back. Unlike the reports on the diary and the risk taking, the discussion of readings focused entirely on the intellectual content of the material. From time to time, the facilitator intervened to ensure that the discussion remained focused on the intellectual aspects of the reading or to promote discussion by asking questions that returned to the fundamentals of the issue.

After a ten-minute break, during which members paid up their debts on the honor system to the pickle jar, the facilitator explained how bad intellectual habits, particularly how the fear of error and of appearing foolish, create barriers to establishing more desirable habits (see chapter 2). In an open back-and-forth, the facilitator and the group discussed the role that such habits as the fear of error play in their lives.

Then, the facilitator introduced a therapeutic exercise to the group. Everyone picked an envelope out of a box passed around by the facilitator. As each member's turn to do the exercise arrived, she turned on her tape recorder and moved into the center of the group circle. Then, still standing, she opened the envelope and retrieved the file card from within.

On each card, the facilitator had written a statement that the member had to read out loud and then address for a full minute on an *emotional* level. That is, she had to address either how the statement itself made her feel and why, or how it felt to be standing up as the center of attention. The presentation was meant to be a one-minute stream of consciousness of the person's emotional reaction either to the topic on the file card or to the process of speaking in front of the group. After the exercise was completed, the member was told to keep the card. Her tape recorder was turned off.

Some of the topics I remember were: "No woman has become a great painter like Picasso"; "Housework is demeaning because there is no thought involved in performing it"; "It is as important to 'know other people' as to 'know thyself'; "If science discovered there were differences in the brains of men and women, how would that new information change your opinions?"; and, "Women around the world share certain traits regardless of the culture influences."

Again, the group member could not assess the truth or falsehood of the statement, only some aspect of how it made her feel to read or think about it. For example:

• "This confuses me because I haven't given it any thought, and I don't like people watching me think about something for the first time."

• "My father used to say things like that and it still makes me so mad because anyone who says that is just baiting you."

• "I always freeze when I have to speak in public . . . right now my palms are sweating."

• "One of the first things running through my mind was whether I would read it correctly. When I pick something up and read it in front of people, I have difficulty. I have a tendency to stumble. I think I did and that bothers me."

• "I wish I could speak about the topic because it would be easier for me to pick it apart intellectually than to talk about my emotions."

After every member had participated, another round of the exercise occurred. This time each member stood in the middle of the circle, read the same topic again, and addressed it on a purely *intellectual* level. That is, she commented on the truth or falsehood of the statement, on its historical context, on its political implications, etc.

At some point in either round of the exercise, the facilitator will encounter resistance from a group member. Roughly the following exchange will occur:

Member: "Maybe we should try someone else, because I'm drawing a blank."

Facilitator: "What are you feeling right this instant?"

M: "I don't know, I'm still blank."

F: "When people don't want to deal with something painful or uncomfortable, they sometimes blank out. What is it you're avoiding?"

M: "I don't know."

F: "If you did know, what would it be?"

In a surprising number of cases, the last question worked—that is, the member started talking. If not, the facilitator had the member close her eyes, and continued to ask questions until the sixty seconds were up. Sometimes the most valuable sessions were those that showed the member precisely how she was shutting off her mind.

Directly after this exercise, the facilitator went into a less pressured one, perhaps to regain a sense of fun. I remember one such exercise vividly: the facilitator asked a question and each person in the circle contributed an answer as the question rotated around. "I pass" was considered a valid response. At one point, the facilitator's question was "What is the title of the first book you intend to write?" One woman bluntly announced: "All About Me!" The next question was

"What is the title of your second book?" She didn't miss a beat: "All About Me, Volume Two!" Shyness wasn't her problem.

Reading material was handed out at the door as members left.

Session Three

The session began with a review of the intellectual diary and of the risk taking, followed by a discussion of the assigned reading material. Again, people were allowed to hang back in silence, if they so chose.

After a ten-minute break, the facilitator explained how to draw up a realistic self-appraisal and handed out forms that consisted of a sheet of paper divided in half by a line down the center (see chapter 4). At the top of one column were the words "Intellectual Limitations": at the top of the other were the words "Intellectual Accomplishments." The form was to be filled out by each member in the coming week as their intellectual risk.

Then, a therapy exercise was introduced. Again, it was a variation of sentence completion, but this time it involved a one-on-one exchange between the facilitator and each member of the group in turn. As each member's turn arrived, she switched on the tape recorder. Each time the member completed a sentence, the facilitator shot another fragment back at the same member. (The facilitator taped each member individually and gave her the cassette to review over the next week.)

Facilitator: One thing I don't like about my mind is . . .

Member: . . . I can't control my thoughts.

F: To me, controlling my thoughts means . . .

M: . . . never looking stupid.

F: If I looked stupid, I would . . .

M: . . . I don't know, I'm blank.

F: I went blank because . . .

M: . . . I can't stand thinking about being stupid.

F: Being stupid means . . .

M: . . . having people laugh at you.

F: I want . . . (a standby sentence fragment)

M: . . . to shut up anyone who laughs at me. To make them sorry. To make them . . . I'm sorry, I don't know why I'm saying this.

F: Don't evaluate. I don't understand myself when . . .

M: . . . I'm out of control.

F: If I give into my feelings . . .

M: . . . I might start crying.

F: Sometimes I want to cry out . . .

M: . . . just leave me alone!

F: If I'm out of control . . . (The facilitator returned to the issue of control, which emerged as a central problem.)

M: . . . something bad is going to happen to me.

F: Mother was always . . . (Abruptly switching topics keeps the flow going.)

M: . . . complaining.

F: That made me feel . . .

M: . . . like nothing I did was right. That I couldn't make anything better.

F: It also made me feel . . .

M: . . . furious, and helpless.

The sentence completion went on for approximately three minutes with each member. Whenever the member blanked out or could not otherwise respond to a particular sentence fragment, the facilitator fell back on certain "standard" fragments that loosened the flow. *The Disowned Self* (p. 136) is the single best source of such standby fragments and on sentence completion itself. In the absence of this book, however, you can get a sense of them from the following:

"I want . . ."

"I can't stand it when . . ."

"All my life, I've been told . . ."

"When I wake up in the morning . . ."

"As a woman, I wish I could . . ."

"Sexually, I wish . . ."

"For me, a woman's body . . ."

"Father was always . . ."

"Mother was always . . ."

"Right now I am feeling . . ."

"Right now I am thinking . . ."

"When I look into the mirror . . ."

"Ever since I was a child, I've wondered . . ."

"The tension in my body is telling me . . ."

The natural tendency of the member will be to revert to emotional statements. It is the facilitator's responsibility to keep all exercises in the session as focused as possible on the psychology of reasoning.

Reading assignments were handed out at the door.

Session Four

The session began with a review of the intellectual diary and risk taking, followed by a discussion of the assigned reading material. During this session, the facilitator began gently to pressure those who had been hanging back in discussions to participate. Instead of allowing them to sit in silence, the facilitator directed questions specifically to them, e.g., "What did you think of the article's central argument?" or "How do you react to what X just said?" or—asked in a gentle manner—"Why is it that you do not speak out during discussions?"

For the first time, members were encouraged to address each other, not merely as a part of the intellectual exchange, but in terms of their emotional reactions to each other during the exchanges. It was absolutely essential, however, that the comments remained respectful and noncombative. All comments must focus on the speaker's reactions, *not* on other members. For example, a member could properly say, "I get confused when X points her finger at me while making a point. Somehow that intimidates me and I shrink back." A member could not properly say, "X babbles when she makes points." Through gentle questioning and instructions, the facilitator must assert control to ensure that every member is respected and every member participates.

(Depending on how productive the above-described process is, the facilitator might add such a "postmortem" at the end of various discussions or exercises. Or not.)

After the ten-minute break, the facilitator explained the practice and purpose of setting intellectual goals, including breaking larger goals down into explicit and manageable units (see chapter 4). Members were then asked to report briefly on a personal, but modest, intellectual goal that included a strong emotional component. For example, if the prospect of raising your hand in class terrified you, that would qualify as an intellectual goal with an emotional component. The goal each person described became her risk for the coming week.

Another exercise was introduced, one that I found particularly difficult. Each member of the group, in turn, stood in the middle of the group circle in silence for sixty seconds, while everyone else stared at them. During that time, the member was to slowly turn 360 degrees, while maintaining eye contact with at least one member of the group. As the member turned, she was to monitor her thoughts and feelings about being the absolute center of attention. The other members were instructed *not* to register any emotions or reactions in their expressions: they were simply to stare back.

After every member had taken a turn, each one reported her reaction to the exercise. As amazing as it may seem, to those of us who veer sharply toward shyness, some reported that they actually enjoyed the exercise and welcomed the group scrutiny.

Then, perhaps to bind the group together after the preceding exercise, another few rounds of sentence completion worked their way around the circle. The first sentence fragment was: "One thing I like about my mind is . . ."

—it works

—it continues to heal

—. . . I draw a blank

—it is going all the time

—it makes strange connections

—it irritates my father

—it is quick

—it is retentive.

The next sentence fragment: "One thing I don't like about my mind is . . ."

—it requires too much care

—I don't think clearly

—that it is disorganized

—my thoughts are fuzzy

—that I don't take risks

—it doesn't work when I want it to

—the way I forget things

—that it skirts around things.

And, finally: "If I thought I were as smart as anyone else in the world . . ."

—I would write a book

—I would help children

—I would become rich and famous

—it wouldn't make any difference

—I would have confidence

—I would try harder

—I would tell my boss where to get off

—I would like myself.

At the end of the exercise, the group spent a few minutes commenting on the exercises. Reading material was handed out at the door.

Session Five

The session began with a review of the intellectual diary and the risk taking, followed by a discussion of the assigned reading material. The discussion this time was not an open format, however. Each member was asked to take a position, for or against some issue that had been stated within the assigned reading and to argue that position vigorously for three minutes, of course switching on the tape recorder beforehand.

(Remember: the same cassette from earlier sessions is to be used but not *re*used. The individualized sentence completion, for example, is not to be taped over. The new material is added onto the end of that material.)

The facilitator briefly sketched what was meant by the technique of visualizing a goal: that is, breaking down (for example) the goal of "being intellectually confident" into small units, such as what a confident person dresses like, how she holds her body, what her voice sounds like (see chapter 5). Then, just before the ten-minute break, the facilitator explained that the session would reopen with everyone stating an intellectual goal they wish to visualize.

After the break, everyone stated their goals and wrote them down on file cards which were handed to the facilitator, who read the first one aloud. As she did, the member responsible for the card turned on the tape recorder and shut her eyes. For three minutes, she visualized out loud what the goal would look like, feel like, taste like . . .

After each member had visualized her goal, group members engaged in an intellectual technique that was discussed earlier—brainstorming. In his book *Learn to Relax*, C. Eugene Walker claims that brainstorming is most naturally a group process. He writes, "Brainstorming is basically a procedure for groups . . . get some people together who are interested and cooperative. Somewhere around five to ten seems to work best, but often two or three are adequate. Specify as clearly as possible exactly what problem the session is to focus on. then start generating ideas . . ." (p. 68).

Walker sets down four basic rules for group brainstorming:

1. Critical judgment of ideas is ruled out. No member should criticize her own ideas or those of other members. Ideas should flow back and forth chaotically, without evaluation.

2. Free-wheeling is encouraged. Try to be off-the-wall, unconventional, and wild. Leave sober reflection where it belongs—as an aftermath.

3. Quantity, not quality, is the goal. Come up with as many ideas as possible. There is always time to evaluate them later.

4. Combination and improvement are sought. As ideas are expressed, every member should think of ways to revise them, combine them with earlier ideas . . . in short, every member should take the ideas expressed and run with them.

Each member recorded the five minutes of brainstorming that related to her own stated goal. The tape recorder was turned on so that she could review the material in the coming week. The facilitator watched to ensure that each member turned her recorder off after her own topic had been discussed. For Walker, group brainstorming works best because, "One person's thoughts and ideas often stir up another person's associations, stimulating him to come up with ideas and thoughts. . . . Also, the social motivation and facilitation of being in a group of people working on a problem enables us to work more diligently and enthusiastically" (p. 69).

For the week to come, the intellectual diary was to focus on the intellectual goal. For example, if the goal had been to "speak more confidently," the member would report to the diary every day on her thoughts or actions regarding that goal.

Reading material was handed out at the door.

Session Six

The session began with a review of the intellectual diary and risk taking, followed by a discussion of the assigned reading material. Again—and for all future sessions—the facilitator gently pressured members who hung back to participate.

The facilitator addressed the benevolent role that books can play in intellectual therapy, reviewing much of the material in chapter 6 of the present volume. The facilitator then handed out a battered paperback book to each member and instructed them to destroy it. (Any popular paperback, purchased for next to nothing at a used bookstore, will do.) Torn pages from the books were tossed into a box in the center of the circle. Afterward, the group discussed their reactions to the exercise.

After the ten-minute break, each member of the group, in turn, participated in a new exercise that had been adapted from Gestalt Therapy. The exercise consisted of each member holding a spoken conversation with herself: the three-minute exchange was between the stupid her and the intelligent her—two different aspects of her intellectual persona. Again, the tape recorder was switched on. Again, the facilitator needed to exercise a great deal of guidance. The following is a typical example of the exercise:

Facilitator: Begin talking as the stupid you, then let the smart you answer. Just go back and forth.

Member: Okay. Well . . . the stupid me would say, "you can never understand anything . . ."

F: That's good. But don't report. Actually speak as the stupid you.

M: You can never understand anything. You never could. (Pause as the member switches.) Well, maybe you never let me understand anything. Maybe if you stopped talking all the time I'd ... (The member starts laughing.)

F: Which one of you is laughing?

M: Neither. I mean, *I'm* laughing because I feel silly.

F: Have the stupid you comment on why you're laughing.

M: Wait. (The member frowns.) Okay. You're laughing because you might as well. Everyone else is going to be laughing at you in a minute. I can't believe you're coming to a therapy session that makes you sit in a chair. Why don't you wear a dunce hat while you're at it, like you did in the second grade that one time?

F: Now let the smart side of you answer.

M: Why are you trying to make me hate myself all the time? I mean, what's in it for you? Does it give you pleasure to ridicule me all the time and never give me a fucking break on anything? (The member is getting angry, so the facilitator guides the exchange back to focus more on the intellectual issues.)

F: Let the stupid side of you answer those questions.

M: Because you make me mad. You are not even mediocre, and you always embarrass me when we're out in public. You don't deserve to be happy. I can't trust you. (Answering as the smart side without instruction) I'm not trying to hurt you. I don't want to fight with you. Why can't we ... (At this point the member reports feeling light-headed.)

F: Open your eyes for a moment. Do you want to go on?

M: Yes. I just ... yes.

F: Good. Let me talk directly to your stupid side.

M: Okay.

F: Tell me why X's smart side doesn't deserve to be happy.

M: I ... I don't know. I'm drawing a blank.

Whenever the dialogue breaks down, the facilitator should switch tactics and assume one side of the dialogue. As soon as possible, however, the member should resume both sides of the exchange.

F: In that case, I'm going to become your stupid side. Are you ready? (The member nods.) You don't deserve to be happy because you don't fight hard enough for it. Every little comment anyone makes, you take inside yourself and brood about. If you grew up, and learned to roll with the punches, maybe I could respect you a bit. As it is, you're pathetic. (Pause) Have your smart side answer me.

M: (Visibly shaken, and almost in tears.) You are too strong. I don't how to fight you, or anything else. If you'd just shut up for a while maybe I'd be able to learn how to stand up for myself and not take everything so seriously.

At some point—either because the three minutes had ticked off, or because the exercise had become too emotional to be productive—the facilitator broke off the exercise. This is one of the few exercises after which other members are encouraged to give the participant a show of support and affection, in the form of a hug or a compliment or a pat on the back. Sometimes the participant badly needs a bit of warmth and approval.

After each member had participated, the group discussed the exercise. Members were asked to review the tape several times during the coming week in order to prepare for another exercise. To reduce any anxieties, the therapist stressed that the new exercise would not be an emotionally trying one, but would help to resolve the conflicts revealed during this session's exercise.

Reading material was handed out at the door.

Session Seven

The session began with a review of the intellectual diary and risk taking, followed by a discussion of the assigned reading material.

The facilitator addressed the subject of definitions and presented the basic material from chapter 10.

After the break, the exercise mentioned in the previous session was introduced. While still seated in the circle, each member was asked to report on what she had learned by listening to the dialogue from her stupid side. Everyone was encouraged to be as specific as possible about the accusations or attacks that had been hurled from the stupid side. Then, the facilitator discussed a technique derived from Windy Dryden's RET groups known as "zigzagging." RET uses zigzagging to counter the irrational statements people make to themselves in order to block self-acceptance.

Dryden describes the zigzag technique: "The group member begins by writing down a rational ego belief and rating her degree of conviction in this belief on a 0 to 100 rating scale. Then she responds to this belief with an irrational argument, which she then rebuts" (p. 121). For example, the group member might write down the statement, "I know how to deal well with people, even strangers," then rate her belief in it as 60 percent, meaning she is slightly convinced the statement is true. The irrational argument might begin, "People actually laugh at me behind my back. . . ." To refute this attack, the member could point to the absolute lack of evidence that the argument's statement was true. Dryden has the member continue in this vein until every single irrational objection to rational ego statements has been dismissed. Then, the group member "re-rates her degree of conviction in her rational ego belief, which is usually increased if the person used the technique properly" (p. 121).

The RET zigzag technique is easily adapted to suit IT purposes. Each member is handed a form on which she is asked to rate several of her intellectual characteristics and skills as objectively as possible, assigning it a score from 0 to 100. The form, which should be altered to fit the facilitator's needs, might look something like this:

(Please note that the form is constructed in such a manner as to encourage high scores. For example, rather than ask about math skills, which most women would rate abysmally low, the form asks about language skills at which most women are above average. The purpose of this bias is a blatant attempt to make the members feel good about themselves after the upset of the prior quasi-Gestalt exercise.)

Score 0-100

Intellectual Characteristics:

Curiosity about ideas   _____

Intellectual honesty   _____

Respect for others   _____

Desire to improve   _____

Interest in books   _____

Intellectual Skills:

Proficiency with language   _____

Music (not necessarily playing,
    perhaps merely appreciating)   _____
Ability to learn new things   _____
Art (not necessarily creating,
    perhaps merely appreciating)   _____

Then each member, in turn, was asked to turn on her tape recorder and recount once more the individual attacks/accusations made by the stupid side of her intellectual persona. After each specific attack, the member was asked to present a reasonable and vigorous refutation of the charge. For example, to the accusation "You don't fight hard enough for it (intellectual self-respect)," the group member replied, "I fight harder than anyone I know, as evidenced by my being willing to talk to you. And being a part of this group is going to make me fight even better." One by one, the self-accusations made by each member were refuted. The facilitator admonished everyone to listen to their participation in the zigzag exercise in the coming week in order to convert their counterstatements into automatic responses that would arise any time their stupid side began to chatter.

Then the members reevaluated themselves on the form, noting in the margin the reason for any substantial shift in the rating. The revised form was filed in the member's binder.

The facilitator explained how the zigzag technique could be used in what is called "tape-recorded disputing." Dryden explains the adaptation of this technique: "Members put the dialogue between their rational and irrational ego beliefs on tape. . . . [K]eep to the point while using this method . . . respond to irrational attacks with force and energy . . . weak rational responses will have little lasting effect" (p. 121).

Group members were encouraged to tape-record zigzag conversations between any two competing aspects of their intellectual personae. But they were admonished to not use the cassette on which session segments had been previously recorded.

Reading material was handed out at the door.

Session Eight

The session began with a review of the intellectual diary and risk taking, followed by an abbreviated discussion of the assigned reading material.

For much of the remaining time, the facilitator presented material on the psychology and strategy of how to argue (see chapters 13, 14, and 15). The presentation continued after the break. Then each member, in turn, was asked to participate in an exercise that was basically a rerun of a prior one.

After turning on her tape recorder, each member picked an envelope out of a box in the middle of the floor. Standing in the middle of the circle, she opened the envelope and retrieved the file card from within. On each card was written a provocative and complicated statement or question, on which almost everyone would have an opinion and usually a strong one. For example, "Abortion is murder because there is no moral difference between a potential human and an actual one." Or, "A pacifist who stands by while someone else is being beaten shares in the moral blame, and ought to be liable for prosecution by the law or through a lawsuit brought by the victim." Or, "If you are one of two survivors in a lifeboat and the only escape from starvation is to eat the other person, would you? If not, why not? And does your answer change depending on who the other person is?"

The member, still standing, read the assigned statement or question out loud. Then, for the next five minutes, she addressed any intellectual aspect of the topic that occurred to her. She could dispute the statement, agree with it, analyze the probable reasons why anyone would believe such a claim, provide a historical context, spin out its implications, review a list of thinkers who have held that opinion, review the circumstances that might make her change her mind. There were no rules, except to stay on the subject and keep talking on an intellectual level for five full minutes. *But* the topic was stated in such a controversial manner as to ensure that the member would take a position.

If a member's mind went absolutely blank with fear or confusion, then she was allowed to talk briefly about that emotional process, until the facilitator instructed her to return to the topic.

During each five-minute segment, the nonparticipating members sat and respectfully listened, trying to keep their minds from wandering. That was their assignment: to practice listening. At the end of each five-minute exercise, the file card was turned into the facilitator who noted the member's name on a corner of it.

Reading material was handed out at the door.

Session Nine

The session began with a review of the intellectual diary and risk taking, followed by a discussion of the assigned reading material. Again, the discussion was shorter than most.

For much of the remaining time, the therapist presented material on how to argue in the absence of good will (see chapter 14). The presentation continued after the break. Then each member, in turn, was asked to participate in an exercise that was basically a rerun of the prior session's, but with a twist.

After turning on her tape recorder, each member was handed back the same card from the week before and instructed to take the opposite position for a full three minutes. She was to argue as vigorously and effectively as she could, trying to refute her own beliefs. Everything else about the exercise remained the same.

With about fifteen or twenty minutes remaining, the group discussed the intellectual therapy experience and reported on what they had received from the sessions. As the last piece of group business, everyone voted on a restaurant and a time at which to meet sometime in the coming week. Typically, by this point the pizza fund was between $125 and 250 and could buy a fairly nice dinner, complete with wine, for the entire group.

No material was handed out at the door.

Pizza Night

There are no rules for the (probably misnamed) pizza night. The evening out provides closure for a unique and, perhaps, unsettling experience. It offers an opportunity for the group members to make plans to stay in touch, if they so choose, or to sketch the formation of another group to carry on with the intellectual therapy. The facilitator herself might decide not to attend in order to give all the power of the dynamics over to the group. Or she may wish to lead an advanced IT group, formed partly from the members of this group and of others. It is a judgment call on the facilitator's part.

In any case, *bon appétit.*

Accept my best wishes.*

SUMMARY

A model eight-week intellectual therapy group is described, session by session. Although the descriptions are altered out of respect for the feelings of the other participants, the sessions are based on my experiences in real groups. The chapter offers a formula for how to function as the facilitator of such a group from the moment the session opens to its conclusion.

Techniques adapted from psychotherapy are examined. Through presenting typical responses of participants to the exercises, an emotional sense of the benefits of intellectual therapy is offered.

Reducing emotional barriers to your intellect, however, does not guarantee excellence in reasoning. This requires a firm grasp of the tools of reasoning.

---

*I recommend not only the books cited but *Gestalt Therapy* by F. S. Perls and associates, which has many ingenuous exercises for getting in touch with the "here and now." Also useful is *A Practitioner's Guide to Rational-Emotive Therapy* by Windy Dryden and associates.

In general, browse through the psychology section of a good bookstore and dip into the techniques of whatever schools of therapy appeal to you personally.

9

The Tools of Reasoning

All the tools with which mankind works upon its fate are dull,
but the sharpest among them is the reason.

Carl Van Doren, *Many Minds*

This book is not about the technical aspects of reasoning. It is about the underlying psychology of reasoning, especially those psychological factors that interfere with a healthy enjoyment of ideas. Yet something must be said about the technical side of reasoning because much of your intellectual self-esteem will come from how satisfying you find your exchanges with other people. This sense of yourself will come, in turn, from how effectively you use the tools of reasoning.

The ensuing discussion does no more than skim the very surface of logical reasoning. It is intended only to provide a general sense of direction and a sense of the wealth of intellectual guidance available from this field of study, which is often dismissed as dry and boring. Yet as the philosopher W. H. Werkmeister remarks in *An Introduction to Critical Thinking*, "In man's arduous and long struggle for existence, reason and thought have been his primary instruments of survival" (p. xv). Werkmeister adds, "It is important to note, however,

179

that the principles of logic do not describe the psychological processes involved in thinking—not even the processes involved in critical thinking" (p. xvii).

It is the psychological process with which we are concerned. And, yet, an intimate relationship exists between how you view yourself intellectually and the feedback you receive from the world. In turn, much of the world's reaction comes from how skilled and comfortable you are with at least some of the technical aspects of reasoning.

Conversation, whether in the form of an argument or of chitchat, seems to be a more important form of feedback to women than it is to men. Perhaps this is true because conversation seems to be the most prevalent means of intellectual exchange and feedback for many women. As a sad comment on our society, women tend to occupy less intellectually demanding and rewarding jobs than men do. Even a cursory inventory of scientists, engineers, medical doctors, and mathematicians will reveal a shocking inequity of gender representation.* Whether such disparities are due to nature or nurture—to an innate tendency within women or merely to their cultural programming—the fact remains that women do not generally derive the same intellectual satisfaction from their employment as men do.

The psychological and intellectual feedback women receive often comes from family situations and whatever social life or further education they pursue outside of work. Under such circumstances, conversation may be the main intellectual outlet and feedback mechanism that many women have. No wonder they sometimes dwell on the nuances of annoying exchanges or of small barbed remarks for weeks.

Usually, adding men to the mix of conversation doesn't make the situation better. Men tend to approach conversations about ideas, not as a way to explore and enjoy the terrain, but as the intellectual equivalent of an athletic event in which there is a winner and a loser. And men don't like to lose.

I've often watched women at gatherings become flustered or defensive and hostile when they try to argue with men who are not more

---

*For insight on this question, I recommend Samuel C. Florman's *Blaming Technology*.

intelligent than they are, but who are more skilled or aggressive in presenting ideas. Often what is lacking is nothing more than a familiarity with the rules of arguing. Not being able to articulate adequately the thoughts in your own mind—especially in public or in the face of an adversary—is an incredibly frustrating experience. Not knowing how to approach an argument can make an otherwise intellectually competent woman feel like a third-rate thinker.

Yet there is no sorcery or gender-bias involved in arguing well. It is a human talent that requires nothing more than practice and the inculcation of good habits. A preliminary step to practicing is learning the appropriate intellectual tools to pick up and use for a specific job. This does not entail taking a university-level course in symbolic logic. Or memorizing all the logical fallacies, complete with their Latin names. Such knowledge of formal logic can be incredibly useful, but it is certainly not necessary.

This chapter presents some informal, though still technical, guidance on how to approach and analyze arguments and statements of fact in order to become more intellectually confident. The following is *not* meant to replace a good introductory text on logic, showing the forms and rules of argumentation. But it may provide a sense of how powerful an understanding of logic can be in clarifying thought and honing your ability to argue.

At this point, you are now engaged in the study of Logic, with a capital L.

VALIDITY AND TRUTH

It is not the business of Logic to make men rational, but rather to teach them in what their being rational consists. . . . Logic, then, is the science which studies the general principles in accordance with which we think about things, whatever things they may be; and so it presupposes that we have thought about things.

H. W. B. Joseph, *An Introduction to Logic*

The philosopher Antony Flew opens his invaluable book *Thinking Straight* with the words, "The first thing to get straight in thinking about thinking is the difference between questions about validity and questions about truth. . . . What is true, or false, is propositions. What is valid, or invalid, is arguments" (p. 9).

As Flew points out, the most essential thing to understand about arguing is the difference between validity and truth. Validity has to do with how an argument is structured, not with propositions, statements that can be shown to be either true or false. An argument will certainly contain propositions—indeed, they are the content of the argument—but the structure of the argument refers to how the series of propositions relate to each other. Do they logically follow, one from the other?

The structure of an argument is like a bookcase, or a framework, that supports tier after tier of book titles. Propositions are like the individual books on the shelves. The books may contain true or false information, but this assessment in no way affects whether or not the structure on which the titles physically rest is sound. The shelving of the bookcase is either structurally sound, or it is not. If it is structurally unsound, it will not support the weight of the books placed upon it however true the information those books contain may be.

So, too, with arguments. The structure of an argument must be valid in order to support the propositions it carries, and that support exists independently of the truth or falsehood of the specific statements being made.

Errors of Logic—Errors of Structure

The traditional example of a valid argument—an argument structured in a logically correct manner—is the time-honored syllogism:

1. All men are mortal.

2. Socrates is/was a man.

3. Therefore, Socrates is/was mortal.

There are three propositions, or statements, presented here. The first statement is a general one, and it is called the *major premise*. The second statement involves a specific instance of the preceding one, and it is called the *minor premise*. The third statement is called the *conclusion*. The argument represented by this syllogism may be said to be valid because the conclusion logically and necessarily follows from the premises. If all men are mortal and if Socrates is a man, then logic constrains us to conclude necessarily that Socrates is mortal as well. If, after asserting the premises, you reached the conclusion that Socrates was *not* mortal, you would be involving yourself in a contradiction.

Stripping the above syllogism down to basics, you could write the three statements it offers in the form of symbols. This gives you the advantage of seeing the flow of the argument without being distracted by whether or not the statements are true or make any sense. Thus, the above syllogism can be written as:

Major Premise: All A is B.

Minor Premise: C is A.

Conclusion: Therefore, C is B.

The validity of the syllogism rests on nothing else but whether the connection being drawn between the three statements is a logically correct one. Is there any instance in which all A is B, C is A, and yet C is not B? By the very structure of the argument, C *must* logically be B. Any statements that you consistently substitute for A, B, and C will result in a valid argument.

But the validity of the argument, of its structure, in no way means that the statements it contains or the conclusion it reaches will be true. For example, consider a syllogism that represents the valid structure presented above, but which substitutes the symbols with the following statements:

Major Premise: All men are Socrates.

Minor Premise: My brother is a man.

Conclusion: Therefore, my brother is Socrates.

This is still a valid argument, because the conclusion necessarily and logically results from the first two premises. In other words, to assert the first two premises while denying the conclusion would involve you in a contradiction. Yet the first premise and the conclusion are clearly false. In other words, the syllogism is valid because it is internally consistent: the conclusion follows naturally from the premises. But the internal logic of the argument says nothing about whether its conclusion is true—whether the conclusion corresponds to reality. Truth and falsehood are external to the structure of the argument and can be ascertained only by stepping into the real world and looking for evidence. When you perform this process, you quickly discover that the first premise and the conclusion are false. All men are not Socrates. And, presumably, your brother is not Socrates either.

This is the difference between validity and truth. Validity involves the logical structure of an argument; truth involves whether or not the statement resting upon the structure of the argument corresponds to reality. Like books on a bookcase.

Although the foregoing may sound academic and seem far divorced from the parlor conversations and party arguments with which you are familiar, the material bears directly upon every intellectual encounter you will experience. Arguments contain at least two elements that are essential for you to analyze: first, is the structure of the argument valid? and, second, are the statements, or propositions, it contains true? If the answer to either question is no, and you have developed the skill to recognize and demonstrate this fact, then you have won the argument.

VALIDITY IN FORMAL ARGUMENTS

It is not only useful to begin the analysis of every argument with the question "Is the structure of the argument valid?" there is also an eminently practical reason for doing so. It can save a great deal of time and effort on your part.

Consider the problems entailed in evaluating the second question, "Are the statements, or propositions, true or false?" Few of the propositions you encounter in an argument will be self-evidently true or false, as the statement "dogs are cats" is self-evidently false. If you are familiar with the subject under discussion, you might be able to verify or dispute a statement with ease. But many arguments—which are no more than connected propositions that lead to a conclusion—will not present themselves as immediately or easily true or false.

Imagine the time and energy required to determine the truth or falsehood of every statement you encounter. We live in a fast-moving age that is flooded with changing information and analysis of information on virtually every subject of interest to humankind. Each day, there is more to know, and seemingly less spare time to absorb it all properly. Checking out statements of fact can take a lot of time. Moreover, if the "facts" are thrown at you in a party situation, the time required to verify them is a luxury you do not have. The party would be over before you've found the book, or Internet site, or magazine article that provides the evidence you need to make an evaluation.

But checking the validity of an argument—checking whether the structure is internally consistent—can be a quick and painless process. It does not require time in the library, a background in the field, or specialized knowledge. Simply by looking at the structure of an argument, you can get a fast read on whether or not its conclusion follows logically from its premises. In short, investigating the validity of an argument's structure is a labor- and time-saving intellectual technique.

So far, we have considered arguments with valid structures, although their propositions may have been false. Let's consider a few other structures to ascertain if they are valid. The first syllogism we considered took the form of: All A is B; C is A; therefore, C is B. Consider another common form of syllogism:

Major Premise: All A is B.

Minor Premise: C is not B.

Conclusion: Therefore, C is not A.

Plugging statements into this structure gives us the following argument:

All women are reasonable.

Carl is not reasonable.

Therefore, Carl is not a woman.

Not only is this argument valid, the proposition that constitutes the conclusion also happens to be true.

Is the next syllogism valid?

Major Premise: All A is C.

Minor Premise: B is C.

Conclusion: Therefore, B is A.

If the symbols are confusing, test the argument's validity by plugging statements into the structure. For example,

All women are reasonable.

Carl is reasonable.

Therefore Carl is a woman.

This is an invalid structure, because the conclusion of the syllogism does not necessarily and logically follow from the premises. For the conclusion to follow validly, it would be necessary for the major premise to read "All women and only women are reasonable." Otherwise, it is quite possible to suppose that (1) all women (and many men) are reasonable; (2) Carl is reasonable; (3) therefore, Carl may be either a woman or a man.

In *Thinking Straight*, Antony Flew points out that, during the anti-Communist, blacklist days, Sen. Joseph McCarthy and the House Committee on Un-American Activities, this type of invalid structure was sometimes called "the Un-American Fallacy." The reason? It was assumed that, because someone possessed a characteristic which was associated with communism—perhaps a commitment to atheism or membership in a labor union—he or she was automatically "proven" to be a

Communist. In essence, McCarthy and his ilk leaped from the statement "All Communists are atheists" to the conclusion "All Atheists are Communists"—a conclusion that can be validly reached only from the statement "All Communists and only Communists are atheists."

Consider whether or not one last form of syllogism is valid.

> All A is B.
>
> C is not A.
>
> Therefore, C is not B.

Again, test this structure by plugging in statements:

> All women are reasonable.
>
> Carl is not a woman.
>
> Therefore, Carl is not reasonable.

Again, this is an invalid conclusion because it does not follow necessarily and logically from the two premises. The fact that all women are reasonable says nothing about whether or not men are reasonable as well, any more than saying that all sugar is sweet precludes other substances, such as honey, from being sweet. For the stated conclusion to follow necessarily, the major premise would have to read "All women and only women are reasonable." Thus, if you had argued "Sugar and only sugar is sweet," then you could have concluded with logic on your side that honey is not sweet. The proposition that constitutes your major premise would have been wrong, of course, but the structure of the argument would have been valid.

The invalid arguments above are called *formal fallacies*. A fallacy is an "error of logic," an error within the structure of the argument. If by plugging statements into the basic structure of the argument, you come up with a statement similar to "My brother is Socrates," you know something dubious is occurring.

Informal Fallacies—or "Errors of Method"

To segue into informal fallacies, consider more syllogisms in terms of the validity of their structure. Consider the "If A, then B" structure.

> If A, then B.
>
> Not B.
>
> Therefore, not A.

Plugging in statements might result in the following argument, "There is no God, because I'm thirty-one and single." Written as a syllogism, the argument would run:

> If there is a God, then I will be married by thirty.
>
> I am now thirty-one and still unmarried.
>
> Therefore, there is no God.

Whatever the truth of the conclusion, this is a valid syllogism. Not-B logically necessitates not-A.

Another example of an "if A, then B" structure is:

> If A, then B.
>
> B.
>
> Therefore, A.

Plugging in a statement might result in the following argument, "He loves me because he stayed home tonight." Written as a syllogism, the argument would run:

> If he loves me, he will stay home tonight.
>
> He stayed home tonight.
>
> Therefore, he loves me.

Whatever the truth of the conclusion, this is *in*valid because B does not necessitate A. In order for it to become a valid syllogism—that is, for B to necessitate A—the major premise would have to read "If and only if he loves me, he will stay home." In this case, if he stays home (B), then he necessarily loves her (A).

The If/Then syllogistic structure may be used to reach a valid conclusion, as seen in the first example, but using an If/Then form of argument is very likely to result in a false conclusion.

Consider the first and valid syllogism regarding the unmarried woman. Is there any reason to believe its conclusion is true? Is a Godless universe the only reason why a woman would remain single past the age of thirty? There might be a God who has determined she should be single until the age of forty, not thirty as she would prefer. There might be a lack of eligible men, or a myriad of other causal factors.

In the second syllogism regarding the man who stays home, there may be other reasons that the man so decided, reasons that have no romantic implications. For example, he may be too tired to go out with the boys, or there may be a basketball game he wants to catch on TV.

In order for the second "If A, then B" structure of an argument to result in a true conclusion, you must be able to make the further statement of "If *and only if* A, then B." Only by eliminating the possibility of any other explanation for a result can you ensure veracity. In applying this qualifier to the second syllogism considered above, the argument would become:

If and only if he loves me, he will stay home tonight.

He stayed home tonight.

Therefore, he loves me.

This is a valid conclusion. If the major premise is true, it is a true conclusion as well.

By contrast, informal fallacies are errors that don't relate to the validity of the structure of an argument. They are errors of method, errors in how you approach an argument. For example, if you attack the character of a person presenting an argument rather than analyzing his argument as valid or true, you are committing what is called the *ad hominem fallacy*. Literally translated, ad hominem means "against the man."

Another more complicated and extremely common fallacy is called *post hoc ergo propter hoc*. It has also been labeled the "Whatever-follows-must-be-the-consequence" Fallacy. The error here is to assume that because a certain event directly follows another, that the second event was caused by the first. For example, it is a fallacy to assume that the rate of employment has risen because a certain labor law was just passed. The rate of employment might have risen in any case. Indeed, it might have risen more had the law not been instituted.

The preceding provides no more than a hint of the power of logic to refine your thoughts and arguments. Expanding on the technical tools of reasoning is inappropriate in a book on the psychology of reasoning. But a knowledge of the technical side is indispensable, and I urge you to continue reading in this area.*

SYLLOGISTIC STRATEGY

> The Athenians do not mind a man being clever, so long as he does not impart his cleverness to others.
>
> Plato, *Euthyphro*

---

*To read more about informal fallacies, I highly recommend an entertaining and imminently readable book by Antony Flew entitled *Thinking about Thinking: (Or, Do I Sincerely Want to Be Right?)* which has been reissued under the title *Thinking Straight.* An equally charming work, which will be difficult to find in bookstores as opposed to libraries, is Stuart Chase's *Guides to Straight Thinking; with Thirteen Common Fallacies.* R. H. Thouless's *Straight and Crooked Thinking* and H. B. Smith's *How the Mind Falls into Error* are also valuable supplements.

M. C. Beardsley's *Practical Logic* and M. H. Hepp's *Thinking Things Through* offer the sort of overview you would receive from a traditional university course on logic and are written on an introductory level.

Much of the remainder of this book will deal with the psychology and the strategy of arguing, but while the subject of syllogisms has arisen, let me make a strategic point in passing. If nothing else, this section may convince you of how powerful a tool of analysis syllogisms can be.

Syllogisms consist of a major premise, a minor premise, and a conclusion. Although many arguments you encounter will have a more complex structure than this, they will almost all have a major premise, which may or may not be stated. For example, you may encounter someone who argues passionately that an accused serial murderer should be executed. Amid the flow of emotion and the many side comments, you discern the following syllogism:

> **Major Premise:** Murderers should be executed.
>
> **Minor Premise:** X is a murderer.
>
> **Conclusion:** X should be executed.

Often this argument will be stated in the form "X is a murderer and should be executed," leaving the major premise unstated but clearly implicit.

If the major premise were "Murderers should be *punished*," leading to the conclusion "X (as a murderer) should be *punished*, few people would be likely to quarrel with the major premise because punishing murderers is an almost universally accepted moral and social principle. Instead, people would zero in on the minor premise and question the evidence that points to X being a murderer.

Generally speaking, unless the major premise (which is often a moral statement or a statement of principle) is a blatantly controversial one, people tend not to focus their criticisms upon it, but leap instead upon the minor premise (which is a statement of fact). This seems to be true even when people do not fully agree with the moral statement of the major premise. Perhaps they feel on safer ground by sticking to the facts, rather than more abstract matters. Perhaps they are not as comfortable with arguing theory as they are with arguing straightforward facts.

Whatever your reason, when you challenge the minor premise of an argument rather than the major one, the other person has an easier time responding as it is much simpler to defend facts than principles. Return to the original form of the above major premise, "Murderers should be executed." Defending this position is a far more complicated matter than offering evidence to support the minor one, "X is a murderer."

It is also a totally different—and, to my mind—a far more interesting argument. Even if X is a murderer, should he be, in turn, killed? If your main objection to the argument rests in the major premise, do not get bogged down in arguing the facts of the minor premise, because the facts may be irrelevant to your disagreement. As well, the statement of moral value is often a more fruitful area for questions.

For one thing, the other person might not be entirely aware of the implications of her own major premise. What about a murderer who manifests the battered-wife syndrome? What about a seven-year-old child who thinks she is protecting her mother from attack? And is it ever wise to give the state the power to kill a citizen? By questioning, you may discover that she is uncomfortable with some of the implications of her own position and, so, the argument will be refined.

As a rule of thumb, when you disagree with an argument, the most productive place to start is to focus on the major premise and to make it as explicit as possible. This means exploring its implications. For example, in his major premise the other person might assume the moral value of majority rule—by which he means that the will of the people should prevail as public policy. His argument might run as follows:

Major Premise: The wishes of the majority should become law.

Minor Premise: The majority wishes higher taxes.

Conclusion: Taxes should be higher.

Again, people who disagree will usually focus upon the statement of fact, the minor premise. They will either argue that the majority really doesn't want higher taxes or that taxes are high enough already. When the other person responds by presenting the evidence in support of his minor premise, they will question the statistics, or cite contradicting studies.

This is a weak way to argue. It is far more effective to attack the major premise by pointing out problems in the arguer's statement of principle. Is it true that the wishes of the majority should rule and become law? In Nazi Germany, the majority of people may have truly wished to have stern racial policies against Jews, and other "undesirables." The fact that Hitler was elected by popular vote would certainly be an indication of this. Moreover, in the antebellum United States, a large majority of Southerners wished to preserve the institution of slavery and their will was, indeed, embodied in the law. Was it wrong to sweep those laws expressing the will of the majority away? What about other systems of governing, such as a constitutional republic which protects principles like freedom of speech from a popular vote? Why are these systems less desirable than the will of the people? And, if the will of the majority is the most desirable system of government, is there any place where a line should be drawn to protect the dissenting individual, such as freedom of religion?

Clearly, it will be far more difficult for the other person to defend the moral values of his major premises than to deal with the facts of his minor one. And, in questioning him, you will have assumed the upper hand as it is easier to challenge a moral position than it is to defend one.

For this reason alone, whenever you are defending a value statement in your major premise, state it in as uncontroversial a manner as possible. For example, few people will quarrel with the major premise in the following syllogism:

Major Premise: Stolen property should be returned to its owner.

Minor Premise: Mary's watch is stolen property.

Conclusion: Mary's watch should be returned to its owner.

Anyone challenging this argument is likely to focus on the minor premise, on the statement of fact. Is the watch, in fact, stolen? In other words, your argument rests on unchallenged moral ground, and you are confronted with the comparatively easy task of defending factual claims. Of course, not all major premises can be stated in such socially acceptable terms, but get as close as you can without distorting the statement.

Another very effective approach in arguing—and one which leads into the next chapter—is to ask the other person for clarification or for a definition of what he means by key terms in his major premise. For example, in the case of "The wishes of the majority should become law," you could demand to know what precisely constitutes a majority for purposes of defining policies. Should the population of every city or state constitute separate majorities who can determine separate, and perhaps contradictory, municipal policies, depending on the will of the people of that geographically limited area? Should the general will of the American people determine the policies of citizens living in a specific state?

In the vast majority of cases, the more definition you demand of the arguer, the more trouble he will have defending his statements. Again, this observation leads directly to the next chapter on "The Power of Definitions."*

SUMMARY

Much of your intellectual self-esteem comes from how satisfying you find your exchanges with other people. This satisfaction will increase dramatically as you grow comfortable with some of the technical aspects of reasoning, like the difference between validity and truth.

The tools of reasoning can be used not only to clarify and empower your own thought process, but also to dissect the arguments of others. For example, attacking the major premise of an argument rather than its minor premise(s) can be a powerful strategy.

One of the most effective tools of reasoning is yet to be discussed —the ability to define.

---

*For those readers who wish to reap more of the rewards of logic that are merely hinted at in the cursory chapter above, I highly recommend two further standard, though somewhat technical, works: *An Introduction to Logic* by H. W. B. Joseph and *A Preface to Logic* by Morris R. Cohen. Also highly recommended are Stanley Jevons's *Elementary Lessons in Logic,* which is considered a standard text, and A. Wolf's *Textbook of Logic*, which is written on the introductory level.

10

The Power of Definitions

"When *I* use a word," Humpty Dumpty said, in a rather scornful tone, "it means just what I choose it to mean—neither more nor less."

"The question is," said Alice, "whether you *can* make words mean so many different things."

"The question is," said Humpty Dumpty, "which is to be master—that's all."

Lewis Carroll, Through the Looking Glass

Although definitions may seem like dry matters, they provide you with the inestimable benefit of knowing precisely what you are talking about. They help you to avoid one of the most common intellectual pitfalls: namely, not being able to explain clearly what you mean, even to yourself. Simply being able to define your terms can give you a tremendous intellectual advantage in communicating your ideas.

Certainly George Orwell in his dystopian novel of the future, *1984*, realized the intimate connection between being able to use clearly defined words and being able to think clearly. One of the main ways Orwell's totalitarian state, Oceania, controls its citizenry is through Newspeak, a fictional language called Ingsoc (English Socialism). This highly abbreviated form of language strips words of all the subtle meaning, all the shades of distinction and evocative power that definitions and a wide vocabulary so richly provide.

By minimizing the number of words available to people and substituting contrived compounds of words, the government guides their minds toward "goodthinkful" (politically correct) thoughts. Instead of hundreds of words to describe a positive experience or thing, Newspeak recognizes only the word "good." To describe something extremely positive, Newspeak uses "doubleplusgood." Experiences or things that are bad are "ungood," or "doubleplusungood." Ingsoc seeks to control thought by controlling speech.

Although sophisticated subverbal thinking is possible when dealing with images and emotions—e.g., an artist conceptualizing a painting—only primitive thought about ideas can exist without using the clarifying lens of words. Moreover, on a subverbal level, we can easily deceive ourselves about what we really think and feel. For example, a person might be anti-Semitic without consciously knowing it. In fact, she might profess to be a great fan of Jewish culture. The act of evasion can almost be defined as a refusal to verbalize something, a refusal to translate subverbal thoughts into words where they are held in a fully conscious form. By refusing to name her real beliefs, the person is able to avoid them.

Other verbal tactics offer the same advantage of obscuring your thoughts so that you don't have to acknowledge them. Obfuscation is the use of flowery, metaphorical, loose, or mixed-up words in order to confuse thought. For example, describing someone as "vulnerable, highly tuned to her emotions and environment, like a delicate flower" when what you truly mean is that she is afraid of her own shadow.

Thus, Newspeak is only one manifestation of a deeply held human belief: words can change reality, words are magic. Ali Baba utters "Open Sesame" and the cave door to riches admits him. A witch incants a spell and reality conforms to her syllables. Gamblers bet on horses with "lucky" names, and call out to Lady Luck before throwing the dice. Actors are appalled by those who say "have a good show" rather than "break a leg." Your neighbor sneezes and you say "God bless you" so the devil can't enter that opening. We end our prayers with "Amen."

And some religions find the true name of God to be so powerful that speaking it aloud is a heinous sin, once punishable by stoning.

Words are veiled in magic, and almost all of us believe in their power on some level. Perhaps this is inevitable. For, although words do not reshape reality, they do define how we think about it. To some degree, they do define us.

THE PSYCHOLOGICAL IMPACT OF DEFINITIONS

> Every definition is dangerous.
> Erasmus, *Adagia*

Consider a scenario. You know only Newspeak. Although you have a visceral sense of what it is to taste flavorful food, to laugh at a joke, to enjoy a flower, and to revel in a kiss, the only way you can verbally describe such pleasures to yourself is with the word "good." The only way to distinguish between these and a myriad of other pleasures is to add the word "double" or "plus" onto the single term "good." Without words to shape your thoughts, how clearly would you be able to realize the complex psychological reactions that are possible to human beings? In *1984*, the citizenry have no adequate words with which to express, even to themselves, their own unhappiness and oppression.

Ayn Rand's novelette *Anthem* dramatizes the emotional impact of the power of words. Rand portrays a dystopian future in which the word "I" has been eradicated, so that everyone refers to himself and herself as "we." The hero, named Equality 7-2521, is tormented by an inability to reconcile his thoughts and emotions in a united front against the gray culture that almost engulfs him. Equality 7-2521 cries out silently, "May knowledge come to us! What is the secret our heart has understood and yet will not reveal to us, although it seems to beat as if it were endeavoring to tell it?" (p. 93).

The secret is revealed when Equality discovers the words that can express it. "I am. I think. I will. My hands. . . . My spirit. . . . My sky. . . . My forest. . . . This earth of mine. What must I say besides? There are the words. This is the answer" (p. 94).

Definitions and words are more than dry academic matters. They lie at the heart of your ability to think clearly and to express your emotions in a subtle, exploratory fashion so that a healthy union is forged between your thoughts and feelings. It is only upon discovering the forgotten syllable "I," that Rand's hero is able to name himself, and with that name become a free man. He is able to listen to the secrets of his heart.

As Stuart Chase so eloquently expresses it in *Power of Words*, "Words link together all human activities, and form a connecting bond in every human relation. They have a physical existence on stone, paper, and microfilm, and probably in flesh and blood as well, by virtue of verbal habits built into the brain and nervous system" (p. 3).

DEFINITIONS AS A TOOL IN ARGUING

If you wish to converse with me, define your terms.
Voltaire

If you still doubt the power of definitions to clarify or to confuse, try a practical experiment. The next time you are in a discussion with someone who uses a high-level abstraction like "social justice," "obscenity," "common good," or "freedom" ask them for a clear definition of what they mean by the term. This request is not a ploy on your part. It is a valid and, perhaps, a necessary piece of information to ensure a productive exchange. The meaning of such vague and emotionally charged terms vary dramatically from person to person and, without asking, you have no idea what the person is actually saying. It is not uncommon for people to talk at cross-purposes for no other reason than that they are using the same term to mean entirely different things.

The speaker may be able to provide a definition along the lines that Lionel Ruby suggests in a chapter entitled "Define Your Terms!" in *The Art of Making Sense*. According to Ruby, "A definition is a statement that says, 'For this word *A*, substitute these words, *X, Y, Z*.' For the word 'perjury,' substitute its legal definition 'the willful and voluntary giving of false testimony under oath or affirmation with regard to a material matter, in a judicial proceeding' " (p. 53). The word "perjury" and its legal definition should be interchangeable.

The other person may offer a traditional definition of her term, as above, or she may stipulate a different one, that is, she may arbitrarily define the term in such a manner as to support her argument. As Ruby warns, however, "great caution should be used in stipulating new meanings . . . for old habits are hard to get rid of and we usually persist in giving familiar words their customary meanings" (p. 53). The key is for everyone in the discussion to understand what is being said and for words to be used consistently. Without a common understanding of what is meant by the term "social justice," for example, it is extraordinarily difficult to discuss whether Communist China or the United States embodies this concept.

In all probability, however, the person will be caught off guard by your request for a definition and will either not be able to respond or will answer in a clearly unsatisfactory manner. She might counter with the defensive comment, "Don't you know what 'social justice' means?" At which point you should respond, "I know what *I* mean by that term, but I'm not certain you are using it in the same way."

Or the other person might give you a restatement of the term that tells you nothing. For example, she might define "social justice" in flowery obscuring terms such as "the pinnacle of valid civilization," or in equally vague terms such as "fairness in a social context." The latter rephrasing, although it may seem to be a definition, is useless since you are no more clear on what she means by "fairness" than you were about "justice." Ask her to provide concrete examples.

While you gently pursue these definitions make sure to concentrate on the main purpose of this intellectual exercise: observe the psychological impact of your questioning upon the person. If she has been using words loosely, without clearly knowing the meanings themselves, the reaction will probably be defensive and, perhaps, angry. You cannot expect most people to show the charm and self-awareness of Oscar Wilde's character Lord Darlington in the play *Lady Windemere's Fan,* who responds to a request for definition with the words, "I think I had better not. Nowadays to be intelligible is to be found out."

Whatever the other person's reaction, unless a clear definition trips off her tongue, an interesting phenomenon is likely to have occurred. As the person casts about to explain herself, you will have gained the upper hand in the argument.

The lack of definition can destroy an argument; clear definitions can give it power. When you are engaged in an informal, friendly discussion it may be sufficient to define a word or concept by using synonyms or examples. But in a more rigorous argument, and certainly when defining terms to clarify your own thoughts, the best form of definition is an analytic one—one that classifies the thing being defined and, then, differentiates it from all other things in that class.

WHICH WORDS SHOULD BE X, Y, Z?

In order to build a definition, you need to know what it consists of, even if that process seems a tad on the dry side. The two basic components of a definition are:

Definiendum: The word or concept being defined. In the definition "woman is a rational animal," the term "woman" is the definiendum.

Definiens: The defining part of the definition. In "woman is a rational animal," the term "rational animal" is the definiens.

Thus, you have the two sides of a definition: the *A* and the *X,Y,Z* which can be substituted for *A*. But how do you ascertain which *X,Y,Z*s are appropriate?

The process of deciding which words may be substituted for *A* involves analyzing *A* in several ways.

The first question to ask yourself is "What is the genus of *A*?" The genus is the general class, or category, to which *A*, the definiendum, belongs. In other words, the genus is the broader category of which *A* is a subcategory. The genus of the word "blue" would be "color." The genus of the word "chair" would be "furniture." Thus, in the definition "woman is a rational animal," the term "animal" is the genus. It is the wider category to which "woman" belongs.

Determine the broader category of which the word you are defining is a subcategory.

Second, ask yourself what characteristics distinguish the word you
are defining from every other subcategory within the same genus. For
example, what distinguishes a chair from any other piece of furniture,
such as a table or bed? Concerning the word "woman," what makes
that concept different from every other subcategory of the genus
"animal"? What characteristic makes "woman" different than "dog" or
"bear" or "horse"? What is the essential characteristic of "woman"
that separates her from every other animal? In the definition "woman
is a rational animal," the word "rational" is the essential distinguishing
feature, which is called the *differentia.*

Try analyzing various words in order to get comfortable with the
process of defining your ideas. Use the structure provided below in
analyzing the word "triangle" and substitute in your particular *A* and
X,Y,Z.

A triangle is a plane figure having three straight sides.

"plane figure" = the genus
"having three straight sides" = the differentia
"triangle" = a species of the genus "plane figure"

COMMONSENSE RULES FOR
DEFINING YOUR TERMS

He shall be as a god to me, who can rightly define and divide.
Ralph Waldo Emerson,
Representative Men: Plato Quoted

Here are some basic rules for defining your terms:

1. *Definitions should not be too broad.* For example, the definition
"Woman is the animal that shows good sense" is too broad, because
certain men also manifest this trait.

More seriously, and in recognition of the fact that I am using the
term "woman" instead of the traditional "man" to mean "human
being," consider the definition of a "circle." The following *X,Y,Z*

cannot successfully substitute for the *A* since it is an unsuccessful definition of "circle": "a figure, all of whose points are equidistant from a given point" is too broad because it includes the severed arc of the circle. Thus, another and more specific *X,Y,Z* is required. "A circle is a closed, plane figure, all of whose points are equidistant from a given point." This definition excludes arcs and other spheres, referring exclusively to circles.

2. *Definitions should not be too narrow.* They should not exclude some instances of the word being defined, the definiendum. For example, the definition "Woman is the animal that gives birth to human beings" is too narrow since some women are childless. The definition excludes certain instances of the word "woman."

Otherwise stated: A definition must apply to *all* possible cases of the definiendum. If it does not apply to *all* instances, then it is too narrow.

3. *A definition should state the essential characteristic of the definiendum:* that is, it should state the characteristic that best explains any other unique characteristics of "woman." The definition "Woman is the animal who can laugh" or "who can build a computer" is neither too broad nor too narrow. All women have that capacity, and only women have that capacity. But woman's ability to laugh or to build computers does not, in itself, explain her ability to paint a picture, or drive a car, or cook a gourmet meal. Woman's rational faculties do explain all these capacities. Thus, "rational" is a more essential characteristic and a better differentia.

4. *A definition should not be circular.* A circular definition is one that makes use of the very word being defined. Thus, "A carpenter is a craftsman who practices carpentry" is circular. Only if you have an understanding of the word "carpenter" in the first place will that supposed definition make sense to you. A definition should not require a prior understanding of the word in order to acquire an understanding.

5. *Definitions should not be obscure.* State the *X,Y,Z* in as clear and simple a fashion as possible. Avoid jargon and specialized language. The purpose of a definition is to give you access to the meaning of a word, not to obscure it. Consider the following definition of a computer, which uses obscuring language: "A mechanism for the sequential and nonsequential execution of stored programs." Translated into

clear language, this definition becomes: "A machine that can follow a list of instructions and make decisions."

6. *Definitions should not be negative.* Thus, a chair should not be defined as "a piece of furniture that is *not* a table." Although this description is true of chairs, it is also true of beds, and other nontable furniture. The exception to this rule are words that inherently require a negative: e.g., an orphan is a child with no parents.

7. *The more abstract the word being defined, the more precise the definition should be.* It is difficult if not impossible to check the validity of abstract definitions, such as justice, against objects in the real world. As the concept being defined moves further away from real objects, sloppiness and error often creep in. Greater care must be taken with high-level abstractions.

Using these rules and the structure provided in the analysis of the word "triangle," sit down and try to define some of the words you use and take for granted every day. Start with simple definitions, like cat or dog. Then move up the ladder to complicated terms like "social justice," "fairness," "equality," etc.

CONTEXTUAL DEFINITIONS

> Defining night by darkness, death by dust.
>
> P. J. Bailey

One of the books I found invaluable in clarifying a commonsense approach to definitions—indeed, in clarifying concept formation itself—was Ayn Rand's small and rather Aristotelian book *Introduction to Objectivist Epistemology.* The most important message I derived from the introduction about definitions is that they are not carved in stone. By this I mean that the way we define a term is a direct result of our context of knowledge. The reason this insight was so important is that it went a long way toward removing the fear of "getting the definition wrong."

In essence, Rand explains that definitions—in particular, the *X,Y,Z* or essential differentiating characteristics of a definition—depend on your state of knowledge at any given time. For instance, a child who has never encountered any living beings except human beings might implicitly define "woman" as a "thing that walks." Within that child's experience, the ability of women to walk may serve perfectly well to distinguish the concept of "woman" from other concepts such as "table" and "plant." Since the only thing the child has seen that walks is woman, for this child, the ability to walk would be the essential characteristic. Given its framework of knowledge, this is a successful and fully satisfactory definition.

What happens when the child encounters a cat or dog? Cats and dogs also walk, but they are not "woman." Therefore, the child has to select a new essential characteristic in order to distinguish the concept of "woman" from the concept of "nonwoman things that walk." At this point, the child might say "Woman is a thing that walks on two legs." After all, this characteristic perfectly isolates "woman" from all the other things in the child's current experience. Then the child sees a documentary on bears. Another essential characteristic is required. And so on, and so on.

Given this perspective, the definition "Woman is a rational animal" is no more than the best definition available to us, given our current framework of knowledge. If scientists are able to prove that dolphins think, or if a UFO lands on the White House lawn, we may well have to refine the essential characteristic of "woman" in light of the fact that other animals think.

Saying that definitions are contextual does not mean that to define "woman as a rational animal" is just a matter of whim or convention. At our current state of knowledge, rationality is the best essential characteristic serving to distinguish the concept of "woman" from our concept of other animals. But the introduction of context highlights the fact that definitions are not carved in stone, but processes of discovery. In other words, don't worry if you get it wrong. Rather than view definitions as objectively true or false, it is useful to view them as better or worse, more or less useful.

Although, at one point in the discussion of definitions, I focused upon the conversational advantage that can derive from defining your own terms, the true beauty of definitions lies elsewhere. Definitions allow you to think clearly. They are like the focus on a camera lens. Indeed, it is doubtful whether clear thinking is possible without definitions.

The first piece of advice regarding definitions and the richness of words is to own at least two standard dictionaries, a thesaurus, and as many books on English usage as catch your fancy. When in doubt about the meaning of a word you have encountered, never look it up in only one dictionary. Compare the definitions offered by at least two sources.*

SUMMARY

Definitions provide you with the inestimable benefit of knowing precisely what you are talking about. And clearly defined words are a cornerstone of clear thinking.

The basic structure of a definition and the rules of how to define a word are presented in discussion and through examples. Definitions can give you a great advantage in arguments, not only because of the lucidity they provide, but also because you will be prepared to request them from the other person. When she gropes to define how she is using the term "justice," for example, the advantage adheres to your argument.

With precisely defined words, you are ready to "Apply Reason to Theory."

---

*Should you wish to follow up on this chapter, I recommend not only the books cited within it, but also Stuart Chase's entertaining *The Tyranny of Words*. Dr. Rudolph Flesch's classic work *The Art of Plain Talk* is an antidote to bureaucratic jargon, but must be read skeptically. Most overviews of logic, including the books recommended in the last chapter, will include a section on definitions. One of the best introductions to the general area of semantics—the study of language and meaning—is S. I. Hayakawa's *Language in Thought and Action*.

For a more casual and accessible approach, there are many self-help books on English usage, such as Robert Claiborne's entertaining *Saying What You Mean: A Commonsense Guide to American Usage*. And while you are at it, pick up some of the dozens of books on American slang or the evolution of language. Any book that makes words come alive for you should be on your shelf.

11

Applying Reason to Theory

THE CACOPHONY OF THEORY

> There is no squabbling so violent as that between people who accepted an idea yesterday and those who will accept the same idea tomorrow.
>
> Christopher Morley

A theory is a connected body of ideas that are expressed as statements or propositions. Reasoning offers a powerful tool to analyze the many and conflicting theories that bombard you every day in the news, in the classroom, on the street, and in heated discussions over dinner at the kitchen table. Theories—be they political, psychological, economic, religious, aesthetic, or otherwise—constantly confront you, though sometimes they are expressed in such popular terms that you may not reflect upon them. Because you have heard them repeatedly, you may simply consider the theories to be above reproach rather than as a series of propositions and assumptions to be tested. Yet almost every issue discussed on the television news can not only be expressed as a theory, it usually has a complicated network of other theories underpinning it.

207

Consider the politically popular and, thus, relatively uncontroversial attempt to prevent teenagers from becoming "addicted" to cigarettes by restricting advertising. Although this attempt may seem to be nothing more than a combination of common sense and benevolence, backing a ban on cigarette advertisements and cigarette sales to teenagers involves taking a position on many other associated theories. For example, whether you consciously realize it or not, prohibiting a sixteen-year-old from smoking involves taking a position about when the age of consent is reached, the age at which a teenager is considered to be a legal adult who is responsible for her own decisions. It entails taking a position on whether the government, rather than parents, should oversee the health of teenagers. In calling for the ban on cigarette advertisement, you are drawing a line that establishes one of the boundaries of freedom of speech. You are also accepting the scientific studies that claim a cause-and-effect link between smoking tobacco and cancer as opposed to accepting the theory that smoking is merely one contributing factor among many others. These are merely some of the theories and positions you are adopting when you agree with the ostensibly undisputed campaign to protect teenagers from tobacco.

Or consider the simple and laudable statement "Women should be equal to men." For this simple statement to even make sense, you need to have a theory of what constitutes equality. Do you advocate equality under the law, socioeconomic equality, equal representation in legislatures ... ? You cannot advocate all three forms of equality, as the socioeconomic form requires unequal treatment under the law as embodied in such preferential policies as affirmative action. Depending on your theory of equality, what you mean by the original statement will vary dramatically.

The arduous task of unpacking the unspoken implications of the slew of statements you hear, so that their theoretical underpinnings are visible to be examined and evaluated, could well occupy most of your day. Even when the theories are explicitly spelled out, the presentation may not be clear enough to allow you to assess them adequately. As a timesaving measure, you have to develop general approaches to ideas. You need guiding principles by which to swiftly weigh the worth of the theories you encounter.

Some theories can be rebutted simply by reducing them to their syllogistic form. The formal fallacies covered all too briefly in chapter 9 dealt with validity and truth, and the difference between them. Validity refers to whether or not an argument's structure is internally consistent. Truth refers to whether a proposition or claim within an argument corresponds to reality. A theory can be dismissed either on the basis of being invalid or of being untrue—that is, at least one of the propositions within it is seen to be untrue.

Without question, the easiest way to assess most arguments is with reference to their validity. For example, remember the "if A, then B" fallacy that ran:

> If he loves me, he will stay home tonight.
>
> He stayed home tonight.
>
> Therefore, he loves me.

This was seen to be an invalid form of syllogism because the conclusion did not follow necessarily from the major and minor premises. B does not necessitate A. Many factors other than love could explain the man's decision to stay home that particular night. To be valid, the above syllogism would have to be phrased as "If and only if he loves me, he will stay home tonight," thus logically eliminating all other causal factors. The premises of the syllogism may not be true, but its structure is valid.

By putting theories into a syllogistic form, you can quickly evaluate them as either valid or invalid. This process can save you a great deal of time.

So much for validity. How do you evaluate the truth of a theory—that is, of a series of connected propositions? It is a relatively simple matter to evaluate the truth of a straightforward proposition such as "The sky is blue." You go outside and look upward: the evidence either confirms or falsifies the claim. Yet even this simple proposition may turn out to be more complex than it appears. Over the period of a year, you notice the sky is occasionally an unmistakable gray. You amend the proposition accordingly: "The sky is blue, except for when it is gray." Then you live through a tornado, which is often preceded by the sky taking on an ominous green tint. You amend the assertion again: "The sky is normally blue, occasionally gray, and rarely green." The process of evaluating the truth of the proposition involves observing the evidence, drawing a conclusion, and revising it as necessary to integrate new facts.

But how do you evaluate truths that cannot be directly observed? For example, you cannot directly observe whether or not the majority of American voters—a group composed of millions of individuals—is apathetic toward politics. You can speak to individual people and ascertain their specific reasons for not casting a ballot, but it would be a lifetime pursuit. Of course, this is the point at which research firms enter with statistic-gathering techniques such as random sampling. The statistics these firms provide can be quite valuable, but they can also be severely biased and flawed. Before you use them to evaluate a theory, you must evaluate the statistics themselves. (A section on how to evaluate statistics follows in chapter 12.)

But the situation is not as grim as might now be suspected. Although the truth of a theory can be difficult to ascertain, principles of evaluation exist and offer you a way to approach theories. One of the most effective tools for quickly assessing theories is what the philosopher Karl Popper termed "falsification."

THE FALSIFICATION PRINCIPLE

> Some circumstantial evidence is very strong, as when you find a trout in the milk.
>
> Henry David Thoreau

It is difficult to dismiss the factual evidence of a trout in the milk, but you will rarely encounter such a clear indication that theories are either true or false. Indeed, it can be extraordinarily hard work to confirm or disprove a theory. Fortunately, principles for evaluating theories can save a great deal of time and effort.*

---

*Antony Flew's *Thinking Straight* addresses many of these principles in an entertaining manner.

The most useful principle I have found is called *falsification,* so named by the philosopher Karl Popper. Popper developed an intriguing approach by which to evaluate scientific claims. He disputed the notion that scientists should form a hypothesis (a proposition set forth to explain a phenomenon) and, then, go out and try to verify it. He claimed that scientists should go out and try to falsify a hypothesis rather than to verify it. In other words, instead of looking for evidence to support your claim, you should look for evidence disproving it. The difference between these two approaches is immense.

Popper's reason for pursuing falsification was compelling. He observed that you could never conclusively verify a scientific theory, no matter how many confirming cases you observe. To speak in terms of logic, you would be running up against a fallacy known as *affirming the consequent.* In other words, you would be trapped in an invalid form of syllogism that would run as follows: If P, then Q; Q, therefore P. To translate this into common English, you would be arguing along the lines of:

If my theory is correct, then all swans are black.

Here is a black swan.

Therefore, my theory is correct.

This is the fallacy of affirming the consequent. And no matter how many black swans (Qs) you observe, you cannot derive the truth of the theory "swans are black birds" (P) from that process, because there might be a swan out of view that is not black.

But! Popper pointed out, you can disprove the theory by observing one single white swan. Therefore, a theory that cannot be conclusively verified can be absolutely disproven. All it takes to falsify a theory, such as "Swans are black birds," is the presence of one swan that isn't black.

Popper concluded that scientific investigation is a process of *conjecture* and *refutation.* When scientists are confronted with a question, they offer a conjecture—that is, an opinion without sufficient evidence for proof—about what they think the solution might be. Then, they search for ways to refute or falsify the very solution they have suggested. For example, when confronted with the question of why they have no women students, physicists at a university might offer the conjecture, "Women are just not interested in the hard sciences." Then, if they are honest researchers, they should make inquiries at other universities in an attempt to find female students who are studying mathematics and physics.

Of course, as a theory resists falsification over years and years of being tested, it becomes more and more likely to be a correct theory, though its truth can never be absolutely established.

Falsification is a powerful tool in evaluating facts and theories. And it has the charm of reversing the approach people normally take toward their own theories, thus the charm of offering a fresh perspective. People commonly look only for confirming cases. They sift through history or the newspaper and take note only of the evidence supporting what they believe to be true. Or what they want to be true. Evidence that might falsify their beliefs is often ignored, or dismissed. For example, if you believe all pro-lifers are religious zealots or all women seeking abortions are indifferent to human life, you might ignore any human-interest interviews that clearly demonstrate the opposite. You might dismiss them as biased reporting. Yet seeking out such disconfirming cases can be a powerful intellectual tool because they tell you right away if there is something wrong with a theory.

Another way of shutting out disconfirming cases is by presenting arguments which, by their very nature, cannot be refuted. There is an old joke in philosophy about a man who says to his doctor, "Doctor, doctor, I'm dead." The doctor replies, "No, you are not." The man persists, "Yes, I am; I am dead." The doctor argues with the fellow, "Would you agree with me that dead men don't bleed?" The man agrees. The doctor then pricks his patient's finger and he bleeds. "Aha," the doctor proclaims. "See, dead men don't bleed and here is blood, therefore, you are alive." The man reflects on this and concludes, "I was obviously wrong. Dead men do bleed."

The moral is: when people do not want to have a theory refuted, they often construct their arguments in such a manner as to make them unfalsifiable. They construct theories in such a way that no amount of evidence will disconfirm them. In doing so, they make evidence irrelevant to their intellectual beliefs.

As a caveat about the theory of falsifiability, Popper specifically dealt with scientific theory rather than the verification of simple and limited claims, such as the statement "A car is in the driveway." Such statements can be verified by direct observation. Moreover, Popper's critics have been quick to point out that the theory of falsifiability is, in and of itself, unfalsifiable. The claim that theories cannot be verified is, in and of itself, not open to verification.

Nevertheless, falsifiability remains a useful technique to give a quick, rough sense of whether a theory is being honestly presented—that is, presented in such a manner as to include, rather than to exclude, all relevant evidence.*

THEORY IS A RISKY BUSINESS

Without danger, the game grows cold.
George Chapman, *All Fools*, act 3

To advance a theory is to take a risk that the real-world evidence might prove you are wrong. Even in making simple factual statements such as "A trout is in the milk," wherever there is a possibility of verification, there is also the possibility of falsification. Or, logically, there should be. After all, when you go to check your claims against the evidence, it either supports or disproves what you say.

For example, when you say, "If my theory is correct, all swans are black" and wander down to the local pond to check the evidence, you risk seeing a white swan and disproving your theory. Only by an intellectual sleight of hand, e.g., by relabeling any white swan you see as a duck, can you eschew the risk. A person who claims to respect evidence, but doesn't want to take the risk of being proven wrong, is not being intellectually honest.

Falsifying a theory is a more complicated matter but the same principle applies: a theory must be falsifiable in order to be verifiable. It must be vulnerable to evidence.

---

*For those ambitious enough to tackle the work—and it will take persistence—Karl Popper's *The Logic of Scientific Discovery* is highly recommended.

While he was a student in Vienna, Karl Popper took special note of a school of thought that was popular in his day: Freudianism. In analyzing Freudian theory, Popper encountered a strange and insurmountable obstacle. Namely, it seemed immune to refutation. It was not that Freudian theory could not be refuted because it was correct, but that the system of theory was constructed in such a manner as to eliminate the very possibility of disconfirming cases. Consider the Freudian psychological phenomenon called the Oedipal (Electra) complex—the sexual attachment that every child is alleged to feel toward a parent of the opposite sex. Freud claimed this phenomenon was "universal." It was a stage of development that everyone went through. Popper would point out that a great many well-adjusted people, who had happy and apparently unrepressed childhoods, have no memory, no feeling, no indication whatsoever of ever having had such a desire. Surely such recurring evidence seems to disconfirm the claim that the Oedipal complex is universal.

To put Popper's objection in more logical terms:

If Freudian theory is correct, all people have experienced an Oedipal complex.

But many people claim not to have had such an experience.

Therefore, the theory is not correct.

Yet when Freudians were confronted with cases that falsified their theory, they simply defined those cases out of existence, rather as the white swan was redefined as a duck. They said, "People who don't manifest any sign whatsoever of an Oedipal complex are merely repressing it." In other words, Freudians produced a companion theory to define out of existence any counterevidence. In essence they stated: "If there is evidence present, this confirms an Oedipal complex; if there is no evidence present, this confirms an Oedipal complex." The position was so constructed as to preclude falsification. And so, by Popper's standards, it also precluded verification.

And what about Freudian psychoanalysis, a well-defined and lengthy therapeutic process by which psychological problems are said to be cured? After all, Freud claimed to be dealing with universal phenomena so everyone should be covered by his theories. Yet some people have gone through many years of psychoanalysis without experiencing benefits. Some claim to have been harmed by the process. In such cases, the syllogistic form that confronts the Freudian therapist is:

If my theory is correct, this process will cure the problem.

People who underwent the process were not cured.

Therefore, my theory is not (or, at least, may not be) correct.

Yet, typically, psychiatrists and psychologists blame their failures on the patient and not on the theory or the process. They construct a circular argument that runs as follows: the theory/process is valid and true, therefore the patient must not have been really sincere about being cured. This argument is circular because, when trying to establish whether or not the theory is true, it appeals to the truth of the theory in its defense.

Freudianism, as a body of interconnected theories, claims to be scientific, but scientists experimenting in a laboratory will not blame their failures on the things upon which they are experimenting. A research psychologist will not claim that the rats were uncooperative about acting as they should have in the maze.

(Note: I chose Freudian psychology as an example, as opposed to any other school, only because it was the object of Popper's analysis. Although I agree with Popper on this one point regarding psycho-analysis, on a more personal level I find Freudian analysis to be intriguing and Freud's contribution to our understanding of phenomena such as dreams and childhood sexuality to be immensely useful.)

Consider an example other than Freudianism that almost everyone encounters sooner or later. You are trapped in a situation—e.g., a subway ride—with an evangelical fundamentalist Christian who is not content to respect your differences on religion, but feels compelled to save you. She clutches a Bible to her chest and asks "Have you read the good book?" You answer curtly, yes, and stare pointedly at a newspaper in your hand. "Have you been saved?" she persists. Your silence does not dissuade her from her course, and she continues, "God loves you. If you will only open your heart to Him, He will fill you with peace and His love."

At this point, if you are annoyed enough at this intrusion upon and criticism of your personal religious beliefs, you might want to take her up on the challenge. You might turn to her and say, "Okay, I agree to open my heart to God right here and now as sincerely as possible. *But* if I do so, and God does not enter my heart in the manner you describe, are you willing to admit that God does not love me?"

In other words, the fundamentalist has asked you to conduct a religious experiment. She has claimed that, if you do X, Y will happen because God loves you. As a point of intellectual honesty on her part, if you sincerely do X and Y does not occur, she should be willing to call into question the statement "God loves you." I've not yet met an evangelical sort who is willing to accept this challenge.

Yet such zealots, whether religious or political, try to appear reasonable by asking: "Just give it a try," or "Test this hypothesis." In reality, they are anything but reasonable because they want you to assume the risk of being convinced to leave your current position while their position assumes no risk at all from the evidence.

To rephrase this point, whenever you attempt to prove something, you must assume the risk of your claim being disproven. If the evangelist did take you up on the challenge and you were not saved by the process, it is almost certain she would blame the failure on you and not on her version of God. Her theory is then revealed as being immune to falsification. It becomes the type of theory you have to accept as true before you can discover its truth.

Theories must be dealt with on a theoretical level. They must be analyzed and tested according to the logic of their internal structure, and the evidence supporting them—not according to the sincerity, sweetness, or any other characteristic of the people debating the theory.

THE FALLACY OF THE STOLEN CONCEPT

> Little would be left you, I'm afraid,
> If all your debts to Greece and Rome were paid.
>   Alexander Pope

The Fallacy of the Stolen Concept is a phrase originated by Ayn Rand and spelled out in her book *Introduction to Objectivist Epistemology*, which I recommended elsewhere and to which I am greatly indebted.

The psychologist Nathaniel Branden—a former associate of Rand's—defines this fallacy: "The fallacy of the stolen concept is the fallacy of using a concept while ignoring, contradicting or denying the concepts on which it logically and genetically relies."

Imagine that your ideas are constructed in a hierarchy, looking like a pyramid. The most basic of your ideas—the laws of logic and axioms—form the pyramid's broad base. All of your other concepts rest upon this base and are supported by it. In other words, the higher levels of the pyramid of ideas depend upon the basic ones to give them meaning. The fallacy of the stolen concept amounts to using a high-level idea while denying the validity of other more basic ideas on which it depends in order to have meaning. In her *Introduction to Objectivist Epistemology*, Rand defines axioms as "the identification of a primary fact of reality, which cannot be analyzed, i.e., reduced to other facts or broken into component parts."

What constitutes an axiomatic concept? According to Rand, "The first and primary axiomatic concepts are 'existence,' 'identity' (which is a corollary of 'existence') and 'consciousness.' . . . These are irreducible primaries. An attempt to 'prove' them is self-contradictory . . ." (p. 52). For example, any attempt to disprove consciousness presupposes consciousness in the form of some intelligence posing the question.

A common example of this fallacy is the famous political maxim uttered by the French anarchist Pierre Proudhon, "All property is theft." In order to know what theft is, you must have a concept of rightful property because theft is property taken from its rightful owner. If there is no such thing as rightful property, there is also no such thing as theft.

Inevitably, you will encounter someone who will attack the absolute base of your hierarchy of ideas, namely, the laws of logic. The doubting Thomas or Thomasina will say, "Prove the laws of logic." This demand for the proof of logic is, in and of itself, an example of a stolen concept because unless you accept the principles of logic at the outset, the words "*prove* this to me" are stripped of any meaning.

All you can reasonably reply to such a person is that the concept of proof, which he is using, has no meaning without the prior laws of logic. In essence, he is asking you to use logic to prove that logic exists. In other words, the words "Prove the laws of logic" may make linguistic sense, but they make no conceptual sense since the laws of logic are presupposed by the very concept of proof.

For example, if it is the case that A can be both A and not-A, then *true* does not have to be true; true can be both true and false at the same time and in the same respect. What you mean to say and what you don't mean to say can exist simultaneously. All communication would break down, for we can communicate only on the assumption that words have meaning.

Thoughts are in a similar position. You could not even think to yourself without presupposing that your thoughts have a certain identity—that they mean what they mean and are not something else. But if the thought of a car could mean both car and non-car (non-car = everything else besides a car), then your thoughts are not possible.

USING THE ABOVE PRINCIPLES IN APPROACHING IDEAS

> If you will not hear Reason, she will surely rap your knuckles.
> Benjamin Franklin, *Poor Richard*

Approaching ideas well requires nothing more than common sense and a respect for the truth. Here are some questions you should have in mind whenever you examine an idea or a theory (a connected body of ideas). They'll help to point you in the right direction.

1. What Would Falsify This Idea or Theory?

Remember that falsification means that ideas, in order to be true, must run the risk of being false. In other words, when you state an idea or fact—such as "My car is in the driveway with engine trouble"—you run the risk of being proven wrong. You make yourself vulnerable, because the facts may not back you up. Perhaps the car has been stolen since you parked it; or perhaps the engine works fine.

When you ask "What would falsify the above statement about the car?" the answer is clear. You can check the driveway; you can take the car to a mechanic. These empirical, real-world tests will either verify or falsify your claim.

Many times, however, people will make statements that are impossible to falsify. This means they are also impossible to verify. If an idea is immune from being contradicted by facts, it is also immune from being confirmed by them.

Some religious arguments are immune from being tested by the facts. For example, arguments based on God's will—e.g.,women should obey their husbands—are virtually impossible to falsify, since God's will is not available for us to examine. The Bible is available, but you must first accept that it is God's will if you are to accept it as a source of authority. This puts you into a dilemma. You cannot appeal to the Bible as the established record of God's will in order to prove God's will. The argument is circular. You are assuming the truth of what is in question. (This is often referred to as "Begging the Question.")

Always be suspicious of arguments that are impossible to falsify. Always ask the person presenting them, "What, in principle, would cast doubt on what you are saying?" If the person cannot answer—if nothing on earth could invalidate the argument—then consider walking away from the discussion.

2. Precisely What Do We Not Have?

This is a useful question to ask in conversations in which you have presented a knockdown well-structured argument, yet the other person does not budge one inch in maintaining the opposite position.

Most often, the other person will glibly ignore or dismiss your evidence out of hand. Rather than argue on with anyone who shows such intellectual discourtesy, it is useful to ask him "Precisely what do we not have?" In essence, you are calling his bluff. He is saying to you that your arguments and evidence have not convinced him. You are well within your rights to demand: "Then what would convince you? What evidence or statistics could I present that would persuade you?"

Perhaps you are claiming that a woman can do calculus as well, or better, than a man. The other person might reply "I would be convinced if I actually saw a woman solve a problem in calculus that had stumped a man." This is a reasonable request, which means you are probably dealing with a reasonable person who respects evidence. You just haven't presented the right piece of evidence yet.

And, because you took the trouble to ask, you now know what precisely is missing.

3. Is There Another Explanation?

This question is similar to the one discussed in the syllogism, in which a woman believed a man loved her because he stayed home (chapter 9). Yet many other things could have motivated his behavior. You should always look for competing explanations. Then you can decide, on the evidence, which explanation is most likely to be true. Consider the husband who stayed home. The woman happily assumes he did so because he wanted to be with her. There are competing explanations. For example, there may have been a baseball game on the TV.

Armed with two competing explanations, you can now examine the evidence and decide which one is most likely true. Sorting through the facts, you discover that a ball game was indeed being aired. You see a pattern of behavior on the man's part: namely, he usually stays home during prime baseball season. Then you find he spent next to no time talking to his wife, nor did he pay any attention whatsoever to her. His focus was riveted on the television.

Which of the two competing theories do you think is most likely to be true?

Always judge the likelihood of your explanation against the likelihood of competing ones. Which one best explains the facts?

4. What Definition Is Being Used?

There are some conversations in which you don't seem to connect with the other person. Although you are using the same words, you seem to be talking about totally different things. When this is the case, stop and ask for some definitions. For example, you may be discussing whether a court verdict in the news is "just." When you use the word "justice," you mean the classically accepted definition of "to each according to what they deserve." But when the other person uses this word, he means "according to the divine will of Allah." This difference in definitions dooms you to talk all night at cross-purposes with each other—unless, of course, the differences are made explicit.

The next time you are in a conversation with someone who uses words in a confusing manner, ask her to define those words. What does she mean by "economic prosperity," "political justice," or "social good"? And be prepared to answer the same questions yourself.

SUMMARY

We are constantly bombarded not only with information, but also by theories that require time and energy to evaluate. Some general approaches will allow you to assess theories with far greater ease and swiftness.

One of the most useful approaches is called *falsification*. Whenever you advance a theory, you take a risk that evidence in the real world might prove you wrong: you risk falsification. Yet many theories are constructed in a manner that precludes contradicting evidence. Always ask "What will falsify this theory?" If nothing could, be suspicious.

Equally, approach statistics with skepticism.

12

Applying Reason to Statistics

As is your sort of mind,
So is your sort of search: you'll find
What you desire.
                    Robert Browning, *Easter Day*

A friend of mine named David Friedman has accomplished a feat I would have formerly denied was possible: he has written a thoroughly entertaining book on economics entitled *Hidden Order: The Economics of Everyday Life*. The first sentences of the introduction set Friedman's tone for the book, "I once had a colleague whose very popular performances included undressing in the middle of his lecture. In advertising, this approach is known as vampire video."

Vampire video, the reader is informed, is an advertisement which features a breathtakingly beautiful woman upon whom the audience concentrates instead of critically evaluating the information being presented to them. David is drawing an obvious parallel to the nude professor entertaining what would be an otherwise critical and, perhaps, bored audience. Nevertheless, Friedman assures his readers that properly presented economic theory "is both more interesting and more entertaining than naked professors" (p. xi).

I would like to make a similar point about statistics. In arguing, many people flash statistics, controlled studies, random samplings, and double-blind studies in an attempt to dazzle their listeners into a silence that bypasses critical thinking. As Darrell Huff in the *must-read* book *How to Lie with Statistics* observes, "The secret language of statistics, so appealing in a fact-minded culture, is employed to sensationalize, inflate, confuse, and oversimplify" (p. 8). Statistics are the sizzle of the steak, something else that advertisers are admonished to sell rather than the substance of the meat itself.

I used to be intimidated by statistics because of what Huff dubbed the "secret language," which consists of terms such as median, mean, average, probability, zone of acceptance, and sampling. Part of my reaction undoubtedly harks back to a distaste for mathematics that I acquired in grade school.

One of the best ways to overcome the natural intimidation that many women feel toward statistics is to buy one of the several basic self-help books on the subject that are issued as part of a series. The one I used several years ago was issued by Barron's Educational Series—*Statistics the Easy Way*. Short of this, an understanding of the following terms and concepts will take you a long distance in dealing with statistics and those who throw them about with wild abandon.

MY DISILLUSIONMENT WITH POPULAR RESEARCH

About five years ago I wrote a feminist analysis of pornography, which disputed a great many of the conclusions/accusations I had heard from the feminist movement. I took the empirical statements— the statements of fact—that I had heard and went in person to the porn industry to check out whether the accusations were grounded in fact. One result: I found that the so-called undisputed studies and clear evidence were anything but clear or undisputed. The sticky fingerprints of ideology seemed to be everywhere. And, frankly, the distortion was on both sides of the issue. Theories are paraded as facts. Ad hominems take the place of arguments.

Thus, you must learn how to . . .

PROTECT YOURSELF FROM STATISTICS

Self-defense is Nature's eldest law.
John Dryden,
Absalom and Achitophel

The following guidelines for interpreting what is being said should give you an advantage over at least 90 percent of the people with whom you argue. More or less.

1. The "Average" Is Virtually Meaningless

One of the most common statistical terms is the "average," but this term is almost meaningless without knowing how the average has been calculated. For example, imagine going to a job interview at which the recruiter informs you that the average yearly income of an employee of the corporation is $50,000. Duly impressed, you later enthuse about the high pay rate to a friend in personnel at that same corporation, who pointedly contradicts you, and swears that the average income is $20,000. "No, no," pipes in a clerk from accounting who is passing by, "the average yearly income here is $29,000." It is entirely possible that all three sources are quoting correct averages that have been calculated in different manners.

The $50,000 average yearly income may have been calculated by the recruiter in such a way as to impress you with the richness of the income you are likely to earn as an employee. His method of calculation: all incomes of corporate "employees," including the astronomical earnings of the chairman of the board and his like, were totaled up and divided by the number of people working there. Although the figure of $50,000 sounds wonderfully high, it may be that 90 percent of the employees make less than half of that amount. An average calculated in this manner is called the "mean."

Your friend in personnel may have used the "median" as his method of calculation to arrive at an average. According to this reckoning, the yearly income of $20,000 is the figure that lies at the exact middle of the earning range of the corporation's employees. Fifty percent of all employees make more than $20,000, and 50 percent of them make less. In this case, the median may be far removed from the mean because the distribution of corporate income is markedly skewed toward the very top.

The passing clerk from accounting may have used yet another method, the "mode," for producing an average. The mode is nothing more than the most frequently encountered figure in a series. Thus, if there are one thousand employees and more of them make precisely $29,000 than make any other yearly income, then $29,000 can validly be stated as the average income. The *modal* average income, that is, not the *mean* or the *median* average income.

Statistical averages may be correctly expressed in any of the three above forms and, clearly, the method of calculation plays a large role in how you will interpret the results. In general, the most informative sort of average is usually the median—the average that falls directly in the middle of the spread of data, so that 50 percent are above that line and 50 percent are below.

Make sure you ask which method of calculation was employed to produce the average.

2. A Correlation Is Not a Cause-and-Effect Relationship

A correlation is a "mutual relationship between two or more things, parts, etc." A cause-and-effect relationship exists when the mutual relationship is such that the presence of A causes the presence of B.

One of the most common misuses of statistics is to establish a correlation between two events or things and, then, to claim that one thing in some way causes the other. It is an outright fallacy to assume that if A can be correlated with B, then A causes B. Such a correlation might indicate nothing more than that both are caused by another factor C. For example, there is a high correlation between the number of doctors in a city (A) and the number of alcoholics located there (B). But one doesn't cause the other; both statistics are proportional to the size of the city's population (C).

There is also a high correlation between acts of violence (A) and the sale of ice cream (B). Both are related to the soaring temperature in the summer (C) which causes people to become both easily enraged and desirous of cooling off.

When you see a correlation, be skeptical.

3. The Sampling Should Be Random

A random sampling is a representative sampling that is large and diverse enough to render significant results. Such a sampling is designed to save time. If you want to know the ratio of single men to single women who live in your city, you could individually ask every one of the 500,000 residents this question, assuming, of course, they would agree not to change their marital status before your research was concluded. Or, you could randomly phone X number of residents and ask them the same question. In theory, if the number of people phoned is large enough and randomly chosen, your research will render a fair approximation of the ratio you're seeking, with a small probability of error on either side.

A sampling that is too small or not random may well be of less value than an educated guess based on personal experience.

HOW TO INTERROGATE A STATISTIC

> I keep six honest serving-men
> (They taught me all I knew):
> Their names are What and Why and When
> And How and Where and Who.
> Rudyard Kipling, *The Serving-Men*

In his book *How to Lie with Statistics*, Darrell Huff suggests testing the statistics you encounter by asking five simple questions: Who says so? How does he know? What's missing? Did somebody change the subject? Does it make sense?

Who Says So?

The purpose of this question is to seek out possible bias on the part of the researcher or agency offering a statistic. The bias may be conscious. For example, a tobacco manufacturer may support research and may issue reports that support claims favorable to the product it markets. Although the manufacturer's clear bias should make you suspicious, the mere fact that it has a vested interest does not invalidate its statistics. But the bias *does* mean you should carefully examine the evidence and hold it up to the light.

Has there been a shift in measurement during the research? For example, has the researcher used a median instead of a mean in order to make the statistic more favorable to tobacco interests? After all, when the word "average" is used, it covers a multitude of ambiguity.

Unconscious bias may also exist. Even an honest researcher carries all her assumptions with her into the research, and this will greatly influence key factors such as the phrasing of the questions that are asked. For example, a Freudian psychiatrist who accepts the Oedipal complex as being pivotal in a psychological development will ask a patient different questions about her childhood than a Skinnerian who believes behavior modification explains a child's evolution. The data each receives will reflect the bias with which it was gathered.

Look for the researcher's bias, conscious or unconscious, and permit your skepticism to increase a notch if you find it.

How Does He Know?

The purpose of this question is to ferret out sloppiness or bias in the research process, as opposed to bias in the researcher herself. The two forms of bias often go hand in hand, but sloppy research can easily result from laziness or inappropriate methodology rather than from dishonesty.

For example, imagine a researcher who rings doorbells at random in order to ask the occupant, "Have you committed a crime lately?" or even the much milder question "Do you fart in public?" The researcher is likely to discover that her sampling is both crime- and fart-free, not necessarily because this finding is accurate but because few people will look a stranger in the eye and admit either to committing a crime or to performing a socially stigmatized act. Although this may be a random sampling, the researcher's methodology is inappropriate.

Perhaps the most common methodological mistake, however, is to rely upon a biased or unrepresentative sampling. Consider the notorious 1936 survey conducted by the popular *Literary Digest*. In order to predict which candidate would win the 1936 presidential election, millions of people were polled, using phone calls and subscription lists of the magazine. The results were overwhelming: the Republican candidate Alf Landon would garner almost three times the vote total of the Democratic candidate Roosevelt. Of course, Roosevelt won the election. The survey had been biased by the fact that, in 1936, people who could afford telephones and subscriptions to *Literary Digest* were the economically advantaged, who also tended to be Republican.

What's Missing?

Just as the term "average" is virtually meaningless if you don't know whether the average is a mean, a median, or a mode, so, too, are other calculations of little value without knowing their context. "Seventy-five percent of Americans prefer milk to lemonade" is an impressive statistic until you realize that only twelve people were involved in the study, all of whom were Wisconsin dairy farmers. At this point, the surprising result is that 25 percent of them preferred lemonade.

Whenever you note that a small group of people have been surveyed, your suspicions should be roused, and not only because of the statistical insignificance of the sampling. It is quite possible, and, perhaps, quite common, for a company to conduct a multitude of small surveys until one of them produces the desired results. After all, poll enough groups of twelve people and you will find eleven who love your product, even if the mean average of *everyone* you surveyed indicates that only 30 percent would buy it again. Huff reports an experiment he conducted: after numerous tries at tossing a penny ten times in a row, one of the attempts produced eight heads and two tails. On the basis of this survey, he concluded that a tossed penny comes up heads 80 percent of the time. The question becomes: how likely is it that the result of one single reported experiment indicates something significant, other than merely the laws of probability?

Did Someone Change the Subject?

You are undoubtedly familiar with the sort of newscast that quotes a rise in "reported cases" of something and, then, concludes that this something itself is on the increase. The findings of the newscast are not justified, however, because the broadcaster has confused the raw data with the conclusion. The two are very different statements. For example, the reported cases of domestic violence have soared over the past ten years, but this does not mean domestic violence itself is on the rise. Rather, it may indicate a greater willingness on the part of wives to report such battery, and a greater sensitivity on the part of the police who answer the calls and do the paperwork.

Consider another example of changing the subject. A newspaper accurately states, "According to a phone survey of 10,000 American homes, men have sex 4 times a week, whereas women have sex only 2 times a week." The newspaper falsely concludes that American men have sex more often than American women. Besides raising the provocative question of exactly who these men are sleeping with, the conclusion is not justified. All the phone survey really demonstrates is that men *claim* to have sex twice as often as women. It is far from clear whether the claim corresponds to anything factual.

Does It Make Sense?

Never allow a statistical finding to automatically override your good common sense. Don't allow data to substitute for your own judgment.

My husband learned a valuable technique from one of his physics professors at Bradley University called *estimating*. The technique involves taking a statistic to its logical conclusion and seeing if it reduces to absurdity. Consider the alarming statement, over 3,000,000 teenage girls on welfare became pregnant this year.

Start with the total population of the United States—roughly 300,000,000 people. Assume that roughly half of the population is male, leaving you with 150,000,000 people. Bump up the number of females to 160,000,000 to reflect that men generally die a few years earlier than women. Assume the age spread of the female population is approximately one to seventy-five years, of which the teenage years (13–19) constitute 10.7 percent (75 divided by 7 [19 – 12 = 7]).

(Note: two factors make the estimate of 10.7 percent a generous one. First, some significant portion of girls from 13 to 19 will not yet be menstrual and able to bear children. Second, the baby boom has assured the numerical spread of women from 1 to 75 is not even, but bulges toward the ages of 40 and 50.)

Now multiply 160,000,000 by 10.7 percent to produce the figure 17,120,000 which should roughly approximate the number of teenage girls in America. Divide this figure by 3,000,000—the reported number of teenage mothers-to-be on welfare—and the number you get is 5.7. In other words, according to the logic of the quoted statistic, approximately one in every six teenage girls in America must not only be on welfare, but she must have become pregnant in the last twelve months.

Does this make sense to you? Or does it contradict your direct experience, as well as other statistics you've heard, such as the total number of people on welfare?

Never allow the pseudoscientific air of a statistic to short-circuit old-fashioned horse sense. Estimate for yourself.*

---

*For those who wish to pursue the subject of statistics in a more formal manner than that presented by *How to Lie with Statistics*, I recommend *Elementary Statistical Methods* by Helen M. Walker.

WHILE I HAVE YOUR ATTENTION . . .
A GOOD WORD FOR MATH

> Mathematics, rightly viewed, possesses not only truth, but supreme beauty . . . sublimely pure, and capable of a stern perfection such as only the greatest art can show . . .
>   Bertrand Russell, "The Study of Mathematics"

Let me put in a good word for math, especially for women pursuing math in almost any form. It is almost trite to declare math to be the language in which the universe is written, the common language through which human beings and any other intelligence in the universe are likely to communicate should we ever encounter each other. Math is also the wheels that make the mundane basics of daily life roll on. You cannot buy a carton of milk without using math to sort through the change in your purse. You can't fill out a tax return, decide which apartment you can afford, plan for retirement, or write a check without enlisting its aid.

Yet there is a fundamental difference between math as the grand principle of the universe and math as you practice it in your checkbook. The latter might best be called arithmetic, which, according to the *Random House Dictionary,* is "the method or process of computation with figures," rather than mathematics, which is "the systematic treatment of magnitude, relationships between figures and forms, and relations between quantities expressed symbolically." Arithmetic is the most basic branch and expression of mathematics, but it offers few of the real benefits that more advanced math can provide to the reasoning process. In essence, the greatest benefit of studying math is acquiring the skill of *thinking mathematically* about a problem.

For me, a stumbling sense of this skill was acquired when I finally decided to teach myself calculus by using "The Easy Way" series on mathematics issued by Barron's. Until then, I had shunned math as being indecipherable, irrelevant, and a general pain in the neck. Like most women, I shied away from symbolic equations because they represented a hard-edged linear world that might as well be posted "For Men Only." This is a world in which women are often considered second-class citizens.

Like most innumerate people—those who cannot understand math and who form the mirror image of those who are illiterate—I simply believed that the dawning new century would have plenty of room for twentieth-century sorts who wished to use computers without learning how to program, and who throw a calculator into their purses so that even basic arithmetic skills atrophied. The truth is, there almost certainly will be room for those who consume mathematics and hard science without understanding its principles. But those who do understand even the fundamentals of mathematics will have an immense advantage in the twenty-first century over those who do not.

I wish my motive for learning calculus had been a noble one, but I was driven to math by arrogance—not my own, but the arrogance of a man who confidently challenged my ability to understand equations. In short, I did it on a dare. At the outset, I didn't have a clue how difficult calculus would turn out to be. Not because mathematics is intrinsically hard to understand, but because mathematical thinking runs against my natural method of reasoning, which is more intuitive.

I look at the Product Rule of differential calculus, which says: if $f(x) = F(x) S(x)$, then $f'(x) = F(x) S'(x) + F'(x) S(x)$. The intuitive portion of my brain switches off. No matter how often I have worked the equation before, I have to take a pencil in hand and laboriously plug in values, look up formulas, slog through the calculations. It is hard work.

I doubt if I would have persisted in this pursuit had it not been for a Eureka! experience that occurred one night—a sudden realization of the elegance and beauty of which mathematics is capable. The realization came when I put down the text of derivative equations with which I had been struggling halfheartedly and began browsing through *A History of Mathematics* by Carl B. Boyer instead.

I had been grappling with the prosaic nomenclature of differentiation—the rate of change—that is called a "derivative" and is expressed through mind-numbing symbols. In differentiation, rate of change of a y or x is written as a derivative of y with regard to x—dy/dx, or of x with respect to y—dx/dy. Learning how to manipulate the relationships between these symbols was worse than learning how to manipulate the grammar of a foreign language. At least I knew that

Spanish or French could serve a practical purpose in my life. I was close to giving up on calculus, even if that meant letting the arrogant fellow win hands down.

Then, the book on mathematical history sent a shock through my system. As an amateur philosopher—*amateur* meaning "one who engages in something for the love of it"—I knew that the phenomenon of change, how a river never remains the same from instant to instant, had baffled philosophers since Greek times. The phenomenon of change had also haunted mathematics, which was then considered to be a branch of philosophy. How could math accurately reflect reality when reality itself was a shifting chaos of change, and mathematics dealt almost entirely with shapes and numbers that stood still?

Then Sir Isaac Newton and his contemporary Gottlieb Liebnitz developed calculus and, for the first time, the world could truly measure rates of motion and change. The laws of gravitation, of the solar system, of physics became measurable and, thus, accessible to man. They ceased to be mysteries. By probing the fleeting phenomenon of change, dy/dx became a mathematical lever that moved the world, and changed not only the context of human knowledge but also our power to control circumstances.

Suddenly, calculus was not so boring to me. Suddenly, it was a means by which I could learn to think in terms of the relationship between changing forces in a way that reflected the physical world rather than in terms of absolute, static truths. Galileo claimed that it was impossible to understand the universe unless you comprehended the language in which it was written. "It is written in the language of mathematics, and its characters are triangles, circles, and other geometric figures, without which it is humanly impossible to understand a single word of it; without these, one is wandering about in a dark labyrinth."

At that point, I had the emotional fuel necessary to understand and to overcome my resistance to math. In Adler's *How to Read a Book*, there is a useful chapter entitled "How to Read Science and Mathematics." There, he comments on how many people fear mathematics and how psychologists have speculated that there might be a phenomenon called "symbol blindness." Yet, in my experience, people often overcome their blindness in a hurry when the math has to do with matters of intense interest, such as personal finances.*

SUMMARY

Many people use statistics without having any sense of what their own data mean. Often it is far from clear what even seemingly simple statistics actually mean. For example, the content of the statement "the average house on Main Street costs $100,000" may change dramatically depending on whether the method of calculation is based on the mean, the median, or the mode.

The language of statistics need not intimidate you. Indeed, learning it—along with some guidelines on how to handle statistics—will give you an enormous advantage in arguing.

The greatest advantage, however, may well derive from a firm grasp on the psychology of arguing.

---

*To creep up on mathematics in an entertaining manner, I recommend Theoni Pappas's *The Joy of Mathematics: Discovering Mathematics All Around You* and, once again, Bart Kosko's *Fuzzy Thinking*. Also, just as a way to play with numbers and get more friendly with mathematical terms such as "probability," another book by Darrell Huff is delightful, *How to Take a Chance*.

David Bergamini offers an extremely accessible introduction to mathematics in *Mathematics*, which is part of the Time-Life Science Library series. Or leaf through several of the series of self-study workbooks on mathematics which should be available in any bookstore of size, and see if any of them appeal to you. Although taking a college course on math might seem to be the obvious solution, I would recommend against it. Poor teachers who make the mysteries of the universe seem like cold lumpy oatmeal have alienated more people from mathematics than any other factor. And, in my experience, math teachers tend toward oatmeal.

To give a better sense of the true wit and passion that can underlie the mathematical view of the world, read Samuel C. Florman's *The Existential Pleasures of Engineering*.

13

The Psychology of Arguing

To "get out of my house" and "what do you want with my
wife?" there's no answer.

Cervantes, *Don Quixote*

Following my own advice, I want to open the first chapter on the
psychology of arguing by offering a definition of what I mean by
that term. By the word "argue," I am referring to what is often called
argumentation—that is, offering an argument, providing your reasoning for a position or claim. I mean an intellectual exchange or discussion in which beliefs are supported by reason and evidence.

Under the word "argument" the *Random House Dictionary* (1980)
provides this primary definition: "disagreement; verbal opposition or
contention; altercation; a violent argument." Clearly, the words "argue"
and "argument" are emotionally charged and in need of clarification.

In common usage, arguing often refers to contests of reasoning—
almost contests of will—with winners and losers, and during which
the participants attempt to prove each other wrong. These exchanges
are not expressions of reasoning, which has nothing to do with defeating an opponent or winning.

Remember the analogy drawn in chapter 1 to the process of arguing. You are one of the surgeons operating on a patient. An intense discussion breaks out between the two of you because, instead of operating on the heart as you had planned, the other surgeon says, "Look, I think we should explore his stomach." In other words, she disputes your diagnosis and then goes on to provide compelling evidence for her position. In the face of such evidence, would you insist upon operating on the heart, even though you secretly agree with the other surgeon's arguments? Or would the health of the patient override all other considerations? If you are a good surgeon, the health of your patient will take priority.

An argument is similar to surgery. Two of you are dissecting an issue in order to reach the truth. The other person says, "I think you are mistaken; the truth lies elsewhere," and she presents what she believes to be compelling reasons. If you are a reasonable person—a good arguer—your first concern will be with what is true or false. Just as the surgeon does not endanger her patient in order to win, people engaged in a proper argument will not abandon reason.

To rephrase, an argument is a purposeful intellectual exchange between parties with a dispute. The purpose is to resolve whatever differences exist, or at least to reach an understanding of where the irresolvable differences lie. An argument does not involve shouting, violence, accusations, or emotional outbursts. Indeed, whenever such unreasoning behavior rears its head, argumentation has broken down and has been replaced by a verbal brawl.

LISTENING: HOW SINCERELY DO YOU WISH TO HEAR?

> And this cuff was but to knock at your ear, and beseech listening.
>
> Shakespeare, *Taming of the Shrew*

Argumentation—indeed, all human communication—consists of two processes: speaking and listening. Just as some people have difficulty in speaking out, others may be uncomfortable in assuming the role of a listener. Perhaps their minds wander when others expound their views. Perhaps the listener's thinking clouds over and she can't understand what is being said. Or she becomes impatient and interrupts constantly so that the speaker is unable to finish sentences. Bad listening habits are as destructive to a productive exchange as are bad manners in the speaker. Moreover, acquiring the skill of listening well is something you owe to yourself: it is the main method by which you learn what the world is trying to tell you.

The ensuing chapters deal more with the art of arguing well rather than with the skill of listening. Nevertheless, no discussion of how to argue would be complete without a cursory examination of how to listen.

The art of listening deserves a book of its own. In the absence of such a volume, let me offer a personal illustration that highlights the importance of developing the skill of listening.

For about three years I was involved in a fractious organization which revolved around a specific and controversial feminist cause. It finally dawned on me that there was so much personal animosity between the organization's founding activists that I could achieve nothing positive by staying. Whatever I was likely to achieve through the organization would be vastly outweighed by the energy I sank into it. It was time to resign in as graceful a manner as possible in order to avoid ill will.

Part of this attempt at grace involved explaining the situation to a close friend who had nominated me for membership in the first place. Her reaction to my resignation was almost certain to be negative since I was widely and correctly seen as being in her camp and as taking her side on various organizational issues. But broaching the subject with her was a complicated matter because of an earlier exchange.

Some months prior, I had discussed a personal problem with her at length. The two of us talked for hours. Not over the phone, but in her kitchen over endless cups of coffee. When I broached the subject with her about a month later, she remembered having had the conversation with me and many of the circumstances of the particularly perplexing event. But she had utterly forgotten what my response had been and now ascribed an entirely different one to me—namely, the one she would have had in similar circumstances. When I patiently ran over the initial conversation, it didn't seem to spark remembrance. It confused her.

For that matter, her response confused me, and there were too many possible explanations for me to understand her behavior. Perhaps my friend simply had "a deaf spot," like many people have emotional blind spots. When she heard something distressing, she filtered it—either then, or later on in her memory—so that it was more palatable. Or perhaps I hit against one of the emotional prejudices that everyone possesses. Again, she would have distorted the intended meaning of my words, however clearly I spoke, because I was crashing head-on into a vigilant prejudice. Or perhaps we each used words to mean entirely different things.

I wanted to be unforgettably and unmistakably clear about my reasons for resigning from the organization. Accordingly, I carefully composed a long e-mail letter that was as explicit as possible and in which I rephrased the key points in two or three different ways. My reasoning: by putting my words in writing, my meaning would be preserved because the words would be right there for her to check.

The next day I phoned and asked that she make a printout of the e-mail so we could discuss it. Since she would undoubtedly be confronted by other members of the organization about my resignation, I asked her to go over the e-mail with me, line by line. The ensuing exchange literally shocked me. She read the e-mail aloud—or, rather, scanned it aloud, skipping over all but key phrases as she went along. That in and of itself is not unusual. Scanning a document for its essential meaning is often a sign of being busy, nothing more. But in two of the key phrases she automatically and unconsciously inserted a "not" before the verb, thus inverting the meaning of my sentence. Clearly, the "nots" were either in the sentences as she would have written them, or they were what she expected to see and she was reading according to her expectations.

The two incidents described above had a dramatic influence on our relationship. I have never discussed anything personally sensitive with her since then, simply because I do not believe she will hear what

I'm saying. I still like her, I still admire her. But I don't trust her ability to listen to what I say and remember with anything vaguely akin to accuracy. Indeed, her inability to listen, or her unwillingness to take the time necessary to do so, led to yet another problem. Because she had no insight into her own behavior, she would blithely report distorted conversations to others.

In turn, my distrust of her reports has caused her to feel ill will toward me. Recently, she was embroiled in a messy controversy involving a professional academic of mutual acquaintance. In phone conversations with me, she complained vehemently, "He said X, then did Y; he lied to me; he breached our verbal contract." My response must have bitterly disappointed her. I refused to take sides because I had no confidence that she remembered the exchanges with the person any more reliably than she had remembered ours. It is no exaggeration to say that her inability to listen has destroyed a valuable friendship.

Yet anyone can learn to listen, if she so wishes. It is largely a matter of being aware of the process.

WHAT DOES LISTENING ENTAIL?

> Were we are eloquent as angels, yet we should please some
> men, some women, and some children much more by listen-
> ing, than by talking.
>
> C. C. Colton, *Lacon*, No. 13

The art of hearing a person out and sincerely trying to see things through their eyes requires great practice and skill. It requires patience, because we live in a competitive culture that puts a high value on self-expression. Often, when a person appears to be silently absorbing a conversation, she is actually inwardly preparing her next comment, or merely waiting for the speaker to pause. There is a natural tendency to grab onto the conversation, as though it were a prize in hot dispute, and run away with it.

Our culture is so competitive that people who do listen attentively and forego opportunities to interrupt a speaker's flow are sometimes criticized as being too passive. Yet listening well is as active a process as arguing well, and one skill is unlikely to be acquired without the other. When you truly listen to an argument, your mind is anything but inactive. Questions and connections flow as a silent undercurrent to the spoken words you are hearing.

Some of the undercurrents flowing through your mind as you listen will concern the literal content of the argument: "How does the speaker know this? Is this true in my experience? That statistic is different than what I read in the newspaper. What does she mean by the words 'common good'?" Another significant part of your reaction will be in response to the body language and vocal inflection of the speaker: "He is standing too close. What is his motive in speaking to me? The last comment was obviously meant in jest. Why is he so agitated about this issue?" Your thought process is anything but passive as you listen.

These are the two levels on which most people listen: to the literal content of the words, and to the emotional content of how the words are being communicated. Attention shifts back and forth with the speaker's emphasis. If the speaker is screaming his opinion into your ear, you may concentrate entirely on the emotional content. If he is dispassionately sketching a complicated theory, you might concentrate entirely on the literal meaning of his words. A shift of focus between the two messages you are receiving is a natural aspect of good listening.

People block their ability to listen in various ways. A common one is by having and maintaining a deaf spot, an emotional block to hearing something. Everyone has such blocks. For example, I still have difficulty absorbing anything mathematical. Even if a theorem is explained to me repeatedly, even if I finally understand its logic, I forget it within a few days. Some people have similar blocks about sexual or religious matters, and their minds literally go blank when the subjects arise.

Others are so fanatically devoted to an ideology or cause that they are incapable of hearing their beliefs critiqued without distorting the criticism in light of their own views. For example, when talking to a dogmatic socialist you might mention that you believe a free-market system creates the most wealth and results in a relatively class-free society. Because your words are filtered through the ideological assumptions of the socialist, he may entirely distort your words and hear only that you do not care a whit for the poor. Or, if you express even a mild reservation about abortion to a feminist who is zealous on the issue, she might respond, "So you think women should be forced to use coat hangers in a back alley?" Of course, you have said nothing of the sort.

The most effective way to overcome deaf spots is to become consciously aware of them. Many of your blocks may not be worth overcoming: I have learned to listen and to live productively with no knowledge of physics, which would be excruciatingly difficult for me to absorb. Whenever a conversation stumbles over any of my particular blocks, I simply admit that I'm out of my depth and save time— especially if the deaf spot reflects a deep psychological problem.

If you wish to overcome the block rather than simply acknowledging and working around it, an effective method is to sit down with a piece of paper and construct precisely the sort of argument or comment you would normally block out. Make your presentation of the argument a sympathetic one.

As you become more psychologically comfortable in dealing with an intellectual issue, you will be able to concentrate better whenever it arises in conversation. Nevertheless, momentary lapses happen to everyone. Don't apologize, just stop the other person and ask, "Could you repeat that please?" If you are finding it difficult to piece together what is being said to you, say something like, "I'm just not following you. Can you rephrase that?" Merely wanting to understand someone and letting them see that you are making this effort will go a long way toward establishing the atmosphere of good will that, in turn, encourages good listening. After all, it is far easier to concentrate on the words of people you like than of people who irritate you.

Earlier, I mentioned our culturally competitive urge to interrupt and take charge of virtually every conversation, even ones we are enjoying. There is also a natural tendency to want to interrupt whenever we hear something we believe to be wrong or that annoys us. The more we disagree with the statement, the stronger becomes the urge to intrude.

One of the keys to blunting this natural tendency is to cultivate a sincere desire to understand other people's points of view. This requires that you consider those views to be of value, not merely as potential weapons to be turned against the other person, but as ideas in and of themselves. Most people do not approach unpalatable ideas in such a manner.

Yet when you examine opposing ideas and arguments only in order to discover their flaws, you miss one of the primary benefits offered by a good argument: namely, the possibility of learning something. Even if your position is substantially correct, the other person might have facts or perspectives that you haven't encountered before. In fact, some may be superior to your own, and worth adopting. The possibility of learning from an argument becomes more probable if two factors are present: the other person is a generally reasonable human being who is familiar with the issue or area, and the subject is a controversial one that has attracted intelligent advocates on either side. Indeed, if both circumstances are present, it is unlikely that you won't have something to learn from hearing the other person out.

It is a good rule of thumb: if a person you know to be generally reasonable makes a claim or an argument you consider to be ridiculous, have the patience to ask for her reasons and for her evidence. It could be that she is not saying what you think you've heard. Or, the position might not be as ridiculous as you assume.

At this point, the listening reader might well counter with this question: "But what if the point of view is so patently absurd/offensive as to not bear listening to any longer?" For example, a co-worker who has been quite reasonable in all your business dealings together may also be an Islamic fundamentalist who believes all women should cover their faces and never speak out in public. Why give his opinions the time of day?

There are several reasons you might want to hear him out, to listen rather than plunge into arguing vehemently, or simply walk away. A good reason is that he represents an opportunity to better understand one of the most powerful views affecting women on this planet. Ask him questions, not to be hostile, but to understand. Ask him how women respond to such restrictions. Surely his mother, his sisters, and other female relatives have said something on the subject over the years.

Don't ask him the standard confrontational questions. Instead, try to get insight into the psychology of why a man would hold such a position. Would he change his stance if you could prove to him that enforced silence might hurt the people he loves, such as a daughter? Does that mean he doesn't respect you as a co-worker? You don't have to agree with a perspective in order for there to be value in understanding it.*

ARGUING—THE OTHER SIDE OF LISTENING

> Be calm in arguing: for fierceness makes
> Error a fault and truth discourtesy . . .
> George Herbert, *The Church-Porch*

I want to be absolutely clear on what I mean by words like "argue" and "argument." By "argue" I mean a verbal exchange between two or more people that involves a disagreement. An "argument" is a purposeful intellectual exchange between people who disagree and base their disagreement on evidence. The purpose of a good argument is to resolve whatever conflict exists or, at least, to reach an understanding of where the irresolvable differences lie.

The ideal argument is a cooperative venture in which both people attempt to arrive at the truth. This is far from the view of arguments many of us have, or of the view of arguing upheld by our society. For most of us, arguments are loud shrill exchanges in which there are winners and losers. As in physical contests, the winner of such an argument is assumed to be the intellectual victor when, actually, nothing much intellectual has occurred.

To a large extent, we live in an anti-intellectual culture that places a low value on reasoning. Yet we also live in a culture where, to use Henry David Thoreau's phrase, most of us are living lives of quiet desperation. We are cut off from what most philosophers throughout the

---

*Fortunately, a variety of books will help you follow up on the art of listening. I recommend E. Atwater's *"I Hear You": Listening Skills to Make You a Better Manager* and R. Bolton's *People Skills: How to Assert Yourself, Listen to Others and Resolve Conflicts.* R. Lakoff's *Language and Woman's Place* and N. Henley's *Body Politics: Power, Sex, and Nonverbal Communication* offer perspective on the impact of language (both body and verbal) upon women.

ages have considered to be our defining characteristic as human beings: the ability to reason. No wonder the art of arguing has been reduced to a slugfest in which an opponent is pummeled into defeat.

This is a strange way to view arguments. After all, the "loser" is the one who actually benefits the most from the exchange. Presumably, the "loser" is the one who gained knowledge and eliminated an error so that his beliefs are more solid than before. The "winner" may well walk away from the argument no richer—not necessarily with any more information or insight—than when she entered it.

Being good at arguing doesn't mean never having to concede a point, or never losing the exchange. Quite the opposite. A skilled arguer will always admit when she is wrong, and will listen closely to opposing viewpoints, not merely to detect their flaws but to honestly evaluate them. Arguing well means respecting reason and evidence.

The ensuing two chapters address the two basic categories of argument that you are most likely to encounter: one conducted with good will on both sides; and, one conducted with good will only on your side. Being reasonable requires that you admit errors, but intellectual self-esteem requires you to stand up for yourself. These two aspects of arguing are not in conflict with each other, as many people believe. To admit an error or to acknowledge the worth of another person's argument is not a sign of intellectual weakness or of losing the argument. It is a sign of intellectual confidence and honesty.

Having defined what I mean by "argument" and having introduced the two basic contexts in which you are likely to argue, one last step remains.

PREPARING TO ARGUE

> To be prepared for war is one of the most effective means of preserving peace.
>
> George Washington, Address to Congress

A lot of people cause themselves headaches and grief by getting into conversations that, upon reflection, they know should have been avoided. They get into arguments they cannot win and in which nothing can be accomplished. They go away with pounding temples or an upset stomach, and a lurking sense of unease. People do harm to themselves, because they go away with a bad self-image as one who is intellectually inept.

In preparing to argue—and, perhaps, as an argument commences —the most important question you can ask yourself is "What do I want out of this exchange?" Stop for a second and ask yourself what you expect to accomplish from this discussion. Instead of taking a "what the hell" attitude and plunging thoughtlessly into the fray, clarify for yourself why you are there, why you are talking to this particular person.

It may well be that the discussion is just "for the hell of it." If so, make that purpose clear to yourself. Afterward, reflect on whether you actually did enjoy the exchange and why, or why not. Maybe your goal was to acquire information. Did you get the data you wished? If not, why not? It could be that the argument deteriorated into a bitter quarrel that defeated your original purpose. It could be that you wished to convince the other person, or to show him to be a fool in front of a third party. Your purpose in arguing will define how you approach the exchange and the point at which you have been successful, and, so, should stop arguing.

Be realistic about what you can accomplish in any one intellectual encounter. And be specific about your goal. Perhaps you want to learn what the other person's position is. Perhaps you want to practice a specific technique—e.g., the Socratic method of posing probing questions. Or perhaps you want to plant a solitary seed of doubt in the other person's mind.

Here are some additional principles and techniques I have used to good advantage in preparing to argue and in reflecting upon arguments that left me unsatisfied with myself. I have phrased them in the form of questions:

How Important to Me Is It to Convince the Other Person?

Too often the unacknowledged and unconscious goal of arguing is to convince the other person that he is wrong and you are right. The unstated goal is "to win" the argument. This may be an unavoidable consequence of living in a highly competitive society. But focusing on the goal of winning, of convincing the other person, is self-destructive because other people's reactions are not under your control.

No matter how effective or elegant your arguments may be, there are situations in which you will *never* convince the person to whom you are speaking. For example, the other person might have an unshakable emotional investment in what seems like a purely intellectual position. In arguing with him, you are confronting not only ideas but emotional barriers that an experienced psychiatrist would have difficulty scaling. For example, you might be arguing for the theory of evolution with a fundamentalist Christian. Agreeing with any part of what you say would constitute relinquishing his religion and, perhaps, the structure of his social and family life, which may be held together by a common faith. The other person's emotional stake in his position is too deep for any argument to convince him on the spot.

Or your "failure" to convince the other person might be due entirely to circumstances. You are at a crowded party, replete with loud music, constant interruptions, and with only ten minutes before dinner to construct a complicated argument. It is destructive to enter the conversation with the presumption that, despite these handicaps, if you are good enough you *should* be able to convince the other person.

As ridiculous as it sounds, convincing the other person is a common standard by which people judge whether or not they have conducted a successful argument. Did I convert someone from a Democrat to a Republican over coffee and a Danish? Did I make a fundamentalist accept the theory of evolution during the elevator ride this morning? Did my feminist co-worker finally admit affirmative action has failed? Using a conversion experience as a standard of success is unrealistic and only serves to establish a contest of wills, rather than an exchange of ideas, between you and the other person.

Successfully contradicting factual beliefs is a relatively trivial matter that happens constantly in conversation. But to change deep-seated beliefs is rare. For the very best of debaters, it happens once in a blue moon. To realize the futility of this goal, ask yourself one question: What ten-minute discussion at a party would entirely destroy any significant conviction you hold?

Answering for myself: a single argument could never convert me from a deeply held belief which I have tested over the course of years. I don't care if the other person used unassailable statistics, impressive flow charts, quotations from God, the latest CNN poll, or naked brute force. I've arrived at my core beliefs over a long period of time and through a complex process of reasoning. They were not adopted capriciously; they won't be abandoned in that manner either. *But* a ten-minute conversation can shake my confidence in a belief and cause me to read and think further about whether I am right or wrong. It can make me doubt and question. After a long process of reflection, I may come to agree with the person who planted the doubt in the first place.

Unfortunately, unless I make a point of tracking the other person down to inform her of my conversion, she will never receive the acknowledgment that is due. Few people are willing to go out of their way to offer such acknowledgment because it means that, in the contest of wills, they are the losers. Ironically, a consequence of trying so vigorously to convince the other person is that she may be less willing to admit if you have been successful.

Don't set yourself up for failure by establishing a contest.

Your first concern in an argument should be what is true and false. Ideally, rather than being an opponent, the other person should be viewed as the other half of a cooperative effort to find the truth.

Do Circumstances Favor the Achievement of Your Goal?

What constitutes favorable circumstances will vary with the goal of the exchange. If you simply wish to discover the other person's point of view on a single issue, for instance, ten minutes might be sufficient. If you want to debate the issue, ten minutes will almost certainly not be enough time.

Whatever your goal, consider whether the circumstances favor achieving it.

The Environment

Where will the argument take place? Will it occur at a loud and crowded party, where the other person will be drinking and greeting friends as they pass by in the hallway? Or will your discussion take place over a fifteen-minute coffee break at work, with half your co-workers listening? Maybe it will unfold in the car on the ride home, when the two of you have half an hour of uninterrupted time.

When will the argument be taking place? Will it be in the morning over your first cup of coffee, when you are groggy and usually a bit irritable? Maybe it will happen after work in a bar, when you are more relaxed but not necessarily more alert, due to two mugs of beer?

Choose an environment that promotes success.

Your Level of Skill

How much experience do you have in arguing? How much does the other person have? She may be a university professor who lectures on a daily basis, or she may be used to giving presentations at work. If so, then you should not be surprised at being outmaneuvered in the argument. This does not reflect on the worth of your position, merely on your skill at presenting it.

If your goal in arguing is to hone your skill, seek out people who are better at arguing than you are. Watch how they approach issues and blatantly steal some of their techniques.

Your Level of Knowledge

How much do you know about the subject under discussion? Are you comfortable arguing the issue with this particular person? If she is an expert on genetics and you have read only one book in this area, you are probably not prepared to debate the technical aspects of the subject. But the conversation might be a shining opportunity to practice the skill of asking questions.

Try steering the conversation into areas where your level of knowledge is more comparable, such as the ethics of genetic experimentation. Although the other person may well have given more thought to the issue, her reasoning on ethics is based on the kind of observations about human nature that any person can make. Moral issues—e.g., is murder justified?—are not based on specialized information beyond the reach of the average person, as may be the case with scientific data revealed by laboratory experiments.

The Psychology of the Other Person

Is this someone from whom you are ever likely to get whatever acknowledgment or response you wish? Is he able to argue without becoming hostile or abusive?

Many people cannot recognize a good argument when they hear one, let alone give you good feedback for having presented an issue well. Other people may be genuinely dazzled by your presentation and, yet, be totally unable to give interesting responses, letting the "argument" become a monologue on your part. Or they may become defensive and hostile, creating an unpleasant scene.

Ask yourself: Is arguing with this person worth your while? Can he offer what you wish to gain from the process?

What Constitutes a Satisfactory Ending to the Argument?

As previously discussed, the ideal ending for most of us is for the other person to humbly acknowledge his error and salute our brilliance. Short of this, what would satisfy you? Do you wish this person's respect? Or is your goal merely to have stated your own position clearly?

When you have either accomplished your purpose or ascertained that it cannot be achieved, stop arguing. You don't have to break off the conversation in a huff, or even stop talking to the other person. But you should consciously cease pursuing the goal, otherwise the discussion is likely to result in a headache.

Know when to end the argument.

A FINAL CAVEAT

It is a great advantage to be comfortable with dissecting an argument, which is often referred to as "critical thinking." Although comfort may come only with practice, at least be familiar with the process. It consists of finding and explicitly stating the conclusion being offered, and then evaluating the evidence or reasons supporting the conclusion. If the argument is being presented in a confusing tangle, like a stream of consciousness, you might interrupt the other person and inquire, "What is the bottom line? What is your conclusion?"

It is also useful to practice dissecting written arguments because they allow you to dwell and puzzle over their structure without the distractions of a verbal exchange.*

SUMMARY

An argument is an intellectual exchange in which beliefs are supported by reason and evidence. The purpose of arguing is to resolve the disagreements or to discover where irresolvable areas lie. The two keys to excelling during such exchanges are: knowing how to listen and knowing how to argue effectively. Learning these skills is as much a matter of adopting psychological guidelines as it is of practice.

Many people jump into arguments without asking the most basic of questions—"What do I want out of this situation?" The answer is one of the factors that will define the strategy and effectiveness with which you argue.

Another factor is the behavior of the other person(s). Ideally, the argument will occur in an atmosphere of good will.

---

*The excellent *An Introduction to Critical Thinking: A Beginner's Text in Logic* by W. H. Werkmeister will be extremely helpful in this regard.

14

Arguing in an Atmosphere of Good Will

What is civilization? I answer, the power of good women.
Ralph Waldo Emerson, *Miscellanies: Woman*

One reason verbal arguments become adversarial is that few people know how to argue well. Even when you become skilled at argumentation, your exchanges will be complicated by the fact that arguing is not a solitary pastime. In other words, you have to deal with the other person's psychology and with the fact that she will probably not be as skilled as you are, or embody the habit of reason.

This is where showing respect for the other person comes in. You should enter every argument by assuming that the other person is a reasonable human being and an intellectual equal. Extend the same courtesy to her that you hope to receive in return. If the courtesy doesn't flow both ways, you can always cut off the conversation after giving it a good try.

But, don't walk away simply because you have a bad emotional response to something that was said. How you feel about a statement says nothing about whether it was said in a hurtful manner, or whether it was a proper remark. And rejecting statements simply because they disturb you is a habit you need to break. Try to view the exchange as a search for truth and the other person as a partner in the journey.

Perhaps the largest barrier to open and honest debate between otherwise benevolent people is what Freud termed "the ego," but which I am using in the more popular sense. Your ego is the self-opinion you possess. Human beings invest a great deal of ego in their beliefs, so that their beliefs become a part of their self-esteem. The more people identify with what they believe, the deeper and wider this investment becomes. For example, some devoutly religious people cannot tolerate a hint of doubt concerning whether every word in the Bible is divinely inspired. Some chauvinistic men cannot bear to concede a single point during an argument with a woman, viewing that prospect on the same level as losing at arm wrestling with her. Ideas that violate someone's worldview will be difficult for that person to listen to, or tolerate.

People are not emotionless automatons, nor should they be. Whenever you argue with someone, you are dealing with her emotions as well as with her intellect. In some cases, getting past her ego barrier may be the most difficult part of having a productive argument. Indeed, you may well decide the process is more trouble than it's worth. This is particularly true when the person's ego barriers constitute an insult to you. For example, the chauvinist who feels intellectually superior to women, or the racist whose self-esteem requires him to patronize you because of your ethnic background.

If you decide to press on with the argument, however, remember that scaling the ego barrier is nothing more than an acquired skill.

THE STRATEGY OF PRESERVING GOOD WILL

The main feature of this skill is good will, or a display of fair play on your part. Although good will can be expressed in many ways, the following rules of argument etiquette will certainly help to establish it.

1. Never Purposely Embarrass Anyone

As you become skilled at arguing, there will be abundant opportunity to embarrass those with whom you argue, especially those who are not able to argue well and who are not able to defend themselves intellectually. They may contradict themselves, make unsupported and insupportable claims, pretend to know more than they do, and become agitated. By having an intellectual advantage, you will acquire an emotional one as well.

Don't abuse it. By doing so, you will lose the respect of your partner in the argument and of whoever else is within earshot. If the other person has become so irritating that you cannot continue to talk without launching into personal attacks, then simply walk away. The joy you feel at humiliating an adversary reflects poorly upon you and will win you no points from onlookers who can recognize an act of gratuitous cruelty when they see one. Moreover, making such an attack means that you are backsliding into bad intellectual habits. Brute reason is as inexcusable as brute force.

2. Give the Other Person Time to Consider the Argument

Do not badger her for an immediate response or immediately to concede a point you have clearly established. After all, accepting what you say may mean that she has to question other beliefs, and such a process can be extremely uncomfortable, especially if performed in public or under duress. Conceding your point might mean opening an emotional Pandora's box. Give her room to think and change her mind gracefully.

For example, if you have backed a Marxist into a corner on a point about oppression in Cuba, don't press your advantage by going in for the quick kill. You won't convince either her or neutral listeners of anything other than the fact that you are shrill in arguments. Don't listen to sympathetic sideliners who egg you on to "put her in her place." They don't have to live with the possible consequences that might come from causing an ugly public scene. They don't have to live with the intellectual bad habit you would be nurturing. If squelching your opponent is so important to someone on the sidelines, let her do it. Your purpose in arguing is not to punish; it is to explore ideas and, one hopes, to persuade.

(Note: The exception to this rule is when you leap into an already ugly confrontation in order to defend someone who is being badly bludgeoned.)

3. When Someone Has Conceded a Point, Move On

Do not keep hammering away at it simply for the satisfaction of being right over and over again. Don't return to it later in the conversation with remarks like, "Are you sure about X? After all, you were wrong about Y," or, "I hope you have more evidence for that than for your other claim." This tactic is a formula for convincing her never to concede a point to you again.

A person who openly admits being wrong deserves your respect, not punishment for being intellectually honest.

4. Freely Acknowledge When You Have Made an Error

Honesty works two ways. When you misquote a statistic or date, for example, admit the mistake immediately and without embarrassment, then go on from there. Don't dwell on the mistake. At most, indicate that the slipup doesn't really affect your main point, which you should then restate.

If you "stick by your guns" and refuse to acknowledge an obvious error, the other person is likely to focus the rest of the argument on that weak spot. Moreover, your unreasonable obstinacy will tend to discredit every other claim you have made.

But once you have admitted an error, don't allow the other person to gloat or hammer away on it. If he attempts to do so, cut him short and demand, "Is this how you treat someone who admits a mistake? What would you do if I conceded your main point—ridicule me for agreeing with you?"

5. When You Are Uncertain of Something, Say So

If you are asked a question for which you don't have the answer, say "I don't know." This is not only a sign of intellectual honesty, but, more importantly, it is a way to keep from making a fool of yourself. Be willing freely to admit, "I haven't given the subject much thought, but, off the top of my head. . . ." When you *do* claim certainty, people will take that claim more seriously.

6. Be Candid about the Reliability of Your Information

For example, if you were an eyewitness to an event, your statements will be more reliable than if you had heard about it secondhand from a friend. If your information is secondhand, preface what you say with, "I wasn't there myself, but I've been told by someone who was. . . ." Discriminate between what you feel certain about and what you doubt. Admit your limitations by saying: "I got this information from X's latest book, but I can't vouch for it beyond that."

The last thing you want to do is to claim certainty on the basis of someone else's research and end up defending their errors.

7. Be Tolerant of Small Slips

Don't jump on the occasional silly statement or inane question. We all make foolish remarks at some time or other. Instead of using this slip of the intellect to score points on the other person, let her escape with grace. Perhaps you can pave the way by asking, "I'm not sure I understand that remark/question. Can you rephrase it?"

This one strategy alone can create tremendous good will in the other person, who probably expects you to treat her with the discourtesy to which she has become accustomed. The next time you make a slip—and there will be a next time—she will be far more likely to be gracious in return.

8. Show an Interest in What the Other Person Says

Of course, this assumes you *are* interested, otherwise do not fake it out of politeness. Dishonesty is not courtesy, and it is best to simply excuse yourself from an exchange that bores you. You can usually create interest, however, by assuming that you have something to learn from the other person. Be willing to ask questions. This is not a sign of weakness: it is evidence of confidence and healthy curiosity.

9. Acknowledge Good Points

If the other person scores a point in the argument, acknowledge it. Even if she doesn't change your mind on the main issue, give her the credit she deserves by saying, "That's an interesting perspective. I'll have to think about it." Or, "You're obviously right about that."

This level of courtesy within an argument is so rare that you will acquire a reputation for fairness based on such remarks alone.

10. Avoid an Ostentatious Display of Knowledge

Never argue just to display your own cleverness. This is as offensive to most people as an ostentatious display of wealth, which usually causes resentment rather than admiration.

WINNING THE RESPECT OF THE OTHER PERSON

> Virtue is a habit of the mind, consistent with nature and moderation and reason.
>
> Cicero

The key to winning the respect of others—and to winning your own self-respect—lies in what I call "the intellectual virtues." These virtues include: intellectual honesty, intellectual courage, intellectual responsibility, intellectual humility, intellectual simplicity, intellectual self-restraint, and dispassionate thinking.

Intellectual Honesty

The most important intellectual virtue is honesty. Its main characteristics are:

- never pretending to know more than you do;
- always admitting an error;
- always admitting uncertainty;
- always acknowledging other people's good arguments.

Another aspect of intellectual honesty is accepting the fact that saying something is true means taking an intellectual risk. If you are attempting to reach out into the real world and prove a point, then you are making yourself vulnerable to having that point disproven. Whenever there is a possibility of verification, there is a possibility of falsification, or (logically) there should be.

Intellectual Courage

Dealing honestly with ideas requires the courage and willingness to test every belief you hold by comparing it to the evidence of reality and withstanding the onslaught of other people's skepticism. The mere act of questioning deeply held beliefs can be unsettling: the act of changing such beliefs in the face of compelling arguments or evidence can be intensely distressing. Yet this is what intellectual courage requires you to do.

Consider one example offered earlier. Adults are often afraid of embarrassing themselves at tasks that children have mastered. A forty-year-old woman who longs to play the piano may dread learning the same musical scales her five-year-old daughter is working on. Instead of taking the risk of feeling foolish, the woman may hide behind the convenient conviction, "You can't teach an old dog new tricks."

The fear of intellectual embarrassment is at the root of many lost opportunities. Yet life requires nothing so much as courage.

Intellectual Responsibility

Intellectually, you are responsible for what happens to you and for who you are. Although people may go out of their way to make you feel inadequate, you are not a helpless pawn of circumstances and, in the end, you can't blame others for persisting in bad habits.

Intellectual responsibility can be frightening because it leaves no room for passivity on your part. Instead of cursing fate or other people, you have to be introspective and ask, "What am I doing to prevent myself from thinking or arguing clearly?" Sometimes circumstances may be temporarily out of your control, and the best you can do is stand back and analyze how to prevent this situation from ever occurring again.

But even when the situation is irredeemably hostile, there is at least one aspect of it that you do control: your reaction to it.

Intellectual Humility

The word "humility" does not mean "false modesty." You should always be proud of your accomplishments. But all of us are familiar with the sort of man who speaks as though his thoughts were jewels, dropping from the lips of a god. As you become more skilled in arguing and in your general dealings with ideas, it will become easier for you to make others feel inadequate or otherwise bested.

Remember how it felt when you were treated with such intellectual disrespect, and refuse to treat others in the same manner. It is always wise to realize how much you have to learn about the world and from the people around you. And keep firmly in mind: at any given time, you could always be wrong about what you are saying.

Intellectual Simplicity

This virtue is similar to humility. Be as simple and direct as possible about your beliefs and in the language you use. Don't try to become intellectually elite. Ideas and language are tools of communication, not of status.

Some professions, schools of therapy, and certain religions establish their own vocabularies, which only those who are part of the group really understand. They speak in catch phrases and toss them back and forth, more to exclude the unenlightened from understanding than to communicate with them.

Be as simple as you can be without stripping your thoughts and words of subtlety.

Intellectual Self-Restraint

People have a natural tendency to believe in what makes them feel good. Many cults exist for no other reason than people wish the cults' beliefs were true. Using the standard of "what feels good," people allow themselves to become intellectual hedonists. Their beliefs are dictated by what they would like to be true.

When hedonism takes over, concern for truth and falsehood flees the scene and people are put on a collision course with reality.

Dispassionate Thinking

The stereotype of an intellectual is of someone who is dispassionate. Some people translate this to mean cold and unemotional, but that's a totally inaccurate and unfair caricature. Being dispassionate simply means that, when assessing intellectual matters, you try to be guided by the evidence and the arguments, not by your feelings. You don't let emotions temper your judgment of what is true and false.

It doesn't mean that you don't enjoy laughing at jokes, have wild love affairs, cry at sad movies, or have sharp pangs of nostalgia at the sound of certain music. It merely means that you realize the central goal of reasoning is understanding and truth.

Giving emotions a back seat to truth in this context is not a sign of psychological repression. Putting emotions in their proper context is not evidence of psychological pathology. It is evidence of health, of the ability to balance passion and reason, which may be the secret to happiness itself.

AND, YET, A GOOD WORD FOR PASSION

It is with our passions, as with fire and water, they are good servants but bad masters.

Roger L'Estrange, *Aesop*

Being guided by evidence and facts when drawing conclusions and making arguments—in other words, being dispassionate—is not at all the same thing as suppressing emotional reactions. After all, you want to laugh if an idea delights you, to cry if a poignant story touches your heart, and to be dismayed by the advocacy of cruelty. You don't want to strip ideas of joy. These reactions are part of being a more healthy and integrated human being, who expresses thoughts and emotions in a partnership rather than as a dichotomy.

Being dispassionate merely means that, when you evaluate ideas and arguments, emotions are strapped into the passenger seat. Emotional reactions are present, but you handle them with discretion so as not to short-circuit your intellectual functioning.

At a recent conference, I came as close as I can remember to utterly losing my composure in public. I was speaking at a conference in Aspen, Colorado. Or, rather, I was sitting in the audience, half-listening to the speaker who preceded me, while reviewing my notes. Then, he captured my full attention by bringing out a map of North America divided into four brightly colored regions. With a pointer he indicated the region in which—under his political agenda—all Hispanics would live, then the region for blacks, for whites, and (as I remember it) Asiatics. "The races are happier living among their own kind," he assured the audience and backed up his statement with an academically impressive array of statistics.

The flash of rage I experienced made my skin tingle. My husband is Hispanic and the arrogant professorial miscreant at the lecture podium was blithely "assigning" he and me to live in separate regions of the world. The reason: by the speaker's standards, we would be happier with our own kind. If he had pulled out the map during a personal conversation, I am not sure I could have controlled my temper and not torn it in half on the spot.

Fortunately, I was in a crowded hall and all I could do was pace back and forth near the doorway and the tables of authors' books. I used the time to seek out his work, to leaf through them and confirm that his views were every bit as hideous as they appeared to be on the surface. Then, I registered a request with the conference organizer, who also introduced all the speakers. For the first time in my life, I insisted on being introduced by my Hispanic married name, even though I have never used it professionally. The organizer attempted to dissuade me. He seemed to think I was overreacting, but he acceded to my request.

Later in the evening, when the conference attendees retired to a huge party being thrown some distance from the hotel, I made a point to ask for a lift from the speaker who had occasioned my anger. During the fifteen-minute ride, I vigorously disputed every single assumption, fact, and argument he presented. In a neutral tone, I asked whether he was ready to shoot me to enforce his political vision, because nothing short of such a measure would separate me from my husband.

The response was surprising. Not in terms of the answers he offered in the car, but in terms of his behavior the next day. He left the conference early, but only after crossing a crowded room in order to tell me it had been a pleasure to meet me. Apparently, I had been the only person at the conference to take his ideas seriously enough to argue with him, rather than just turn away or hurl abuse.

I cannot imagine feeling good will toward anyone who promotes public policies which would have such vicious consequences. But, apparently, I was able to accomplish what the next chapter addresses: arguing in the absence of good will.

SUMMARY

Even friendly arguments can deteriorate into contentious ones, largely because you are dealing with the other person's emotions and ego as much as with her intellect. Fortunately, there are rules of intellectual etiquette that can preserve good will if followed, such as admitting when you are in error and acknowledging the other person's good points.

There is also a philosophy of arguing that will not only inspire self-respect but also will win the respect of the other person. It embraces what I call the "intellectual virtues," which include intellectual courage and dispassionate thinking.

Some arguments will resist your best efforts to establish and to maintain goodwill. These exchanges require you to adopt a different strategy.

15

Arguing in the Absence of Good Will

I once knew a man who supplemented his income by forging the signature of a well-known novelist on the frontispiece of first editions of her books and, then, selling them as autographed collector's items. I uncovered the scam when I found page after page of practice signatures lying on his kitchen table. Apparently, he warmed up before each autograph session. Upon being confronted, he vowed to stop—though, years later, it occurred to me that someone who forged signatures would also lie about continuing to do so.

He also offered an intriguing defense of his past antics. Rather than harming anyone, he claimed to be providing a service. More people wanted signed editions of the author than were available, especially at the slightly below-market price he was charging. When I objected that "they are paying for a fraud, for books that are worth a small fraction of your price," he disagreed. "It is not a fraud," he insisted, "so long as they believe it is the author's signature and the book makes them happy. And the book is worth what I charge because they can always sell it to a book dealer for at least that much." He knew, because several book dealers were among his customers.

His argument puzzled me, but it did not shake my lurking conviction that something here was fishy. For one thing, when he spoke of the customers whom he made so happy, there was a hint of contempt in his voice as though they were fools. I expect he viewed my puzzlement with the same emotion. "If you are providing such a wonderful service, then you shouldn't mind me telling people," I countered. That's when he promised to stop.

The preceding tale has two morals. The first one I was to learn repeatedly from this particular fellow whom I once saw argue a mutual friend out of a deeply held political belief—a belief all three of us shared—just to prove he could do so. The first moral is: people who argue well can be persuasive without either being right or respecting the truth. Whenever you feel that some intellectual sleight of hand or some ill intent is present, don't dismiss your intuition just because you can't verbalize it. Give yourself, not the other person, the benefit of the doubt and allow yourself to become suspicious. Intuitions are a form of information.

The second moral is that intellectual exchanges are not quite as simple as this chapter and the preceding one might lead you to assume. Often, there is not a clearly drawn division between arguments of good and ill will. People's motivations in intellectual exchanges can be as tangled as in their emotional ones. Indeed, the two are often interwoven.

Even within the broad category addressed by this chapter, you should be sensitive to degrees of ill will, and to the motives underlying it. In my experience, arguments involving ill will are most often expressions of three mental states: defensiveness, aggressiveness, and malice. Although you should always stand up for yourself intellectually, the manner in which you do so should be tempered by the sort of opposition that confronts you.

Defensiveness. In our culture, it is natural for people to become defensive during the most gentle of disagreements and for their reaction to be manifested as mild antagonism. In former arguments, the other person has undoubtedly been treated as discourteously as you have been, and probably expects more of the same. My advice is to be patient. Treat her with the same consideration that you wish others had shown to you.

Aggressiveness. In our culture, it is also natural for people—especially men—to prize highly the act of winning. Many people will argue a point, like a bulldog clenching a bone in its teeth, simply because letting go of it would mean losing. This sort of argument, should you wish to engage in it, is nothing so much as an exercise in skill.

Malice. Some people seem to enjoy being brutal. Newspapers brim over with reports of adults abusing children, spouses beating each other, and other senseless acts of violence. In the course of daily life, we all encounter bitter people who enjoy directing gratuitously mean comments and criticisms to others, and are never happier than when someone else is made miserable. When you encounter such a person in an argument, walk away from her.

DEALING WITH A MALICIOUS EXCHANGE

> Our disputants put me in mind of the scuttlefish, that when he
> is unable to extricate himself, blackens the water about him
> until he becomes invisible.
>
> Joseph Addison, *The Spectator,* No. 476

If you are confronted with open malice, walk away. The interaction has ceased to be—if it ever was—a valuable exchange of ideas or information and has deteriorated into outright intellectual warfare. Just as there are people in the world who physically pick fights, bully others, and enjoy inflicting pain, so, too, are there people who intellectually humiliate others, and enjoy making fools of them for the sheer sense of power it brings. In my experience, such unalloyed intellectual malice is rare but, in the course of a lifetime, you are bound to encounter it now and then.

One of the most blatant examples I have encountered occurred at a scholars' conference I was attending in New York City some years ago. As I stood outside the hotel with two other attendees, waiting for a fourth member of our dinner party, a young man drew closer and halted beside us. His clothes were clean but shabby, his manner was hesitant but respectful. In his hand, he held a slip of paper with an address and other information printed neatly across it. Offering the slip to one of the men with whom I was waiting, he asked, "How much farther down the street do I have to go?"

The man was clearly a bit retarded and more than a bit confused. Someone (perhaps a social worker) had written down the name of a clinic, its location, and an appointment time on a piece of paper, probably with the verbal instruction "If you get lost, ask someone on the street for directions." He chose the wrong person to ask. The day before I had seen the fellow to whom he handed the slip of paper—a respected legal scholar—almost reduce an audience member to tears because her innocuous question had been phrased badly. As my associate examined the paper, the young man pointed down the street and added, "I have to go farther but I don't know how far."

For no other reason than the malicious fun of it, the legal scholar replied, "No, no. You don't want to go that way. You're going the wrong direction. You need to go back the way you came."

Now more confused than ever, the man insisted that "they" had told him the clinic was on the north end of the street and that's the direction he was going in: he knew this because he'd followed the street signs. My associate persisted in contradicting him. By the time the fourth member of our party had arrived, the poor man was close to being distraught. As we piled into a cab, I heard him approach the hotel doorman and ask, "Which way is north and south?"

It is frightening enough for a retarded person to venture out alone into the shifting chaos of big city streets. Imagine how terrifying it must have been to such a person to have his one source of safety yanked away from him, for him to no longer be able to trust the street signs or the instructions on his slip of paper. If he had taken my associate at face value, he might have become hopelessly lost and, perhaps, ended up in a dangerous situation. He certainly would have missed whatever appointment was important enough for him to venture out into the confusion of "the real world."

The incident from the scholars' conference is an example of pure malice. The legal scholar had nothing tangible to gain by taking advantage of the vulnerability of someone weaker than himself. The young man approached him with good will and trust: as a result, he became the brunt of a cruel practical joke and lost confidence in information by which he had been previously and correctly guided.

When you encounter such gratuitous intellectual cruelty, there are two responses possible. If it is directed at you, leave at the first possible opportunity and avoid that dubious human being forever thereafter. He may try to bait you into continuing or resuming an abusive exchange, but resist the temptation. To accept it would be the intellectual equivalent of walking into a sucker punch.

If it is directed at someone else, come to their defense. In this, I am telling you to follow my advice, not my example. I stood mutely by during the two or three minutes of the above-described incident, embarrassed and awkward, at first not knowing what was going on, and then not knowing what to do. Part of my response was confusion: part of it was cowardice. As a senior fellow at the institute hosting the conference, the man held a position of advantage over me, a mere speaker, and I did not wish his omnipresent malice to be directed my way. Cowardice was a bad choice on my part. Whatever retaliation he indulged in could not have made me feel worse about myself than the memory of how I allowed a retarded human being to be made into a laughingstock.

Fortunately, as I mentioned, such clear cases of cruelty-for-cruelty's sake are rare in most people's daily life. In certain contexts, however, they occur more frequently than in others. For example, within the halls of academia and especially during interdepartmental conflicts, gratuitous meanness seems much more common than in normal life. As a friend of mine remarked, "The fights are so bitter because so little is at stake." Try raising your stakes, and your standards.

DEALING WITH AN AGGRESSIVE OPPONENT

Especially when you are discussing emotionally charged issues, such as racial discrimination, abortion, or religion, arguments can easily deteriorate into disputes. In some sense, this reflects a healthy aspect of ideas. Namely, we are intimately involved with and affected by the ideas we hold and hear. They are not free-floating abstractions that have no emotional connection to our lives, and it is reasonable for us to respond with passion, humor, excitement, compassion, annoyance —the full range of emotions—during our discussions of ideas.

But having an emotional response to an issue is very different from becoming abusive to another human being. Perhaps no one was more zealous about or dedicated to an ideal than Mohandas Gandhi, who treated everyone he met—even his bitter opponents—with both respect and humanity. Not everyone can be Gandhi, of course: if we could be, our names might all be prefaced by the title "Mahatma," the Great One. I refer to him only as one example, among many, of how it is possible to be both passionate and civilized in our treatment of other human beings. It is an intellectual balancing act that almost all of us have yet to perfect.

Precisely because of this—because all of us know how easy it is to become emotionally overwrought during a conversation—it is important to show some patience with those who become offensive during a discussion. Show *some* patience, but not necessarily a great deal.

IN THE ABSENCE OF GOOD WILL

> Ah yet, we cannot be kind to each other
> here for an hour;
> We whisper and hint, and chuckle,
> and grin at a brother's shame.
> Alfred, Lord Tennyson, *Maud*

The first and key question to answer about an aggressive exchange that borders on abuse is whether this is a discussion in which you wish to be involved. Should you continue to argue and reason with a blatantly hostile person? In general, my advice is to walk away. As Thomas Paine once said, to argue with a person who has renounced the use of reason is like administering medicine to the dead. What is the point?

Moreover it can be psychologically damaging to argue with an opponent who demonstrates no respect for you as a human being. In essence, you are encouraging the person to treat you with disrespect. This is the sort of person who responds to your reasonable arguments with comments such as "What a stupid thing to say" or "Who the hell are you?" or who engages in constant sarcasm. Why stay in such an abusive situation?

On the other hand, there can be overriding reasons why you should continue the sparring. For example, you may be involved in a formal debate or in a confrontation during a business conference, where there is no option of backing away without damage to your reputation or career. Or, the other person may be a relative or loved one, with whom you desperately want to communicate. Absorbing some abuse may be a price you are willing to pay to make that person *finally* understand your perspective.

Perhaps a crowd has gathered around the discussion and the eavesdroppers seem genuinely interested in the substance of the exchange. Although you are directing comments at the hostile arguer, you might be actually addressing these third parties. Then again, you might simply want to practice how to handle hostility in public situations.

If you decide to plunge forward, make sure to exert whatever control you can over the circumstances. The following guidelines will help.

Determine What Kind of Argument You Are Getting Into

Is it a factual dispute? For example, you might be arguing about whether women make good doctors and lawyers. The most effective way to counter the empirical claim that they do not may be with solid statistics, or several good counterinstances, that prove the contrary.

Is it a theoretical dispute? You might be arguing about whether women are less intellectually capable of being doctors and lawyers than men. The quarrel is a theoretical one about the relative intelligence of men versus women and not as easily resolved by statistics, which may well favor the other person's position. After all, there *are* far fewer female doctors, than male. The theoretical point to be resolved, however, resides in whether the apparent genetic difference is actually a cultural difference.

Is it a moral dispute? You might be arguing whether women *should* become doctors and lawyers, which is against God's will, instead of devoting themselves to domesticity and children. Here statistics will be of no avail. The disagreement is on a far more fundamental level. Indeed, even theoretical arguments will only be effective in the unlikely event that the other person does not have a deep emotional investment in his position. Otherwise the best you can expect is to "argue around the edges," that is, to rouse small doubts about peripheral issues. You might ask, for instance, "What about women who, through no fault of their own, don't marry or who are widowed? Should they be able to support themselves?"

Tailor your arguments to the level of the subject under dispute.

Find Out What Would Resolve the Disagreement

Too many arguments wander aimlessly and endlessly with neither side giving an inch on the subject under dispute. You should ask the other person: "What, in principle, would it take to convince you that I am right?" In the last example concerning religious objections, the answer might well come back, "If God gave me a sign." Most evidence should be easier for you to produce.

If nothing short of a sign from God, a conversion experience, or its intellectual equivalent would change the person's opinion, then his beliefs are a matter of dogma. He is not open to evidence or to reason, and the conversation has nowhere to go. After pointing this out to third parties, it is probably best to end the conversation.

Consider another case. If you are arguing with someone who claims Hispanics are intellectually inferior to Caucasians, you should ask what evidence would convince her that this theory was wrong. Don't let her back away from this question: press your point. Would high IQ scores constitute compelling evidence? When you have ascertained the facts or the point of theory that would alter her opinion, you will have isolated the most productive direction in which the conversation can proceed.

But be prepared to answer the same question yourself, because the other person is likely to come back at you. Ask yourself: "What would convince me that my position is wrong?"

Determine Who Has the Burden of Proof

It is a sound principle of logic that the burden of proof lies with whomever is making the positive assertion, not with the person denying or questioning it. It is called the "Onus Principle" and it springs from the fact that it is impossible to prove a negative. To illustrate the principle, try to prove that you are not a murderer. You might claim that every moment of your life from birth to the present has been chaperoned under watchful eyes, and I still might doubt your innocence. After all, perhaps your witnesses—knowing you to be a murderer— vouch for you only out of fear for their lives.

In frustration, you finally throw up your hands and yell at me, "This is crazy. I can't prove I'm *not* a murderer. All I can do is point to the absolute and glaring lack of evidence that I *am* a murderer. Why don't you show me your evidence that I am one?" With this question, you have established that the burden of proof rests squarely on my shoulders. You are demanding the evidence for my implicit statement "You may be a murderer." On what am I basing my supposition?

In the absence of any real evidence for my positive statement, it is reasonable to believe that the negative is true.

If you say "I have no reason to believe Y is true," however, you are not assuming a burden of proof, because you are not making a knowledge claim. It is an epistemological claim: you are just reporting on your state of knowledge. All you are saying is that you are not convinced.

Determine What the End Point of the Argument Should Be

This does *not* mean determining when you have won the argument hands down: that is an unrealistic goal. But it does means one of two things:

1. It means you know what point in the conversation, by your standards, would constitute a satisfactory resolution of the disagreement. For example, if the other person begins by claiming women are less intelligent than men, then, gives some ground and eventually admits that *some* women are more intelligent than some men . . . is this a satisfactory resolution? If not, what would be? Perhaps your goal is to convince third-party onlookers and, when you perceive this event has occurred, you should feel satisfied and end the argument.

2. It means you know the point at which a satisfactory resolution is clearly not possible. This is the point at which further discussion

would be useless, either because of ill will between the two of you or because the argument has deteriorated into repetition. If discussion is pointless, walk away. Don't waste your time and energy.

The importance of knowing when to end an exchange was dramatically illustrated to me at a party one night when I was arguing with a woman. She had announced that a system of morality was not possible without a fundamentalist belief in the Bible.

In my mind, I quickly reviewed possible strategies. I could have pointed out that a long history of moral theory stretched back in history, well before the birth of Christ, and that many nonfundamentalist religious systems exist, such as Buddhism. But I decided not to open the worm-filled can of comparative religion.

Instead I chose a personal appeal. Having observed how happy her homelife seemed, I brought up her two young children and her husband, who was sitting on a couch a few feet to one side of us. I asked, "Are you telling me that the only reason you act morally is because you are a fundamentalist? Are you saying that, if you lost your faith, you might go home tonight and murder your husband and two children?"

I was trying to establish that something else—the bonds of humanity and mutual love, perhaps—keeps human beings from harming each other. After staring at her husband for a long moment, the woman said, "Yes, I might." At this, I experienced a blinding insight. The conversation was over.

Keep a Tight Leash on the Topic

Most people are not skilled at arguing and their conversation resembles a stream of consciousness that wanders almost drunkenly from issue to issue. The two of you may start out with a clear point of disagreement, but then the other person might meander down a strange twisting path that leads nowhere. By the time an hour has passed, you have no sense of where the conversation is going or where it has been.

If you are enjoying the exchange, this is not a problem. But the context of the argument I am presenting now is one that you are conducting solely to convince onlookers, or for some other purpose than enjoyment. The point at which the argument runs wildly in all directions is the point at which you have lost control of the exchange.

Rein in the conversation. Don't let your partner drift off the topic. If you are discussing your company's sexual harassment policies with a co-worker at a business meeting, don't let the conversation deteriorate into whether there should be free doughnuts with coffee in the morning. If the co-worker persists in introducing an irrelevant topic, politely insist, "That's an interesting point, but it's not what we are discussing. Why don't we hash out sexual harassment first and then we can go back to doughnuts?"

Keep returning to the subject under discussion. If your co-worker doesn't alter his or her wandering ways, bluntly ask "Why do you keep changing the subject? Why aren't you willing to talk about sexual harassment?"

Ask Probing Questions of the Other Person

A well-timed, well-delivered question can accomplish a number of goals:

1. It can bring the other person's confused thinking into clear focus. This is especially valuable when you confront a person who is muddleheaded about an issue. Ask politely, "Why do you believe that's true? Were you an eyewitness to the event? What is the source of your information?" If done respectfully, you can make the person realize how ill-formed and unfounded his opinions are without humiliating him. Onlookers will see you as being curious and careful, rather than bitchy.

2. A perceptive question does more than refute an argument; it can uncover the faulty premises from which the argument sprang. Perhaps a co-worker is arguing that Mary did not merit the promotion she received last week. Instead of presenting all the reasons Mary did, indeed, richly deserve her promotion, you might ask, "What has she done that makes you think that?" Her answer might surprise you. For example, she might say "Mary got married last month, which means she'll be getting pregnant and be unable to give enough time to her work."

3. A question can effectively derail an abusive arguer who is trying to press you against the wall intellectually. Imagine that your

co-worker has angrily related an incident for which he was later repri-manded for sexual harassment. He now glares at you and, in a com-manding voice, he demands to know what the hell it is that women want from men?

On one level, his question is not a question at all. At least it is a rhetorical one not meant to elicit information. Your co-worker is merely venting his frustration on you.

Don't try to answer him directly. This will only encourage him to badger you further. Come back with a provocative question of your own, one that demands a response. For example: "Where would *you* draw the line in sexual harassment? At rape?" Put *him* on the defensive.

Take Your Time in Making Points

Don't always jump back with an immediate reply to a statement or question, even if you have one on the tip of your tongue. Count to three before responding to an argument. The pause will make you appear thoughtful and it will create anticipation for what you say. It may also cut off any inappropriate snap reaction, which you might have a tendency to blurt out in an unguarded moment.

Ask a Personal Question

This is a last-ditch strategy before you give up entirely on the other person and walk away from the exchange. Generally speaking, per-sonal questions or attacks are in poor taste when you are trying to sort through the truth and falsehood of ideas. But, in a hostile argument, good taste and proper respect have already been breached. If the other person persists in sarcasm, rudeness, and crude dismissal, you are well within your rights to demand, "Why are you treating me with such dis-respect?" But, if the conversation has deteriorated to that extent, do not expect to salvage it.

The above suggestions are techniques for controlling an argument. But remember: the purpose of controlling an argument is not to take advantage of the other person. It is to prevent him or her from taking advantage of you. The goal of arguing is not to win, but to get closer to the truth. However skilled you become at manipulating the conversation, it is a breach of intellectual honesty to use ideas as weapons against people. Ideas are tools. Employing them to hurt or humiliate anyone is a poor use of truth.

DEALING WITH INTIMIDATION

Malice is pleasure derived from another's evil which brings no advantage to oneself.

Cicero, *Tusculanarum Disputationum*

Not everyone will play by the same honorable rules you are employing. For many people, words and ideas are clubs with which to bloody anyone in their path. This attitude seems especially prevalent in the halls of academia and other specifically intellectual institutions where knowledge is supposed to find sanctuary and respect.

In many cases—in and out of academia—such benign attitudes are not present. Often, intimidation is used in a conscious attempt to gain an emotional or intellectual advantage over you. On an emotional level, intimidating you allows the person to feel superior at your expense. On an intellectual level, it allows her to avoid dealing with a sticky argument that she may not know how to deflect. She wins simply because you are manipulated into silence.

The following are some common methods of intimidation.

Psychologizing the Opponent

This form of intimidation involves ignoring the content of what is being said and, instead, analyzing the psychology of the person speaking. For example, you might offer a dispassionate defense of science and technology, referring to their many benefits such as extending the human life span. Instead of countering your argument with one of her own—perhaps listing some harms, such as the atomic bomb—the other person asks, "Why are you so afraid of death?" She is psychologizing you.

Not surprisingly, this tactic is often used most blatantly by those deeply immersed in psychotherapy. Although psychotherapy plays an invaluable role in many people's lives, it has no place in weighing the worth of ideas.

It does not matter if the person speaking is anal retentive, in conflict with her id, speaking from her inner child, suppressing a primal scream, unable to get past her body armor, or just out of a Skinner box. In argumentation, all that matters is the validity or invalidity of the arguments, the truth or falsehood of the propositions.

When someone psychologizes her opponent by asking "Why are you so defensive?" or "What do you get out of being right?" she is shifting the ground of discussion from the intellectual to the personal. The focus has shifted from your ideas to your emotions and why they are inappropriate. Ironically, this is often a conscious and manipulative ploy. I say ironically because those involved in psychotherapy are supposed to try to eliminate manipulative behavior.

Women are often assailed with a version of this manipulative tactic in the form of a man who exclaims, "You know, women always say that sort of thing," or "Isn't that just like a woman." The purpose of such a remark is clear. It allows him to focus the discussion on *your* inadequacies—psychologically, or as a sex—not on the inadequacies of his own argument. You are no longer dealing with the truth or falsehood of his ideas, but with whether or not you, by virtue of being a woman, are capable of analyzing them. At this point, you have to decide whether you wish to remain civil.

Intellectualizing the Issue

This tactic involves evading the real intellectual issue by using ideas and language to obscure rather than to clarify.

Just because people use intellectual terms doesn't mean they are dealing with intellectual matters. Sometimes they are holding a monologue that does not include the chore of having to listen to a word you say. Sometimes they are using pseudointellectual terms, needlessly technical language, and other sleights of hand to intimidate you.

This ploy is especially common in universities, or among academics. You might raise your hand in class to ask a probing question of a professor. Instead of answering you, he strokes his chin and replies, "I assume, of course, you have read Dr. X's essay on this question in the October '96 issue of *Snob's Journal of Sophistry?*" Of course, you haven't, and there is no reason you should have. There is also no reason for the professor to interpose the title of a scholarly essay between your straightforward question and his answer to it. Except that doing so allows him to appear knowledgeable about the matter under question, without actually having to possess any knowledge about it. He appears to refute your question, without having to answer it. This is rank dishonesty on his part.

Another way to pseudointellectualize is to use bureaucratic language or "gobbledygook," a word which was coined by Congressman Maury Maverick of Texas. It means using ten words when one word would do, or using a polysyllabic word when a single syllable is all that's required. In his work *The Power of Words*, Stuart Chase offers the following example of gobbledygook. "Voucherable expenditures necessary to provide adequate dental treatment required as adjunct to medical treatment being rendered to a pay patient in in-patient status may be incurred as required at the expense of the Public Health Service." Chase translates, "Seems you can charge your dentist bill to the Public Health Service" (p. 251).

Another common means of intellectualizing is the unnecessary use of technical language. Here, the other person is using language not to explain himself, but to shut you out of understanding the discussion. By using terms you will need explained to you, he is appearing to be more knowledgeable than he truly is. And, again, you are placed at an unfair disadvantage.

Hiding behind Authority

This form of intimidation frequently includes quotations and opinions culled from various authorities from Einstein to Mickey Mantle.

Sometimes the appeal to authority is appropriate. For example, sometimes an argument involves specialized information that the average person lacks. In a discussion about genetic medicine, it might be appropriate to quote recent studies in that area, or the opinions of an expert. Or, in a discussion on how Einstein views bikinis, it would be useful to have a quotation from Einstein on that subject.

But too often people quote authorities in nonspecialized areas in order to stack the intellectual deck in their favor. There is a great difference between arguing genetic theory and arguing moral points, such as "Is murder ever justified?" There are no authorities in ethics as there are in the hard sciences. Moral theory, unlike genetic theory, is not based on information that is inaccessible to the average person. The philosopher may have given more thought to moral issues, but her reasoning comes from observing human nature, not DNA strands. This sort of observation and reasoning is open to any human being.

Yet, when discussing nonspecialized topics—ones that are open to observation by everyone—a person will often ignore the specific criticisms you've made of his position on, say, public schooling, and attempt to intimidate you by offering up the names of those whose opinions are in line with hers. The arguments frequently include quotations, statistics, and opinions culled from authorities, ranging from rocket scientists to politicians to newscasters. Suddenly, if you disagree with the other person's arguments, you are also disagreeing with Tolstoy, Louis XIV, Moses, Betsy Ross, and Groucho Marx.

Yet famous thinkers in the past have been notoriously wrong. For example, both Aristotle and Plato defended the institution of slavery. Does the fact of their defense mean we should return to the antebellum South?

Another common form of arguing from authority is an appeal to the majority. This is the argument that runs: *"Everyone* accepts this as true. Thus, it is true." But "the majority" is nothing more than a collection of individuals, all of whom are fallible. Truth is not a matter of popular vote. It is not a democratic process.

Arguing from Shared Experience

This form of argument involves basing your conclusions solely upon experience, and refusing to credit the conclusions of those who do not share that exact experience.

There is no question that the way to know how an apple tastes is to bite into it. Without experiencing the Rocky Mountains in person or pictures, it is not possible to know what they look like. If you haven't skied down a steep slope, you don't understand how the wind makes you veer. In a more political sense, this point is sometimes raised in the form of "You don't know what it *feels* like to be black, or a woman, because you are neither."

In the simplest sense possible, that statement is absolutely true. So is the reverse statement. The person speaking doesn't know what it *feels* like to be me, or you, or any other unique human being with a unique background.

But, usually, this statement is not referring to purely emotional matters. Instead, the person argues that you cannot intellectually *understand* or meaningfully comment on the condition of being black or being a woman because you are neither. You cannot possibly know what it means to be subjected to injustice due to a physical characteristic, e.g., the characteristics of skin color and gender. Only those who have had such an experience have the "right" to comment on it, or saying anything meaningful about it.

This is the claim that you cannot intellectually understand something unless you have experienced that specific thing directly. Let's return to the example of biting into an apple: Even if I do not know the taste of an apple, I may be better informed about its nutritional breakdown than someone who eats a Granny Smith every day. There are many levels upon which things, events, and issues can be discussed. Direct experience is only one of them.

Interestingly, the same people who argue for "shared experience" invariably flinch at saying "You cannot make any meaningful comment about being a drug addict unless you've been hooked on heroin." Somehow you don't have to experience years of drug addiction to understand that being hooked on heroin is an undesirable lifestyle.

Carried to its logical conclusion the argument from shared experience would mean that no one person could ever understand anything anyone else said. Your unique psychology and background would guarantee that you would not experience anything in precisely the same manner as someone else does.

To restate this position: everyone's perceptions and experiences are unique and are not precisely like those possessed by anyone else. This is not a barrier to human communication. It is the reason human communication exists. We need to communicate our unique experiences and have others understand us by relating what we say to similar experiences in their lives.

I may not know exactly how you experience your mother's death, but because I have gone through a similar process we have common ground to discuss the anger, sorrow, and other phases of grief. Similarly, I have never experienced the insults directed at black people, but I've been treated unjustly for other reasons. And there is a commonality to basic human reactions.

In her recent book *True Love Waits*, the iconoclastic Wendy Kaminer comments on the destructiveness of what, in feminism, is often called "identity politics," or arguing from shared identity and experience. Kaminer writes, "Favoring assimilation, advocates of multiculturalism suggested that the boundaries between people with different backgrounds and experiences were nearly impermeable. The promise of trust, empathy, and shared values and interests between different racial and ethnic groups seemed merely illusory" (p. 25).

Kaminer goes on to describe the verbal tactics of those who argue from shared experience. "This insistence on the primacy of feelings and beliefs over political ideas is often cloaked in polysyllabic, academic jargon, but it is essentially anti-intellectual. . . . Labels like 'racist,' 'sexist,' and 'classist' are indispensable to their arguments" (p. 25).

Such labels masquerade as political discussion, but they are often nothing more than a personal attack upon you. Demand that other people respect your common humanity.

Reducing an Argument to the Personal

"Reducing an argument to the personal" does not refer to making a personal attack: rather, it is the process of substituting personal testimony for arguments. For example, if someone goes through a particular school of therapy and says to you, "I really changed; that means the theory behind it is true."

Although this is a common method of intimidation, people rarely identify it as such. With the above remark, the other person has shifted the ground away from the truth or falsehood of a theory and onto his personal reaction to the theory. If you directly argue with the statement, you seem to be arguing with the truth of his experience, rather than the truth of the theory.

Does this mean that personal testimonials should be ignored? No. If a person went through therapy and feels better as a result, then she feels better. That is all that her testimony proves. It doesn't mean the therapy is effective on most people, or more effective than another therapy would have been on her. It says nothing about the soundness of the therapy's underlying theory.

Reducing an argument to the personal allows the other person to appear to make a counterargument without having to address the substance of what you have said. More than this, it gives the person an unassailable and, thus, unfair advantage. How are you to respond to counter the personal testimony? "No, you didn't go to the therapy," or "No, you don't feel better"?

The only counter is to undergo the tedious process of backing up to fundamental principles and pointing out that truth cannot be established by emotions. No matter how carefully you make this argument, however, the other person is likely to take offense.*

---

*To follow up on the "art of argumentation," several books by Suzette Haden Elgin, a retired professor of applied psycholinguistics, may be valuable. They form a series on what Elgin has termed "The Gentle Art of Verbal Self-Defense." Some of the titles are: *The Gentle Art of Verbal Self-Defense, More on the Gentle Art of Verbal Self-Defense, Staying Well with the Gentle Art of Verbal Self-Defense,* and *The Last Word on the Gentle Art of Verbal Self-Defense.*

SUMMARY

If good will is absent from an argument, you should ask yourself if the other person is being malicious, aggressive, or merely defensive. The answer will determine your strategy. Under most circumstances, you should walk away from malice. When the ill will is merely an expression of the other person's intellectual insecurity, treat her with the same patience you would like to receive—at least, to begin with. If good will does not develop, or if the other person is aggressive rather than defensive, you should exert whatever control you can over the circumstances of the argument. For example, you should ask probing questions of the other person.

Finally, commonsense guidelines will prepare you to deal effectively with the intimidation tactics you are likely to encounter. One particular form of intimidation constitutes a philosophical assault and deserves greater attention, as will be addressed in the next chapter.

16

Addressing Philosophical Assaults

Philosophy—the thoughts of men about human thinking, reasoning, and imagining, and the real virtues in human existence.

Charles W. Eliot

Many of the classical Greek philosophers were passionate about the everyday concerns of ordinary people. They addressed practical and haunting questions about the meaning of friendship, the content of the good life, and how to deal with the pain of life. Indeed, two of the most important schools of Greek philosophy, the Stoics and the Epicureans, can be virtually defined by their approaches to pleasure and pain, and to the role those responses play in human happiness. It is not surprising, therefore, to read of common people going to the likes of Socrates for advice on their personal problems.

How many of us today would approach a philosopher for such advice? If we sought out an authority for help with a personal problem, instead of a family member or friend, we would almost certainly choose a psychologist or a religious figure. And when did you last see a philosopher interviewed on the evening news for insight into a news story that did not involve bioethics? Economists, psychiatrists, social workers, political analysts, doctors, scientists, business leaders . . . everyone, except for the philosopher, seems to have something relevant to say on the evening news.

Philosophers and their explanations are seen to have little or no connection to the everyday concerns of ordinary people. Dismissive terms, like "ivory tower," often arise when the woman on the street discusses philosophers—and justifiably so. We may have moved past the Scholastic period during which philosophers actually did discuss how many angels could dance on a pin, but the current philosophical discourse does not seem to be a great deal more relevant.

Today, and indeed for several centuries, most philosophers seem intent on proving that reality (e.g., the table in front of you) does not exist or that truth is to be found only in the linguistic analysis of sentences, not through sense perceptions. The burning lifestyle questions of the human condition have been left almost entirely to psychologists. Formerly philosophical questions, such as the definition of human happiness, of the good life, and the relationship of emotions to reason, seem scarcely to be discussed.

It is time to rescue philosophy from the halls of academia and return it to the streets, where it belongs. Where it is needed. Philosophy sprang from the driving desire of ordinary people to resolve the fundamental questions and dilemmas of their lives. What is friendship? Why should I prefer the good over the bad? What is the good? Philosophy is desperately needed today, by the ordinary people who Henry David Thoreau believes are "living lives of quiet desperation." It is needed by those who are struggling to find meaning every morning.

THINKING PHILOSOPHICALLY

In his book *Aristotle for Everybody*, Mortimer Adler declares, "I have long been of the opinion that philosophy is everybody's business. . . . [P]hilosophy is useful—to help us to understand things we already know, understand them better than we now understand them. That is why I think everyone should learn how to think philosophically" (p. ix).

Philosophy is the area of human knowledge that deals with the fundamental facts and principles of human existence. Accordingly, thinking philosophically is the skill of thinking in fundamental terms about issues, of asking fundamental questions. For example, instead of pondering whether X deserves to be executed for a specific act of murder, a philosophical approach would involve asking "What role does capital punishment play in society?" or, even more fundamentally, "What is justice?"

Philosophy deserves your attention, if not always your respect. After all, when you deal with philosophy, you are in the presence of the oldest intellectual discipline known to man. Even religion was considered to be a branch of philosophy. It is true that almost every conceivable absurd belief has been defended in the name of philosophy. Doctrines without evidence, doctrines that contradict evidence, doctrines for which no evidence can be acquired—all of these positions, and many many more, have been defended in the name of philosophy. But there have also been magnificent attempts to define the fundamental issues of common humanity. There is a wide gap between the academic and the commonsense approaches to philosophy. It is a gap that currently separates philosophy from the practical or the real world.

The average woman feels little connection to philosophical theories that question the existence of the table she sets for dinner each night. A famous philosophical passage may begin with the sentiment, "When I see a tomato, there is much that I can doubt . . . ," but the average woman does not doubt that the tomato she is slicing into the salad is *really* a tomato rather than an elaborate synthetic fraud. Or the product of hallucinogenic drugs she has unknowingly ingested. If what she holds in her hand looks, smells, feels, and tastes like a tomato, she assumes that's what it is. She slices the tomato and makes dinner for her family.

In short, the average woman is what philosophers would call a naive realist. She assumes there is a reality out there, and that her senses give her knowledge of it. Indeed, most of us would probably not get out of bed in the morning if we sincerely doubted those assumptions. Even the philosophers who deny the existence of reality contradict themselves through their actions: they live as though reality were an unquestioned certainty.

It is important to be clear: I do not mean to argue that all sense perceptions—such as the tomato in your hand—are necessarily or automatically true. Based on sense perceptions, the world was once commonly believed to be flat and, to human eyes, the sun still appears to rotate around the earth. One of the most valuable roles philosophy can play is to question commonly held beliefs.

My point here is that the depth and breadth of the division between the world as ordinary people perceive it and the world as philosophy projects it back to them is an indication that something is drastically wrong with one of the positions. The worldview of ordinary people comes from direct observation, while that of philosophy is usually reached only through torturous arguments. Taking what is called Occam's razor—a bias toward accepting the simplest, least-strained explanation—I suspect the woman on the street is more often right than those on academic committees. I side with common sense.

Much of what remains of this chapter deals with how to protect yourself against verbal attacks that masquerade as profound philosophy.

THE SPECTER OF SKEPTICISM

This section deals with two fundamental assaults on your ability to know or to state anything as being "true." One of the attacks is aimed directly at your ability to perceive reality. It is an epistemological attack: that is, it questions the ability of the human mind to *know* anything at all. Whether or not an objective reality exists, you are by nature a fallible being who is incapable of knowing its nature. Or, rather, you can never be certain your perceptions—and the arguments based upon them—are correct. Therefore, nothing you say need be taken seriously.

The second line of attack is a more metaphysical one. This attack focuses on whether or not reality exists, rather than on your inability to perceive it. That is, instead of saying your observations are wrong, the other person tells you that nothing exists to be observed. In essence, the other person tells you—as a matter of fact—there are no facts. There are no truths except, of course, for the true statement now being uttered by him. The only certainty is that there is no certainty: of course, that statement is uttered as a certainty. I could continue on the contradictory nature of such proclamations, but a more serious examination is called for.

To approach the two fundamental attacks in a different manner: the first springs from a philosophical position known as skepticism; the second from a position known as subjectivism.

The word "skepticism" is used in many ways and some are not objectionable. For example, it can refer to an attitude of intellectual cautiousness. That is, a skeptic may be simply someone who refuses to believe anything without sufficient evidence. The desirability of "skepticism" depends on how the word is being used.

Philosophically, the most common sort of skepticism is epistemological skepticism; that is, a skepticism that denies the possibility of human knowledge. Epistemological skeptics share the common belief that reality lies beyond the scope of human perception and reason. In effect, a woman's fallibility precludes the possibility of her ever being certain; it may preclude the possibility of her possessing knowledge altogether.

Subjectivism is the philosophical position that there is no reality apart from consciousness. Reality does not exist divorced from the mind that perceives it. In other words, objective reality does not exist. In such circumstances, human beings can hardly be said to be able to verify or falsify anything.

How does one escape these challenges?

HOW CAN YOU KNOW?

Before dissecting these attacks, however, it is important to admit that there are occasions on which the following questions are valid.

Who Are You to Say That?

There is one context in which the question "Who are you to say that?" is not an insult and should be answered politely. If you make a claim of specialized knowledge, for example, a statement that would require technical knowledge of genetic medicine, the other person can quite reasonably inquire after how you come by the information. Under such circumstances, "Who are you to know?" becomes a proper request which allows him to assess how likely it is that you know what you're talking about. If you are a doctor, a medical researcher, or someone else with specialized training, the likelihood is good.

Equally, you might make an accusation that would require you to have been an eyewitness to an event, such as a crime, in order for you to know your statement is true. In this case, the question "Who are you to say that?" is also proper because it is aimed at ascertaining how you came by knowledge that may not be specialized, but certainly is not shared by others.

But most of the issues discussed at parties, while driving with a friend, or during coffee breaks at work don't involve specialized knowledge. Most of them are issues that everyone grapples with in some form on a daily basis, from taxes to sexual harassment to the condition of public schools. You don't require a university degree, world travel, or dispensation from the church to realize there is something wrong if your teenage children cannot spell common words after eight years of education.

In short, unless you are claiming special knowledge, the question "Who are you to say that?" is an abusive dismissal of your right to have an opinion, a dismissal which you should not tolerate.

How Can You Be Certain?

There is a sense in which this question can be properly asked, and it is similar to the above-described situation in which you have information that is not available to other people. Under these circumstances, the question is a request for evidence or information as to why you think your statements are true. Consider a conversation in which you announce that a neighbor of yours is a thief. The other person, who knows the neighbor as well as you do, falls into a surprised silence. No one else he knows of has ever made this accusation before. There have been no police cars in the neighbor's driveway, no gossip of past arrests. It is quite reasonable for the other person to ask "Do you know this for a fact? How can you be certain?"

This is a request to examine the credibility of the evidence on which your accusation is based, and the intellectual burden is upon you to produce it. Perhaps you have witnessed a theft by your neighbor firsthand; perhaps you have seen a police report; perhaps the neighbor confessed the details of the crime to you. Such evidence would be compelling and the other person would know to take the accusation seriously.

On the other hand, you might respond, "Well, the thefts are common knowledge in the neighborhood." At this point, the other person —who is also from the neighborhood but who has heard nothing of this "common knowledge"—might decide to push the accusation to the back of his mind until he has a chance to make further inquiries. Or he may dismiss your accusation as being "based" on nothing more than rumor. Through the question, "How can you be certain?" the listener is able to evaluate the credibility of the evidence supporting your accusation.

In many instances, however, you will not be dealing with anything so evenhanded. Typically, an outright attack on your ability to know anything will be hurled at you by those who preemptively wish to take control of the discussion without doing the work of presenting a solid argument. These intellectual maneuvers constitute attacks on the possibility of anything being true and of people being able to know anything at all.

This sort of quasi-philosophical attack is often a last-ditch stand of a person who wishes to muddy the waters of an exchange. It is natural to be thrown off balance by such an intellectual maneuver because, on the surface, the attack appears to be a sophisticated one, if only because it can be difficult to answer. After all, being an honest human being, you feel obliged to admit that you are fallible and not omniscient. You might be mistaken and, thus, absolute certainty is not possible.

When you make this type of commonsense admission, however, your honesty is seized upon and immediately used against you. The other person will take the fact of your fallibility as sufficient reason, in and of itself, to dismiss automatically the well-documented evidence and the well-presented logic of your argument.

In other words, because it is possible for you to be wrong, she will not see any reason to acknowledge the extreme probability that you are right. Instead, since all opinions could be wrong, she will assign the same truth value to every opinion—except, of course, hers on this matter. Such an attack is an unfair method of arguing, and it should be treated as such.

There is a powerful tool with which to defend yourself from fundamental attacks upon your ability to "know." It addresses the two fundamental assumptions that underlie such an attack: that of infallibility and that of omniscience.

Infallibility refers to the state of being nonfallible, of never making an error, and, indeed, being incapable of making an error. It is a capacity. An "infallible being" is one with a certain type of mind that renders all its judgments and beliefs correct. The Judeo-Christian God is an example of such a being. It is not merely that God avoids mistakes: God is incapable of making them. Her nature is such that she cannot be wrong.

Omniscience refers to the state of having infinite and absolute knowledge of all things. This refers to the scope of knowledge possessed by a being. An omniscient being is one who knows everything there is to know without expending any effort. Such a being would not acquire knowledge, it would *have* all knowledge by virtue of its nature. Again, the Judeo-Christian God is an example.

DEFENDING THE POSSIBILITY OF HUMAN KNOWLEDGE

When the other person improperly demands, "Who are you to know?" she is requiring you to be infallible before she will take you and your claims seriously. She is refusing to consider the merits of your arguments, and is falling back on the statement "You've been wrong before."

Ask yourself a question: If you were an infallible, omniscient being, how would your reasoning processes differ from what they are now? If you knew everything immediately and simultaneously, what would thinking out a problem entail? You might go through a series of mental processes to come to a conclusion, but how closely would they resemble the human process of reasoning?

Consider just one fact alone. For an omniscient being there is no distinction between what it believes is true and what actually is true. This is what omniscience means. Since there is nothing it did not already know, there would be nothing for its mind to discover, and no need to compare its beliefs against reality to ascertain their validity. From this one fact alone, it is clear that an omniscient being would not "think" in any manner remotely resembling human thought, which is a process of mentally moving from ignorance toward knowledge. An omniscient being would already be entirely knowledgeable. Ignorance would be against its nature.

In *Thinking as a Science*, Henry Hazlitt writes, *"If a man were to know everything he could not think.* Nothing would ever puzzle him, his purposes would never be thwarted, he would never experience perplexity or doubt, he would have no problems. If we are to conceive of God as an All-Knower, we cannot conceive of Him as a Thinking Being. Thinking is reserved for beings of finite intelligence" (p. 9, italics in original).

The crucial point is: all the standards of knowledge that human beings apply to themselves are firmly based on the assumption that we are fallible, nonomniscient creatures. The very words we use to describe our standards of knowledge exist in this context of fallibility. The words "certainty," "truth," "falsehood," "probability," and "possibility" make no sense whatsoever except when referring to fallible beings.

In other words, if people were infallible, then the concepts of truth and falsehood, and all the shades of intellectual likelihood in between, would not exist. Truth—a term which is meant to distinguish a belief or statement as being "not false"—would have no significance. Every belief of an infallible being would be automatically true. The concepts of possibility, probability, and certainty would never have evolved because there would be no need of cognitive yardsticks against which to measure the likelihood of our "knowledge" being true.

The situation would be analogous to that involving an animal who can only see one color. Why would it need to evolve terms that describe a wide range of hues and a spectrum of possibilities? It would have no use for such distinctions. Indeed, the animal would not need a word to describe even the one color it could see, since words—or, at least, their definitions—distinguish how one thing or characteristic is different from some other thing or characteristic. Equally, for an infallible being, the concepts of "evidence" or "reason" would be irrelevant.

Yet, with the entire intellectual structure of human knowledge revolving around our fallibility, someone is now saying that you are excluded from the search for knowledge by the fact that you are fallible. Which is to say "You are a human being." It is an odd thing to set up standards of human knowledge that violate the basis of human nature.

There is an interesting technique you can use with anyone who attacks the possibility of your knowing anything. When someone tells you "You can't be certain about that," ask her what she means by the word "certainty." (You might even ask if she is "certain" that certainty doesn't exist.) Ask her to define the standards by which certainty could be established. In all likelihood, she will require you to be a God before acknowledging that any statement you make is true, however overwhelming the evidence you have presented in support of it.

You should respond: "According to your version of certainty, I would have to be nonhuman, therefore, your objection is entirely irrelevant to human beings."

You might continue, "The mere act of arguing with each other presupposes that we are not omniscient or infallible. What would be the point of an argument otherwise? Moreover, the fact that you have been using terms like 'true' and 'false' presupposes it as well."

Always demand that the person with whom you are arguing examine your evidence, rather than attack you for being human.

THE SPECTER OF SUBJECTIVISM

The arguments against subjectivism are quite similar to those offered above against skepticism, and I won't risk becoming repetitive. Suffice it to say that the average woman believes she is dealing with reality in her daily life. She believes in the cold floor beneath her feet in the morning, in the bitter coffee that wakes her up, and the existence of the children she packs off to school.

The burden of proof remains firmly on the shoulders of the philosophers who wish to tell her differently. Such intellectuals would trap women within the confines of their own consciousnesses over which they could peek to perceive a world existing apart from it. Women would be trapped in what is known as the "egocentric predicament." All they could know would be their own perceptions and ideas. And all assertions would be reduced to statements about their own experiences.

Subjectivists are made, not born. Fortunately, most women adamantly maintain a belief in tomatoes.

WHAT IS TRUTH TO A FALLIBLE BEING IN A WORLD OF SHIFTING FACTS?

You are justified in claiming "the truth" when, having reasonably examined an issue, you find overwhelming evidence that a statement is true, and no evidence contradicting it. The fact that the "information" may be invalidated at some later date does not mean you were unreasonable or hasty in your original judgment that it was true. Revising your beliefs in the face of new facts is part of the context in which you should hold all knowledge. It is reasonable to freeze your beliefs and hold them as absolutes only if you can say of them that "no more relevant evidence can possibly be found." Such a statement would require you to be omniscient.

Consider the following concepts as terms of distinction:

Possibility: This term means that a given assertion *can* be true. There is some evidence to support it, and nothing to contradict it. For example, someone at a party tells you that your car has been stolen. When you demand to know why he says this, the fellow replies, "Well, you've parked in a bad neighborhood which is notorious for car thefts." You look out the window but do not see your car, because a large truck is blocking your view of where it should be. At this point, it is possible your car has been stolen.

Probability: This term means that the preponderance of evidence indicates that a given assertion is true, and that nothing contradicts it. The greater the preponderance, the greater the probability. Return to the above scenario and add one element. The truck pulls away and the parking place where your car should be becomes clearly visible. Your car is not there. It is now probable that it has been stolen. It is *probable* but not certain because there are other possible explanations. For example, you might have absentmindedly parked it elsewhere.

Certainty: This term means that the evidence supporting a given assertion is conclusive. What would this mean regarding your car? After searching the area without finding it, another person at the party reports seeing a man shattering a side window to gain admission to your car, in which he subsequently drove away. It is now certain that your car has been stolen. In other words, there is overwhelming evidence of the theft, which no other theory adequately explains.

Note: the fact that you call the police to report—with certainty—a stolen vehicle doesn't mean that you may not be wrong. Further evidence is always possible. For example, your husband might return to the party in your car with the extra beer he'd run out to purchase. The car with the smashed window might merely be one that closely resembled yours. This additional information does not mean you were wrong to call the police. It merely means that *all* human knowledge—including claims to certainty—are contextual. Do not let the other person use the fact that you are a human being as a reason to dismiss you. As a human being, you deserve respect, not dismissal.

SUMMARY

One form of intimidation consists of making a philosophical assault on your ability to know that anything is actually true or false. This attack comes in two basic forms:

(1) epistemological skepticism, which denies the ability of the human mind to know anything at all; and,

(2) subjectivism, which denies that reality exists apart from consciousness.

With skepticism, the other person is claiming that because you are a fallible human being who has been wrong in the past, she can dismiss arbitrarily the impressive evidence that your present argument is correct. With subjectivism, the other person is claiming that because there is no objective reality, there is no reason to consider seriously the truth or falsehood of your argument.

Providing a context for human knowledge offers a powerful weapon to protect against such assaults.

Afterword

One of my favorite quotations comes from Louisa May Alcott's *Little Women*. It comes when Jo reads a passage from one of her short stories: "And the good fairy said, I won't leave you money or pretty dresses but I will leave you the spirit to seek your fortune from your own efforts."

These are the circumstances into which most women are born. Not naturally beautiful. Not rich through circumstance. But with their wits about them. It is my sincere wish that every woman who reads *The Reasonable Woman* will have an easier time seeking her intellectual fortunes as a result.

Recommended Readings

Adler, Mortimer. *Aristotle for Everybody: Difficult Thought Made Easy*. New York: Macmillan, 1978.

————. *The Difference of Man and the Difference It Makes*. New York: Holt, Rinehart and Winston, 1967.

Adler, Mortimer, and Charles Van Doren. *How to Read a Book*. Rev. ed. New York: Simon and Schuster, 1972.

————. *Great Treasury of Western Thought: A Compendium of Important Statements on Man and His Institutions by the Great Thinkers in Western History*. New York: R. R. Bowker, 1977.

Atwater, E. *"I Hear You": Listening Skills to Make You a Better Manager*. Englewood Cliffs, N.J.: Prentice-Hall, 1981.

Beardsley, Monroe C. *Practical Logic*. Englewood Cliffs, N.J.: Prentice-Hall, 1955.

Bergamini, David. *Mathematics*. Life Science Library, 1963.

Blanshard, Brand. *The Uses of a Liberal Education, and Other Talks to Students*. La Salle, Ill.: Open Court, 1973.

Bolton, R. *People Skills: How to Assert Yourself, Listen to Others and Resolve Conflicts*. Englewood Cliffs, N.J.: Prentice-Hall, 1979.

Boyer, Carl B. *A History of Mathematics*. New York: John Wiley and Sons, 1991.

Branden, Nathaniel. "Breaking Free." In *A Nathaniel Branden Anthology*. Los Angeles: J. P. Tarcher, 1980.

———. "The Disowned Self." In *A Nathaniel Branden Anthology*. Los Angeles: J. P. Tarcher, 1980.

———. *The Psychology of Self-Esteem: A New Concept of Man's Psychological Nature*. Los Angeles: Nash, 1969.

Chase, Stuart. *Guides to Straight Thinking; with Thirteen Common Fallacies*. London: Phoenix House, 1959.

———. *Power of Words*. New York: Harcourt Brace, 1954.

———. *The Tyranny of Words*. New York: Harcourt Brace, 1938.

Claiborne, Robert. *Saying What You Mean: A Commonsense Guide to American Usage*. New York: Ballantine Books, 1986.

Cohen, Morris R. *A Preface to Logic*. New York: Meridian Books, 1956.

De Bono, Edward. *Lateral Thinking: Creativity Step-by-Step*. New York: HarperCollins, 1990.

———. *New Think: The Use of Lateral Thinking and the Generation of New Ideas*. New York: Avon, 1971.

Dowing, Douglas, and Jeff Clark. *Statistics the Easy Way*. 2d ed. New York: Barron's, 1989.

Dryden, Windy. *Inquiries in Rational Emotive Behaviour Therapy*. London: SAGE Publications, 1996.

Elgin, Suzette Haden. *The Gentle Art of Verbal Self-Defense*. Englewood Cliffs, N.J.: Prentice-Hall, 1980.

———. *The Last Word on the Gentle Art of Verbal Self-Defense*. New York: Prentice-Hall, 1987.

———. *More on the Gentle Art of Verbal Self-Defense*. Englewood Cliffs, N.J.: Prentice-Hall, 1983.

———. *Staying Well with the Gentle Art of Self-Defense*. Englewood Cliffs, N.J.: Prentice-Hall, 1990.

Ellis, Albert, and Russell Grieger. *Handbook of Rational-Emotive Therapy*. New York: Springer Publishing Company, 1977.

Ellis, Albert, and R. A. Harper. *A Guide to Rational Living*. Englewood, N.J.: Prentice-Hall, 1961.

Fausto-Sterling, Anne. *Myths of Gender: Biological Theories About Woman and Men.* New York: Basic Books, 1985.

Feynman, Richard. *"Surely You're Joking, Mr. Feynman!": Adventures of a Curious Character.* New York: Norton, 1984.

———. *What Do YOU Care What Other People Think?: Further Adventures of a Curious Character.* New York: Norton, 1988.

Flesch, Rudolf. *The Art of Plain Talk.* New York: Macmillan, 1985.

Flew, Antony. *Thinking Straight.* Amherst, N.Y.: Prometheus Books, 1977.

Florman, Samuel C. *Blaming Technology.* New York: St Martin's, 1981.

———. *The Existential Pleasures of Engineering.* New York: St. Martin's, 1994.

Follett, Wilson. *Modern American Usage.* New York: Hill and Wang, 1966.

Frankl, Viktor. *Man's Search for Meaning: An Introduction to Logotherapy.* New York: Pocket Books, 1963.

Friedman, David. *Hidden Order: The Economics of Everyday Life.* New York: HarperBusiness, 1996.

Gonick, Larry, and Mark Wheelis. *The Cartoon Guide to Genetics.* New York: HarperPerennial, 1991.

Gonick, Larry, and Art Huffman. *The Cartoon Guide to Physics.* New York: HarperPerennial, 1991.

Gonick, Larry, and Woollcott Smith. *The Cartoon Guide to Statistics.* New York: HarperPerennial, 1993.

Hayakawa, S. I. *Language in Thought and Action.* New York: HarcourtBrace, 1949.

Hazlitt, Henry. *Thinking as a Science.* Los Angeles: Nash, 1969.

Henley, N. *Body Politics: Power, Sex, and Nonverbal Communication.* Englewood Cliffs, N.J.: Prentice-Hall, 1977.

Hepp, Maylon H. *Thinking Things Through.* New York: Scribner, 1956.

Hospers, John. *Human Conduct: An Introduction to the Problems of Ethics.* New York: Harcourt, Brace and World, 1961.

———. *Introduction to Philosophical Analysis.* Englewood Cliffs, N.J.: Prentice-Hall, 1988.

Huff, Darrell. *How to Lie with Statistics.* New York: W. W. Norton, 1954.

———. *How to Take a Chance.* New York: W. W. Norton, 1959.

James, William. *Talks to Teachers.* London: Longmans, 1899.

Joseph, H. W. B. *An Introduction to Logic.* Oxford: Clarendon Press, 1967.

Kaminer, Wendy. *I'm Dysfunctional, You're Dysfunctional: The Recovery Movement and Other Self-Help Fashions.* New York: Vintage, 1993.

———. *True Love Waits: Essays and Criticism.* New York: Addison-Wesley, 1996.

Keen, Sam. *To a Dancing God.* New York: Harper and Row, 1970.

Kosko, Bart. *Fuzzy Thinking: The New Science of Fuzzy Logic.* New York: Hyperion, 1993.

Lakein, Alan. *How to Get Control of Your Time and Life.* New York: New American Library, 1996.

Lakoff, R. *Language and Woman's Place.* New York: Harper and Row, 1975.

Molloy, John T. *The Woman's Dress for Success Book.* New York: Warner Books, 1978.

Montaigne, Michel de. *The Essays of Montaigne.* New York: AMS Press, 1967.

Orwell, George. *1984.* San Diego: Harcourt, Brace, Jovanovich, 1977.

Pappas, Theoni. *The Joy of Mathematics: Discovering Mathematics All Around You.* San Carlos, Calif.: Wide World Publishing, 1989.

Partridge, Eric. *Usage and Abusage: A Guide to Good English.* Harmondsworth, England: Penguin Books, 1973.

Perls, Fritz S., R. F. Hefferline, and P. Goodman. *Gestalt Therapy.* N.p.: Julian Press, 1951.

Popper, Karl R. *The Logic of Scientific Discovery.* New York: Harper and Row, 1968.

Rand, Ayn. *Anthem.* Caldwell, Idaho: Caxton Printers, 1977.

———. *Introduction to Objectivist Epistemology.* New York: The Objectivist, Inc., 1967.

Ruby, Lionel. *The Art of Making Sense: A Guide to Logical Thinking.* New York and Philadelphia: J. B. Lippincott, 1954.

Russell, Bertrand. *History of Western Philosophy and Its Connection with Political and Social Circumstances from the Earliest Times to the Present Day*. London: Unwin, 1979.

Walen, S., R. DiGiuseppe, and W. Dryden. *A Practitioner's Guide to Rational-Emotive Therapy*. 2d ed. New York: Oxford University Press, 1992.

Walker, C. Eugene. *Learn to Relax: 13 Ways to Reduce Tension*. Englewood Cliffs, N.J.: Prentice-Hall, 1975.

Walker, Helen M. *Elementary Statistical Methods*. New York: Holt, Rinehart and Winston, 1969.

Werkmeister, W. H. *An Introduction to Critical Thinking: A Beginner's Text in Logic*. Lincoln, Nebr.: Johnsen Publishing, 1969.

Wolf, A. *Textbook of Logic*. London: Allen and Unwin, 1948.

Index

Acton, Lord, 58
Addison, Joseph, 267
Adler, Mortimer, 28, 37, 42, 49, 121, 122, 127, 151, 234, 286
Alcott, Amos Bronson, 123
Alcott, Louisa May, 299
Anthem, 197
argument etiquette, 255–58
argumentation, 31, 33–35, 88, 180–81, 185, 190–94, 198–200, 237–97
Aristotle, 22, 23, 46, 117, 134, 135, 203, 280
Aristotle for Everyone, 28, 42, 286
Art of Making Sense, The, 21, 122, 198–99
Art of Plain Talk, The, 205
Art of Thinking, The, 139–40

Asquith, Lord, 26
Atwater, E., 245
Aurelius, Marcus, 32
authority, 37, 279–80
average, 225–26
axioms, 217

Bacon, Francis, 156
Bailey, P. J., 203
Balfour, Lord, 26
Barron's Educational Series, 224, 232
Beardsley, M. C., 190
behavior modification, 44, 63–69. *See also* Ellis, Albert
Bergamini, David, 235
Biocentric Therapy, 144
Blaming Technology, 180
Blanshard, Brand, 25, 32, 33, 40,

129, 130, 132, 134
Body Politics: Power, Sex, and Nonverbal Communication, 245
Bolton, R., 245
books, 121–34, 141
Bourgeois Gentlemen, The, 21
Boyer, Carl B., 233
brainstorming, 69–73, 169
Branden, Nathaniel, 42, 142, 143, 145, 157, 158, 217
Breaking Free, 142, 144–45, 157
Browning, Robert, 223
Bryant, William Cullen, 56

capacities, 85, 87
Carew, Thomas, 95
Carroll, Lewis, 129, 195
Cartoon Guide to Genetics, The, 139
Cartoon Guide to Physics, The, 139
Cato, 11
Cervantes, Miguel de, 237
Chapman, George, 213
Chase, Stuart, 190, 198, 205, 279
Chesterfield, Lord, 17, 29
Cicero, Marcus Tullius, 11, 36, 258, 277
circumstance, power of, 50–56, 112–15, 249–51, 271–77
Claiborne, Robert, 205
Cohen, Morris R., 194
college, 12
Colton, C. C., 241
concentration, 75–78

contextual definitions, 203–204
correlations, 226–27
cosmetic fixes, 95–99
Cronkite, Walter, 11

Dancing on the Cliff, 58–59
Darwin, Charles, 109
Day, Doris, 117
De Bono, Edward, 74
definitions, 195–205, 221
Dentinger, John, 58–59
Dickens, Charles, 50
Dictionary of Modern English Usage, A, 95
Difference of Man, and the Difference It Makes, The, 42
Disowned Self, The, 142, 165
dispassionate thinking, 261–62
Disraeli, Benjamin, 112
dress, 96–97
Dryden, John, 225
Dryden, Windy, 155, 156, 157, 172–73, 174

eccentricities, 84, 117–19
Edison, Thomas A., 12, 86
Ego-barrier, 254
Einstein, Albert, 12, 109, 279, 280
Elementary Lessons in Logic, 194
Elementary Statistical Methods, 231
Elgin, Suzette Haden, 283
Eliot, Charles W., 285
Ellis, Albert, 44, 64–65, 104, 142, 143. *See also* Rational-Emotive Therapy

Ellis, Havelock, 83
Emerson, Ralph Waldo, 73, 132, 151, 253
Epictetus, 79
equivocation, 93–94
Erasmus, Desiderius, 65, 197
error, 49–59. *See also* fear of error
Essays (Montaigne), 123
estimating, 231
evasion, 93–94
Existential Pleasures of Engineering, The, 235

fallacies, formal, 186–87, 211, 226
fallacies, informal, 188–90, 217–18
falsification, 210–16, 218–19, 221
Fausto-Sterling, Anne, 15
fear of error, 16, 45–46
Feynman, Richard, 139
Flesch, Rudolph, 205
Flew, Antony, 182, 186, 190, 210
Florman, Samuel C., 180, 235
Follett, Wilson, 95
Fowler, F. G., 95
Fowler, H. W., 95
Frankl, Viktor, 116
Franklin, Benjamin, 147, 218
Freud, Sigmund (Freudianism), 40, 43, 214–15, 254
Friedman, David, 223
friends, 52–53, 79–80, 84–85, 134–40

frustration, 17, 46–50, 115–17
Fuzzy Thinking, 74, 235

Galilei, Galileo, 234
Gandhi, Mohandas, 270
Gentle Art of Verbal Self-Defense, The, 283
Gestalt Therapy, 144, 170, 173
Gestalt Therapy, 177
gestures, 97
getting specific, 101–103
Gonick, Larry, 139
good will, arguing with, 253–64
Great Treasury of Western Thought, 151
Greek philosophy, 27–28, 40–41, 285–86
Guide to Rational Living, A, 104
Guides to Straight Thinking, 190

habit, 23–29, 35–38, 43–44, 61–78, 92, 101–19
hair and makeup, 98
Hall, Charles Albert, 25
Handbook of Rational-Emotive Therapy, 44, 64–65, 142
Hayakawa, S. I., 205
Hazlitt, Henry, 95, 147, 150, 293
Henley, N., 245
Hepps, M. H., 190
Herbert, George, 245
Hidden Order: The Economics of Everyday Life, 223–24
History of Mathematics, A, 233
History of Western Philosophy, 151

Holmes, Sherlock, 33–34
Hood, Thomas, 61
Hospers, John, 151
How the Mind Falls into Error,
     190
*How to Get Control of Your Time
     and Life,* 90
How to Lie with Statistics, 81,
     224, 228
How to Read a Book, 49, 121,
     234
How to Take a Chance, 235
Huff, Darrell, 81, 224, 228, 230,
     235
*Human Conduct: An Introduction
     to the Problems of Ethics,* 151

"I Hear You," 245
ill will, arguing in the presence
     of, 265–84
*I'm Dysfunctinal, You're Dys-
     functional,* 42
infallibility, 292–94
*Inquiries in Rational Emotive
     Behavior Therapy,* 155
intellectual diary, 147–50, 160–
     61
intellectual therapy group, 11–12,
     141–77
intellectual virtues, 40, 258–62
intelligence, 25–26, 80–81, 88
intimidation, 113–14, 277–83
*Introduction to Critical Thinking,
     An,* 179–80, 252
Introduction to Logic, 181, 194
Introduction to Objectivist Epis-

temology, 203, 217
*Introduction to Philosophical
     Analysis,* 151
IQ tests, 81

James, William, 36–37
Jefferson, Thomas, 125
Jevons, Stanley, 194
Johnson, Samuel, 69
Joseph, H. W. B., 181, 194
Joy of Mathematics, The, 235

Kaminer, Wendy, 42, 282
Keen, Sam, 45
Kelly, John, 146
King's English, The, 95
Kipling, Rudyard, 227
Knowlson, T. Sharper, 139
Kosko, Bart, 74, 235

Lady Windemere's Fan, 199
Lakein, Alan, 90
Lakoff, R., 245
Language and Woman's Place,
     245
Language in Thought and Action,
     205
*Last Word on the Gentle Art of
     Verbal Self-Defense, The,* 283
*Lateral Thinking: Creativity Step
     by Step,* 74
lateral thought, 73–74
Learn to Relax, 68, 136, 169
Leonardo da Vinci, 106
Lessing, Gotthold E., 45
Levant, Oscar, 117

Liebnitz, Gottlieb, 234
Lincoln, Abraham, 50
linear thought, 73–74
listening, 238–45
Literary Digest, 229
Little Women, 299
logic, 179–94
Logic of Scientific Discovery, The, 213

McCarthy, Sen. Joseph, 186–87
malice, 267–69
Man's Search for Meaning, 116
Mantle, Mickey, 279
Mathematics, 124, 139, 232–35
Mathematics, 235
Maverick, Maury, 279
Menander, 141
Milnes, R. M., 38
Milton, John, 79
Moby Dick, 50
Modern American Usage, 95
Molière (Jean-Baptiste Poquelin), 21
Molloy, John T., 96, 98
Montaigne, 64, 123
More on the Gentle Art of Verbal Self-Defense, 283
Morley, Christopher, 207
Mozart, Wolfgang Amadeus, 117
Myths of Gender, 15

Newspeak, 196–97
New Think, 74
Newton, Sir Isaac, 234
1984, 195–96, 197

obfuscation, 93–94, 196, 199
Occam's razor, 288
omniscience, 292–94
O'Neill, Eugene, 86
Onus Principle, 273
Orwell, George, 195

Paine, Thomas, 125, 270
Pappas, Theoni, 235
Parker, Theodore, 101
Partridge, Eric, 95
People Skills, 245
Perls, F. S., 177
Plato, 64, 190, 280
Pope, Alexander, 88
Popper, Karl, 210–11, 213–15
Power of Words, 198, 279
Practical Logic, 190
Practitioner's Guide to Rational-Emotive Therapy, A, 177
Preface to Logic, A, 194
Proudhon, Pierre, 217
psychology, 29–32, 38–41, 43–44, 48, 62–63, 179–80, 214–15, 228, 277–78, 283. *See also* intellectual therapy group
Psychology of Self-Esteem, The, 42

Rand, Ayn, 197–98, 203, 217
Random House Dictionary, 232, 237
Rational-Emotive Therapy (RET), 64, 104, 142, 144, 155–56, 172–73
reading, 150–51. *See also* books

Reasoner, Harry, 11
Reed, Thomas B., 62
reflectiveness, 33–34
relaxation techniques, 67–69
risks, 91–95, 151–52, 213–16
Roosevelt, Eleanor, 141
Ruby, Lionel, 21, 122, 198–99
rules of defining, 201–203
rules of intellectual etiquette, 17–21
Russell, Bertrand, 151, 232

Saying What You Mean, 205
Schiller, Johann, 91
Scott, George C., 11
Seinfeld, Jerry, 45
self-destructive statements, 104–12
self-evaluation, 79–88
sentence completion, 157–59
Sertorius, Quintus, 43
setting goals, 88–90, 247
Shakespeare, 238
shared experience, 281–82
Shaw, George Bernard, 35
skepticism, 288–97
skills, 86–88
Smith, George, 142
Smith, H. B., 190
Spurgeon, S. H., 75
statistics, 210, 223–31
Statistics the Easy Way, 224
Staying Well with the Gentle Art of Verbal Self-Defense, 283
stereotypes, 14–15
Stolen Concept, 217–18

Straight and Crooked Thinking, 190
subjectivism, 289, 294–95
Surely You're Joking, Mr. Feynman! 139
syllogisms, 182–94
systematic desensitization, 37, 66–69, 103. *See also* behavior modification

Talks to Teachers, 36–37
Taylor, Elizabeth, 117
technical aspects of reasoning, 179–221
Tennyson, Alfred, Lord, 270
Textbook of Logic, 194
theory, 207–16. *See also* falsification
Thinking about Thinking, 190
Thinking as a Science, 147, 150, 293
Thinking Straight, 182, 186, 210
Thinking Things Through, 190
Thoreau, Henry David, 210, 245, 286
Thouless, R. H., 190
To a Dancing God, 45
Transactional Analysis, 144
True Love Waits, 282
truth, 181–85, 189, 209–10, 292–96. *See also* falsification
Tyranny of Words, The, 205

Usage and Abusage, 95
Uses of a Liberal Education, The, 25, 129

validity, 181–90, 209
Vanbrugh, Sir John, 126
Van Doren, Charles, 151, 179
visualization, 68–69, 102–103, 113
voice, 97
Voltaire (François-Marie Arouet), 198

Walker, C. Eugene, 68, 69, 70, 136, 169
Walker, Helen M., 231
Washington, George, 246
Watson, Dr., 33–34

Werkmeister, W. H., 179–80, 252
What Do YOU Care What Other People Think? 139
Wilde, Oscar, 199
Wolf, A., 194
Wolpe, Joseph, 66
Woman's Dress for Success Book, The, 96
Women's Liberation, 142
writing, 76, 89–90, 93–95. *See also* brainstorming; intellectual diary

zigzagging, 172–74